AI for Community

AI for Community explores the transformative potential of technology to bridge cultural divides and responsibly preserve cultural heritage, while thoughtfully considering how to ensure fairness without any ideological or cultural bias. It acknowledges the need for careful scrutiny of traditions so that artificial intelligence (AI) systems can promote comprehensive cultural understanding. This approach underscores the promise of AI as a tool for human flourishing.

Authored by a multigenerational, multicultural team, this book presents real-world examples and ethical insights that are timely, actionable, and deeply human-centered. It introduces pioneering projects like the Indigenous Knowledge Graph, which documented ancestral wisdom; Howard University's Project Elevate Black Voices, funded by Google, which enhanced speech recognition for African American Vernacular English (AAVE); and Laleh AI, which posthumously preserves the insights of a progressive female Islamic thinker. Also, initiatives like UNESCO's work on cultural heritage preservation and NVIDIA's collaboration with Te Hiku Media to safeguard the Māori language showcase AI's vital role in reviving endangered languages.

This book interweaves "Community Voices" sections between chapters, featuring interviews that explore the role and implementation of AI in new arenas. Each chapter is also supported by online resources, accessible as podcasts, videos, and articles, that provide multimedia ways to deepen understanding of culturally aware AI.

AI for Community highlights how community-driven language preservation, storytelling, and inclusive design can empower cultures and protect their heritage. This book is a vital resource for those seeking to create AI that respects and uplifts communities.

AI for Community
Preserving Culture and Tradition

Iran Davar Ardalan, Amir Banifatemi,
Fernando Gonzalez, Myles Ingram,
Reza Moradinezhad, and Lucretia Williams

CRC Press
Taylor & Francis Group
Boca Raton London New York

CRC Press is an imprint of the
Taylor & Francis Group, an **informa** business

A CHAPMAN & HALL BOOK

Designed cover image: © Iran Davar Ardalan. Family quilt from Ohio, passed down by John Oliver Smith's family, husband of Iran Davar Ardalan. It embodies heritage and the preserving of cultural narratives across generations.

First edition published 2025
by CRC Press
2385 NW Executive Center Drive, Suite 320, Boca Raton FL 33431

and by CRC Press
4 Park Square, Milton Park, Abingdon, Oxon, OX14 4RN

CRC Press is an imprint of Taylor & Francis Group, LLC

© 2025 Iran Davar Ardalan, Amir Banifatemi, Fernando Gonzalez, Myles Ingram, Reza Moradinezhad, and Lucretia Williams

ISBN: 978-1-032-85211-9 (hbk)
ISBN: 978-1-032-84662-0 (pbk)
ISBN: 978-1-003-51711-5 (ebk)

DOI: 10.1201/9781003517115

Typeset in Times
by codeMantra

Access the Support Material: http://www.routledge.com/9781032846620

To all communities eager to be part of AI's future, we welcome you. Like tulips breaking through tough soil, your resilience and creativity belong not just at the table but in shaping what comes next.

Contents

Iran Davar Ardalan

Iran Davar Ardalan

Lucretia Williams

Chapter 3   The Role of AI in Language Preservation and Revitalization 55

Myles Ingram

Chapter 4   Building Trustworthy and Culturally Intelligent AI 85

Reza Moradinezhad

Chapter 5   Human Agency and AI.. 122

Amir Banifatemi

Authors

Iran Davar Ardalan is a leading AI Strategist, where she contributes to AI research in the civil sector. Formerly the founder of TulipAI, Ardalan is known for her expertise in Responsible AI, merging AI tools with creative content generation and developing AI-driven solutions such as custom GPTs and virtual assistants. Her career includes leadership roles at National Geographic, NPR News, and the White House Presidential Innovation Fellowship program, where she championed data and AI and health initiatives. Her research in cultural intelligence, which focuses on AI's role in preserving culture, nature, history, and wisdom, was featured in the *New York Times* in March 2022.

Amir Banifatemi is an accomplished technology executive and strategist with over 25 years of experience in AI and emerging technology ventures. As chief innovation officer at XPRIZE and co-founder of the AI for Good Global Summit, Banifatemi has driven human-centered AI advancement. His work with the AI Commons and the Global Partnership on AI's Responsible AI group reflects his dedication to promoting AI as a tool for public empowerment.

Fernando Gonzalez is a professor and chair of the Department of Computing and Software Engineering at Florida Gulf Coast University. His background is in automation, starting with the intelligent control of automated systems such as manufacturing systems and the U.S. electric power grid to the automation of software tasks through the use of intelligent agents for the Semantic Web. His work in the U.S. Department of Energy and various academic institutions underscores his commitment to advancing AI in ways that benefit society.

Myles Ingram is the founder and CEO of MylesAI Consulting, specializing in developing conversational agents for clients across multiple industries. Holding a bachelor's in biophysics from Harvard University and a master's in data science from Columbia University, he advocates for the ethical implementation of AI technologies. While at Harvard, he was particularly interested in classics and Latin—subjects that earned him acceptance into the Georgia Governor's Honors Program during high school. Before founding his company, Myles worked at Columbia University Medical Center, publishing AI models for cancer treatment and public health. He also advises AI-based startups in the academic research sector and presents his research at global conferences like the American Society of Clinical Oncology Annual Meeting.

Reza Moradinezhad is an assistant teaching professor of computer science at Drexel University College of Computing and Informatics and a former AI scientist at TulipAI. His research focuses on designing trustworthy and effective interaction techniques for human-AI collaboration, particularly with embodied virtual agents

(EVAs). Recognized for his contributions to AI research, his work spans collaborations with institutions such as the MIT Media Lab and Harvard University.

Lucretia Williams is a senior research scientist at Howard University's Human-Centered AI Institute. Her work focuses on the lived experiences of underrepresented communities, examining how emerging technologies can improve their access to systems that traditionally overlook their needs. Specializing in designing and evaluating culturally responsive health technologies for underrepresented communities, Williams' research spans international borders. She is one of the first Black women to earn a PhD in informatics at the University of California, Irvine, and is a co-founder of an AI-based startup.

Preface

Welcome to *AI for Community*. At first glance, artificial intelligence (AI) and community might seem at odds—one rooted in technology, the other in human connection. But this book is really a conversation between these two worlds, exploring how they intersect and what we can build together to support human flourishing.

For me, AI is a collaborator, a partner in the creative process that helped shape this very book. From typing on a manual typewriter at Brookline High School in the 1980s to splicing tape at NPR in the 1990s, to championing VR projects and later leading global podcasts at National Geographic in 2020, and now working alongside my AI assistant, I've embraced technology to further fuel my creative work.

However, AI isn't perfect. It makes mistakes, fabricates information, and raises important ethical questions—particularly when it's involved in projects like this one. These challenges remind me that no matter how advanced technology becomes, human oversight, judgment, thoughtful reflection, and transparency remain key.

Every chapter in this book was shaped by a back-and-forth exchange with AI. Whether generating ideas, checking grammar, accessing our archives, or improving language, the process was not automated but guided by human input at every step. Our co-authors shaped and cross-checked the AI's output, creating a collaborative dialogue between us and the technology. We also recognize that, in its current form, AI carries inherent biases. Unlocking its full potential requires a commitment to responsible development, making sure it serves diverse communities ethically and equitably.

As co-authors, we come from varied professional backgrounds—AI researchers, strategists, storytellers, technologists, and academics—which you will notice in the different writing styles throughout the book. Some chapters are more technical, while others offer reflective and narrative-driven content. This range reflects our collaborative approach, exploring how AI intersects with culture, community, and ethics from multiple perspectives.

At the end of each chapter, you'll also hear from our "Community Voices"—a range of contributors who responded to our AI for Community survey. These voices bring their own perspectives to the mix, from a climate storyteller envisioning AI's potential to amplify underrepresented stories, to a Brazilian AI professor exploring how AI can support cultural practices like agroforestry. You'll also hear from a strategist focused on sustainable food systems and an Indigenous technologist who reminds us of the deep responsibility required when handling cultural knowledge.

Finally, make sure to explore the support material available on our book's web page. We have curated materials that further examine how AI intersects with culture and community. Enage with resources like the Project Elevate Black Voices FAIR AI Usage Guideline to discover fair AI practices and the Moorland-Spingarn Research Center's Black News Archives to consider safe practices for cultural preservation using AI. Also, the Navajo Nation AI Flower, a creative exploration of AI-generated representations of Diné culture. These resources, accessible as podcasts, videos, and articles, offer rich, multimedia ways to deepen your understanding of culturally aware AI.

So, what role can AI play in our human story? Each of the authors in this book answers that question from their perspective. I had the privilege of meeting each of them through my journey in the AI community and invited them to join this book project. As you read, I hope you feel inspired not just to think about AI but to engage with it actively. It's vital that communities are involved in shaping this future, so AI development reflects a diversity of voices and addresses the needs of everyone.

Iran Davar Ardalan

Acknowledgments

First, we extend our deepest gratitude to you, our readers, for joining us in exploring the intersection of AI and community.

Special thanks to Taylor & Francis and Commissioning Editor Lucy McClune. We are deeply grateful to our co-authors Iran Davar Ardalan, Dr. Fernando Gonzalez, Dr. Lucretia Williams, Myles Ingram, Dr. Reza Moradinezhad, and Amir Banifatemi. A heartfelt thanks to Benjamin Castro for his research on cultural AI and to the AI for community voices contributors: Chamisa Edmo, Beba García, Dr. Senthil B. Girimurugan, Nishan Chelvachandran, Dr. Leandro de Castro, Dr. Samira Kiani, Doug Mitchell, Dr. Jaye Nias, Sam Ragland, Matt Scott, Stéphanie Camaréna, and Tash Tan, who enriched this work. Six responses from the Community Voices surveys are included in this book, with the full collection available digitally.

Chapter 1: Iran Davar Ardalan

I would like to thank Kee Malesky—whom NPR's Scott Simon has called "the source of all human knowledge"—for reviewing the Introduction and Chapter 1. Special thanks to AI scientists and technologists Victor Yarlott, Rafael Pérez y Pérez, Tracy Monteith, and Chamisa Edmo for our invaluable collaborations through the years. I am especially grateful to Anousheh Ansari, CEO of XPrize and Space Explorer, who opened the door to her AI community in 2018, profoundly shaping this journey. To my husband, John Oliver Smith, whose passion for engineering a sustainable world reflects our shared love for family, and to our beloved children and grandchildren—your hard work, creativity, and love inspire me every day. To my father, Nader Ardalan, whose visionary mind continues to inspire, and to my late mother, Laleh Bakhtiar, whose tenacity and unwavering spirit remain my guiding light.

Chapter 2: Lucretia Williams

I extend my deepest gratitude to Gloria Washington and Jaye Nias for their invaluable insights and dedication to elevating Black voices and advancing ethical AI practices. Thank you to the Google Research team for their unwavering support in making this initiative a success. I am also grateful to Gillian Hayes and the CERES network for the opportunity to contribute to impactful research in South Africa, a life-changing experience. Special thanks to Catherine Draper, Caylee Cook, and Elizabeth Ankrah for your support and friendship during that time. Lastly, I am deeply thankful to Howard University for shaping me into the researcher I am today and to my family for their unwavering love and support.

Chapter 3: Myles Ingram

I would like to thank Jack Weyen, Aitor Juaristi Diez, Kanstantsin Loichyts, Subhan Valiyev, Alex Manuel Martinez Aguilera, Oladeji Eunice, Nuria Samper, Jiefeng Kang, Hacane Hech, and Rishu Kumar for taking the time to participate in my survey and providing very insightful conversations that formed the basis for this chapter. I learned so much from all of you about the role AI could play in language revitalization, and

I hope this chapter can both raise awareness for all of your languages and get more people interested in learning them. I would like to especially thank Jack Weyen for helping edit this chapter and giving his perspective on the chapter as a computational linguist. This chapter wouldn't have been possible without your help!

Chapter 4: Reza Moradinezhad

I'd like to send my love and appreciation to my PhD advisor, Dr. Erin Solovey, who has been a great source of support and inspiration throughout the tumultuous years of my PhD Under Erin's advisory, I learned about her journey in the field of neuroadaptive HCI, and I had the chance to collaborate with amazing scientists from Stanford and UC San Diego to Carnegie Mellon and Harvard University. Many thanks to my PhD thesis mentor, Dr. Nataliya Kos'myna from the MIT Media Lab, whose mentorship broadened my knowledge of brain-computer interfaces and gave me an invaluable understanding of elements of trust in automation and AI. I am also grateful to my other committee members—Drs. Gkatzelis and Kim from Drexel University, Dr. Carrington from Carnegie Mellon, and Dr. John Lee from Wisconsin–Madison. And finally, special thanks to Karina Glik for her invaluable contributions to structuring and editing the chapter and being an amazing source of assistance and support.

Chapter 5: Amir Banifatemi

This chapter owes its depth to the insights and support of many remarkable individuals and organizations. I'm profoundly grateful to Yoshua Bengio, whose unwavering commitment to using AI for Good has been a guiding light. Stuart Russell, Francesca Rossi, and Konstantinos Karachalios have been invaluable, offering diverse expertise and fostering rich dialogues on AI ethics and human alignment. XPRIZE and ITU deserve special mention for providing platforms like the AI for Good Global Summit, enabling crucial conversations. AI Commons has laid much of the conceptual groundwork shaping these reflections. My heartfelt thanks extend to the broader community of AI researchers, policymakers, NGOs, and advocates tirelessly working to ensure AI serves humanity. Your passion, initiatives, and thought-provoking discussions have profoundly influenced my understanding of AI's potential and societal role. This chapter stands as a testament to our collective aspiration for an AI-enabled future that benefits all.

Chapter 6: Fernando Gonzalez

I want to express my gratitude for the open admissions policy at my local community in Miami, Florida, which was called Miami-Dade Community College at that time which, like many community colleges, welcomed students regardless of their educational background. This policy allowed me to continue my education after dropping out of school in the sixth grade due to a learning disability. Without this opportunity, I wouldn't have been able to contribute to the writing of this book. It highlights the importance and impact of effective policies and the institutions that champion them. While this policy gave me the opportunity, it was a difficult journey for which I could not have succeeded without the support of my parents, Rafael and Dulce Gonzalez. I would also like to thank my wife, Afsar Gonzalez, and my three children, Roshanak, Sahbah, and Armon Gonzalez, for making life a wonderful journey.

AI Statement

Our book incorporates AI tools like ChatGPT 4.0, Claude, Gemini, Mistral.ai, Grammarly, and QuillBot for tasks such as idea generation, summarization, language improvement, grammar correction, table creation, abstracts, bibliography formatting, captions, and alt-tags. All AI-enhanced content has been reviewed for accuracy, appropriateness, and with an eye toward avoiding common AI clichés.

Iran Davar Ardalan developed a custom generative pre-trained transformer (GPT) model, ARC-AI, using her writings since 2016. ARC-AI provided instant access to her archives, facilitated idea generation, and enhanced the language, significantly improving the depth and efficiency of her research and writing. It also conveniently converted hyperlinks into in-text citations and references.

Lucretia Williams used AI tools like Grammarly, QuillBot, and ChatGPT-4 for grammar editing and tone consistency in Chapter 2.

Myles Ingram developed MylesAI Writing Aid, based on his writing style, to assist with outlining, interview summarization, drafting, and editing in Chapter 3, ensuring all content was reviewed for accuracy.

Reza Moradinezhad employed AI (Claude and ChatGPT) in Chapter 4 for structuring, summarization, and generating examples, with all AI-enhanced content reviewed for accuracy.

Amir Banifatemi, the author of Chapter 5, used ChatGPT and Claude to help with the review of duplicates and verify grammar and style continuity. ChatGPT was also used to find precise references (title, author, dates).

Fernando Gonzalez's Chapter 6 was supported by ARC-AI, a custom GPT developed specifically for this book. ARC-AI was utilized to review PDFs of earlier chapters and identify where the AI definitions are most relevant within the context of *AI for Community.*

While AI tools like ChatGPT have been invaluable in streamlining our workflow—whether by summarizing content or improving language—you have to be mindful of certain patterns they introduce. These AI clichés often include predictable phrasing and buzzwords like *robust, tapestry, revolutionize, dynamic, delve, dive into, additionally, underscore,* and *harness.* For example, you might see phrases like "Delve into the dynamic landscape of innovation."

AI tools also tend to generate redundant introductions or conclusions, using broad framing statements such as "In today's fast-paced, ever-evolving world..." that can feel generic or formulaic. To maintain clarity and authenticity, we carefully edit AI outputs to ensure our content stays original and aligned with our voice.

If there were an AI watermark, it would be evident throughout this book—yet so would the imprint of human knowledge, editorial insight, and intention. This collaboration between humans and AI is a new frontier, one we're navigating thoughtfully and transparently. While we've made every effort to ensure accuracy and ethical integrity, any errors are simply part of this ongoing journey.

Notes on Online Support Material

The authors have curated an extensive array of resources exploring how AI intersects with culture and community. These materials draw on significant initiatives, such as the Project Elevate Black Voices Fair AI Usage Guidelines, which provide insights into ethical AI practices that respect and amplify Black voices. The Navajo Nation AI Flower, an artistic endeavor, uses AI-generated imagery to eplore and honoe Dine culture and the Navajo Nation AI Flower, an artistic endeavor that uses AI-generated imagery to explore and honor Diné culture. These resources are accessible through a mix of podcasts, videos, and articles, presenting diverse formats to deepen understanding of culturally aware AI and fostering human flourishing through responsible AI applications.

The support material also includes resources such as AI reciting Rumi in Persian, showcasing AI's capacity to bring classical literature into digital spaces and bridge cultural heritage with contemporary technology. Eleven Labs explores advancements in AI-driven voice synthesis, enhancing storytelling with human-like expressiveness. The GOLEM framework (GOld Standard for Learning and Evaluation of Motifs) proves why ethically sourced cultural data is essential for AI. By providing a structured approach to embedding cultural motifs in AI systems, it highlights the gaps that can arise without culturally representative data, reinforcing the need for AI systems that are informed by diverse and ethically sourced cultural inputs. The collection also features Generative AI Misuse: A Taxonomy of Tactics and Insights from Real-World Data, a critical resource for understanding and mitigating risks in generative AI applications.

Expanding the cultural scope, the support material includes resources on language preservation and Indigenous wisdom. Highlights include Te Hiku Media's efforts to support Māori language preservation and tutorials on endangered languages such as Hokkien and Garifuna. Together, these resources underscore the importance of developing AI systems that honor diverse cultural narratives and foster inclusivity, ethics, and respect within AI development. Also, The AI Innovator Collaborative—part of ONA's AI in Journalism Initiative—is a regular gathering for ONA members already using AI in journalism to connect and share ideas.

Introduction

Iran Davar Ardalan

This book is about weaving AI into the heart of our communities. It's about honoring our cultural roots, traditions, and values—making sure that AI reflects us.

This belief in community-driven AI is deeply personal to me. It draws from my own heritage, where my grandmother, Helen Bakhtiar, instilled in me a deep respect for both our American and Iranian roots. Years later, after my mother passed away, I turned to AI to preserve her wisdom—honoring her legacy in a way that even Helen could never have imagined.

Growing up as an Iranian American, I lived through the turbulence of the Iranian Revolution, a turning point that reshaped both my family's journey and my sense of belonging. The displacement and uncertainty it caused deepened my appreciation for the power of tradition and culture to ground us in times of change. The Iranian diaspora, scattered across the globe, has worked tirelessly to preserve its heritage, recognizing that traditions are often what keep us connected when everything else shifts.

My husband, John Oliver Smith, and I, along with our blended family of seven sons and one daughter—spread across Pennsylvania, Maryland, Virginia, and London—continue to embrace this multicultural heritage. Whether through the customs of Nowruz, celebrating the arrival of spring and renewal of life, or family storytelling and poetry events, these traditions remain alive in our homes and communities, passed down from generation to generation.

Working in the media has taught me that while modernity sometimes threatens these traditions, it also offers powerful tools to give them voice. This delicate balance—between heritage and innovation—has led me to explore how AI can play a meaningful role in cultural preservation.

Today, AI-driven tools are helping document endangered languages and create learning experiences, allowing younger generations to engage with the languages and customs of their ancestors. In this way, AI offers an exciting opportunity to ensure that cultural heritage continues to thrive, even in the face of displacement and change.

Bezoku, for example, claims to prioritize low-resource languages by working with communities to design safe, private generative AI tools. Starting with Haitian Creole and scaling to other dialects like Cuban and Honduran, Bezoku is a platform focused on cultural and linguistic preservation while reducing its environmental impact (Bezoku, n.d.).

In this book, "community" refers to the collective group of people who share cultural heritage, traditions, values, and social practices. We emphasize creating a dialogue where community members are not just subjects but active contributors to the AI development process, fostering empowerment and resilience.

However, as we build with AI, it's essential to be proactive about the biases embedded in these technologies. AI systems often reflect human biases because they are trained on imperfect, biased data (IVOW, 2018). Ensuring that data used to train these systems meet responsible and trustworthy standards is key to avoiding harm. When done thoughtfully, this approach can enable AI to align with community values, resulting in successful and ethical adoption that benefits society. Open-source frameworks, in particular, play a crucial role in promoting transparency, inclusivity, and cultural preservation (Ardalan, 2024).

While private and academic initiatives all over the world are working to address biases and enhance cultural relevance, governments and public institutions are also taking steps to promote trustworthy AI. In the Fall of 2024 in the United States, some federal agencies embedded these principles into compliance plans, emphasizing transparency and the fair use of AI technologies. For example, the U.S. Department of the Interior (DOI) emphasized the importance of integrating Indigenous Knowledge into AI systems and models. How this approach will evolve over time remains to be seen.

The 2024 Google report "Generative AI Misuse: A Taxonomy of Tactics and Insights from Real-World Data" highlights the misuse of generative AI technologies in various contexts. The report documents around 200 real-world incidents of GenAI misuse between January 2023 and March 2024, revealing a variety of tactics used to exploit AI capabilities maliciously. For instance, one notable incident involved a group of high school students who created a deepfake video of their school principal making racist statements. This deepfake was circulated widely, causing significant harm to the principal's reputation and illustrating the potential for generative AI to be used in harassment and defamation efforts (Marchal et al., 2024).

While these examples highlight the risks of AI—such as deepfakes, misinformation, biased algorithms, and surveillance—they also serve as a reminder of the critical need for responsible AI. This book focuses on the potential of AI to act as a force for good, particularly when guided by ethics and used to foster cultural preservation.

We expand the discussion of ethics to include cultural intelligence and human agency, emphasizing the need for AI systems to authentically resonate with the communities they serve. Our approach prioritizes collaboration with communities, ensuring they remain in control of how AI supports their cultural heritage and that the technology benefits them directly.

For instance, NVIDIA has partnered with California Black Media (CBM) to assist Black-owned newspapers in preserving nearly 100 years of journalism. Through the use of AI, this initiative safeguards archives that reflect the stories and perspectives of Black journalists in California (People of Color in Tech, 2024). This partnership exemplifies how AI, when developed ethically and in collaboration with communities, can be a powerful tool for both preservation and empowerment.

In shaping this approach, we are inspired by the work of AI pioneers like Dr. Timnit Gebru, founder of DAIR, who advocates for ethical AI and addresses the sociotechnical impacts of AI, and Dr. Joy Buolamwini, founder of the Algorithmic Justice League, who has exposed biases in AI and led efforts for equitable technology and policy reform (DAIR, 2024; AJL, 2024).

UNESCO also continues to lead in exploring the potential of AI to preserve intangible cultural heritage, a vibrant form of heritage that extends beyond physical artifacts to encompass the traditions, skills, and expressions passed down through generations. This kind of heritage—such as oral histories, performing arts, and traditional crafts—anchors people to their roots and is sustained by the communities that practice it. UNESCO emphasizes that intangible cultural heritage thrives not due to exclusivity, but because of the deep connections that communities nurture through shared knowledge and identity (UNESCO, n.d.).

For instance, the traditional carpet weaving of Fars in Iran, inscribed on UNESCO's Representative List of the Intangible Cultural Heritage of Humanity, brings generations together in a practice rich with symbolism. Local communities shear wool, spin, and dye it using natural pigments, each weaver creating designs that tell a story of nomadic life. This practice is more than a technical skill; it is an identity marker that ties people to their history, environment, and each other (UNESCO, n.d.).

In October 2024, UNESCO marked the International Day of Intangible Cultural Heritage with discussions on AI's role in sustaining these kinds of heritage. The organization highlighted how AI could support the preservation and transmission of such traditions while emphasizing the need for community-led input to prevent misrepresentation or commodification. This requires integrating local data and involving cultural experts to capture the true depth and diversity of these traditions. With responsible AI frameworks, UNESCO envisions tools like interactive exhibits and skill-sharing applications that aid in passing down cultural knowledge and maintaining community control over heritage practices (UNESCO, 2024).

Finally, my personal journey with AI and community draws deeply from the legacies of my parents, both of whom have shaped my values and perspective.

In May 1976, my father, Nader Ardalan, an architect, took part in the Habitat Forum in Vancouver and contributed to the first UN Habitat Bill of Rights, setting forth recommendations for designing urban settlements. This moment, in collaboration with thought leaders such as anthropologist Margaret Mead and architect Buckminster Fuller, emphasized the importance of considering local culture alongside economic, environmental, and social criteria in future design (Staley, 2013). Just as my father saw architecture as a blend of culture and community, I see AI as a tool to preserve and amplify the essence of our cultural identities.

My mother, the late Dr. Laleh Bakhtiar, also played a major role in shaping my views on the intersection of technology, culture, and ethics. Before she passed away in Chicago in 2020 from a rare blood disorder, we had been working together to bring her voice and stories to AI, ensuring that her vast knowledge and insights would continue to inspire and guide others. In 2024, I created Laleh AI, a custom GPT in her honor. This project not only reflects my desire to preserve her teachings on Sufism but also highlights the transformative potential of AI in connecting communities with the knowledge that matters most to them (Laleh AI, 2024).

As I finished this manuscript, I moved from the world of startups to my new role as an AI strategist. I'm excited about the opportunities ahead.

HOW TO NAVIGATE THIS BOOK

A central theme throughout this book is the role of cultural intelligence—how AI can integrate diverse narratives, traditions, and knowledge systems to create inclusive and community-centered technologies.

CHAPTER 1: REFLECTIONS ON CULTURAL INTELLIGENCE FOR AI

By Iran Davar Ardalan

My chapter is shaped by personal stories and case studies, including the Indigenous Knowledge Graph (IKG)—a model for building AI systems that capture the depth and diversity of human experience. My background spans journalism at NPR and National Geographic, founding cultural AI startups, and leading data and AI initiatives within the federal government. Throughout these roles, my focus has been on how technology can preserve the stories that shape our identities.

CHAPTER 2: SHAPING AI INNOVATION IN BLACK COMMUNITIES

By Lucretia Williams

Dr. Williams focuses on how AI can address systemic biases through culturally responsive technologies. She highlights Howard University's efforts to digitize Black archives, demonstrating the importance of communities maintaining control over their own narratives. As a senior research scientist at Howard University, Williams blends human-computer interaction and informatics with social justice, ensuring that AI serves underrepresented communities in meaningful ways.

CHAPTER 3: THE ROLE OF AI IN LANGUAGE PRESERVATION AND REVITALIZATION

By Myles Ingram

Ingram focuses on how AI tools like natural language processing (NLP) can help safeguard endangered languages and strengthen cultural identity. His chapter blends technical insights with real-world examples, exploring both the successes and challenges in this field. Founder of MylesAI Consulting, Ingram brings together expertise in biophysics, data science, and a passion for preserving cultural diversity through AI.

CHAPTER 4: TRUST AND AI SYSTEMS

By Reza Moradinezhad

Trust is essential to the adoption of AI, and this chapter explores frameworks for building it through transparency, fairness, and cultural sensitivity. Dr. Moradinezhad, an assistant teaching professor at Drexel University, specializes in human-computer interaction and virtual agents, offering practical models for creating AI systems that communities can adopt with confidence.

CHAPTER 5: HUMAN AGENCY AND AI

By Amir Banifatemi

Banifatemi reflects on the balance between AI and human agency, discussing how AI reshapes societal landscapes while ensuring it empowers, not dominates, human autonomy. His chapter raises critical questions about ethics, empowerment, and autonomy, blending structured tables with data-driven insights. A former chief innovation officer at XPRIZE, Banifatemi has led global initiatives like AI for Good, promoting responsible innovation that serves society.

CHAPTER 6: KEY AI CONCEPTS FOR COMMUNITIES

By Fernando Gonzalez

This chapter offers a practical toolkit, covering essential AI concepts in machine learning, including neural networks and generative AI, while emphasizing the importance of cultural heritage preservation. In this chapter, he compares artificial to natural intelligence and discusses the potential future roles of AI in our society. Gonzalez stresses that AI tools must be community-driven, inclusive, and sustainable. As chair of the Department of Computing and Software Engineering at Florida Gulf Coast University (FGCU), Gonzalez focuses on creating AI applications that serve the public good and meet community needs.

COMMUNITY VOICES

At the end of each chapter, we feature a voice from the community—whether it's someone working in AI, communications, ethics, or even climate storytelling. These firsthand stories come from individuals who responded to a survey we sent on AI for Community, offering grounded perspectives on how AI can make a difference when it's shaped by and for the people it aims to support.

HONORING ROOTS, SHAPING THE FUTURE

We conclude with reflections on how AI can evolve through continuous collaboration between technologists, cultural advocates, and communities.

REFERENCES

Ardalan, D. (2024, April 19). Inside CulturaFX: Riding the wave of generative AI to shape the future of ethical audio. *Medium.* https://medium.com

Bezoku. (n.d.). *Private and safe language technology for everyone.* Bezoku. https://bezoku.ai/

Distributed Artificial Intelligence Research Institute (DAIR). (2024). DAIR. https://www.doi.gov/sites/default/files/documents/2024-09/2024-doi-ai-compliance-plan-final.pdf

IVOW. (2018, July 13). Can artificial intelligence create culturally-conscious stories report. *Issuu.*

LalehAI. (2024). *Customized ChatGPT.* OpenAI. https://chatgpt.com/g/g-mW7hSRU3b-laleh-ai

Marchal, N., et al. (2024). *Generative AI misuse: A taxonomy of tactics and insights from real-world data.* ArXiv. https://arxiv.org

People of Color in Tech. (2024, August 29). *NVIDIA partners with California Black Media to pre-serve Black journalism with AI.* People of Color in Tech. https://peopleofcolorintech.com

Staley, R. (Winter). Vernacular design: Architect Nader Ardalan. *Montecristo Magazine,* Winter 2013.

The Algorithmic Justice League (AJL). (2024). AJL. https://www.ajl.org/

UNESCO. (2024). *Join the webinar on artificial intelligence and intangible cultural heritage.* https://ich.unesco.org/en/news/join-the-webinar-on-artificial-intelligence-and-intangible-cultural-heritage-13534

UNESCO. (n.d.). *Traditional skills of carpet weaving in fars.* https://ich.unesco.org/en/RL/traditional-skills-of-carpet-weaving-in-fars-00382

1 Embedding Cultural Heritage into AI

Iran Davar Ardalan

My journey into the world of AI and community was inspired by an eye-opening interaction with IBM's Chef Watson in 2017.

After returning from a storytelling project in the South Pacific, where I visited Tonga and Fiji, I became curious to see if Chef Watson, a popular AI at the time, could understand the culinary specifics I had experienced. I typed in some ingredients from Samoa, but Watson failed to recognize them. This brief encounter with AI and its lack of cultural intelligence sparked a calling in me—to research how to embed cultural contexts into AI.

That curiosity deepened through my involvement in *Beyond the Stars*, an immersive storytelling project launched across nine schools in Fiji in April 2018. Although it didn't involve AI, this project was deeply embedded in the community, using virtual reality (VR) and gamification to address malnutrition and restore pride in traditional diets. The project, which included a book and curriculum, was inspired by local Fijian stories of using the night sky and constellations to navigate home (Ardalan, 2017). This experience reinforced how crucial it was to embed cultural contexts in AI systems, further leading me to explore how AI could better understand and represent diverse cultural narratives (Figure 1.1).

Supported by the Australian Aid program's InnovationXchange, through the LAUNCH Legends initiative I helped lead at SecondMuse, "Beyond the Stars" responded to a crisis in the Pacific islands, where 40% of the 9.7 million population had been diagnosed with non-communicable diseases (NCDs), consuming 40%–60% of healthcare budgets. Also, many children faced malnutrition, with high obesity rates. The glamorization of imported foods and the decline in traditional diets contributed to these issues. "Beyond the Stars" aimed to promote nutritious eating habits and restore pride in traditional diets in the Pacific region (Ardalan, 2017).

As a journalist who spent two decades at NPR News, producing national and international broadcasts, I had always been passionate about storytelling. But it was in the open innovation space, working with SecondMuse, that I saw how technology could bridge gaps in understanding and bring stories to life in ways that were previously unimaginable.

Tash Tan, the visionary behind "Beyond the Stars," was instrumental in realizing this project. As one of the founding partners of the creative technology agency S1T2 in Sydney, Australia, Tan spent weeks in Fiji collaborating with educators, health and nutrition experts, and the Fijian Health and Education Ministries. Their goal was to ensure the program was a true product of Fiji, for Fiji. Teachers, students, and their

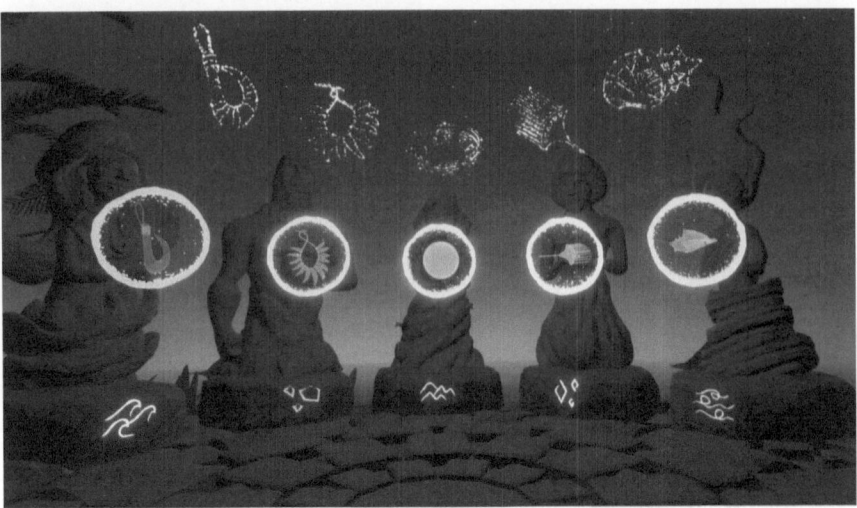

FIGURE 1.1   Beyond the Stars Guardians. In Beyond the Stars, the Guardians of Nature stand tall, each representing a unique element, their symbols glowing with ancestral power. (Credit: Courtesy of Tash Tan SIT2.)

FIGURE 1.2   Beyond the Stars Masi. In Beyond the Stars, Masi, a flying tapa cloth, guides the heroes on their journey. (Credit: Courtesy of Tash Tan SIT2.)

families were equally excited about the program, as it was as much a first for Fiji as it was a world first. The program directly incorporated aspects of the school curriculum and national policies into the interactive story, making it simple and effective in motivating children to learn (Figure 1.2).

One of the key storytelling elements in the VR narrative is Masi, a flying tapa cloth. Masi guides the heroes on their journey, and Tash describes him as cheeky and playful. In one scene, Masi mimics the user's movements, enhancing their sense of control and agency within the VR world. This interaction makes the fictional world feel more real, as the protagonist builds a reciprocal relationship with the VR characters.

Masi art holds significant cultural value in Fiji, traditionally used in ceremonies, clothing, and storytelling. By incorporating Masi into the VR experience, the project not only educates but also celebrates and preserves this important aspect of Fijian heritage.

In a manner similar to the way "Star Wars" and "Harry Potter" share their characters, stories, and universes over multiple mediums, Tan was using transmedia storytelling to imbue a sense of wonder across platforms, from the immersive cutting-edge to the accessible lo-fi. This approach would ensure that the cultural richness and educational value of the project are conveyed effectively across various media, engaging students and fostering a deeper connection with their community and their heritage (Institute for the Future, 2018).

Initial reports and evaluations found that this approach proved to be rewarding in an educational context. Children were not only able to articulate the narrative of "Beyond the Stars," but they also demonstrated an understanding of the program's learnings and impact outcomes behind the narrative. The pilot fostered more ingenuity among the students who wanted their families to cook with local ingredients.

Tan believed that action starts with the empowerment of communities. Through this VR experience, each child becomes a storymaker or storyteller of their own. They are not just watching characters but living and experiencing their history and their universe for themselves. Empowering children in this way could inspire renewed pride in their traditions and encourage healthier dietary habits through an engaging and culturally resonant learning experience (Ardalan, 2017).

"Beyond the Stars" shows how innovative technology, such as VR, could connect communities with their cultural heritage in meaningful ways. While this project was a success, it also highlighted the complexities of using technology to reflect cultural nuances accurately.

As I explored more advanced tools like AI, I began to see both the potential and the limitations of these systems in preserving and representing cultural contexts. Recognizing this challenge, I realized that the key lies in integrating diverse datasets in local languages, especially low-resource ones. This approach enables AI to better support students in these regions by providing more relevant and culturally appropriate educational resources and tools, ultimately making AI more effective globally. I also understood that the data must be ethically sourced, with communities actively involved in the open-source process of creating these datasets, ensuring they benefit from them on their own terms (IVOW, 2020a).

For example, in low-resource languages, AI systems often lack the necessary data to generate accurate chatbots and conversational AIs. This gap leads to significant challenges in providing reliable and culturally relevant services to communities that speak these languages. By incorporating diverse and well-represented datasets,

AI can more effectively serve these communities, ensuring that their voices and cultural nuances are authentically reflected.

Many AI systems are trained on data that has not been ethically sourced, leading to potential biases and misrepresentations. For instance, in healthcare, an AI-driven app designed to offer medical advice might fail to consider culturally specific health practices or symptoms due to a lack of diverse training data. This can result in misdiagnosis or inappropriate recommendations. When AI models are trained on diverse and accurately represented datasets, the resulting content is more authentic and relevant, leading to richer and more immersive experiences that build community trust (IVOW, 2020a).

As we engage in ways that AI can be more culturally intelligent, it's important to keep ethics front and center. To make this clearer, I've put together Table 1.1 that highlights the key ethical considerations we should be mindful of.

Inspired by Masi art, I purchased a Masi cloth in Fiji and took it with me to many of our AI engagements, including some upcoming ones discussed in this chapter. This serves as an example of how cultural expressions can be incorporated into the geometry of data, demonstrating how data from different cultures can be interwoven through relevant cultural visual representations.

By drawing on the rich cultural heritage embodied in traditional art forms like Masi art and quilts, data ecosystems can be crafted to be both intricate and insightful, reflecting the depth and diversity of the data they encompass.

My quest then became a pursuit to ensure that AI does not become a monolithic entity catering to a narrow spectrum of human experiences.

1.1   WHAT IS CULTURAL INTELLIGENCE?

Through our research at IVOW AI, we define cultural intelligence, or cultural IQ, as the ability to recognize, understand, and effectively integrate diverse cultural perspectives, values, and contexts into decision-making. When I first started in the AI space, generative AI had not yet emerged. The focus was on using structured, open-sourced datasets to provide context for AI models. However, it became clear that structured data alone wasn't enough, and our *Women in History Data Ideation Challenge* with Topcoder, launched in Spring 2020, reinforced this realization.

The challenge aimed to explore public data sources on women throughout history and how that information could be used to inform AI products—specifically our cultural AI chatbot, Sina. The results confirmed many of our concerns: we cannot build a culturally rich and meaningful chatbot without better datasets and machine-ready content (Ardalan, 2020).

Most participants in our Topcoder challenge relied on Wikipedia, which, despite being a comprehensive starting point, revealed significant limitations such as biases, lack of cultural diversity, and gaps in global representation. For example, word embeddings trained on Wikipedia often associated male terms with science and female terms with art, reflecting and perpetuating stereotypes. This issue exemplifies how existing datasets can carry historic gender and cultural biases into AI systems, which makes improving data practices essential (Ardalan, 2020).

TABLE 1.1
Ethical Considerations

Ethical Consideration	Importance in AI Development	Example from This Chapter	Strategies for Implementation
Data sourcing	Ensures the data used is accurate, diverse, and representative of the culture being preserved	Using ethically sourced datasets for AI training	Develop guidelines for sourcing diverse and representative datasets
Community involvement	Engages communities as active contributors, ensuring that AI development aligns with their values and needs	Involving Indigenous communities in AI projects like the Indigenous Knowledge Graph	Facilitate community workshops and include community feedback in AI development
Bias mitigation	Reduces the risk of perpetuating biases within AI systems, leading to fairer outcomes	Addressing biases in AI models that may misinterpret cultural narratives	Incorporate bias detection and correction mechanisms in AI algorithms
Transparency	Promotes trust by making AI processes and decision-making clear and understandable	Providing clear documentation on how AI decisions are made	Implement open-access policies and clear documentation for AI processes
Cultural richness	Ensures the inclusion and celebration of diverse cultural narratives, enriching AI outputs	Incorporating cultural elements like Masi art in a way that enhances their value and significance	Work with cultural experts to ensure AI systems respect and accurately represent cultural values
Intellectual property rights	Protects the ownership rights of cultural content, ensuring that it is not misappropriated	Ensuring that cultural content used in AI is properly attributed and protected	Develop and adhere to intellectual property agreements that respect cultural ownership
Sustainability	Ensures that AI practices are environmentally and socially sustainable, benefiting future generations	Using AI in ways that support long-term cultural preservation without harming the environment	Adopt AI practices that prioritize ecological balance and cultural continuity
Monetization	Addresses the ethical implications of monetizing cultural heritage, ensuring that communities benefit fairly from their cultural assets	Developing fair compensation models for cultural content creators when AI is used to generate income from cultural heritage	Create transparent monetization frameworks that ensure fair distribution of profits to cultural heritage stakeholders

Table outlining key ethical considerations in AI development, highlighting their importance, examples from this chapter, and strategies for implementation.

Participants also pointed out that data sources don't sufficiently represent diverse cultural and ethnic backgrounds. While datasets like Pantheon contain information on famous historical figures, they mostly focus on well-known individuals, leaving lesser-known women from various cultures underrepresented.

If AI systems are trained only on these sources, they will continue to miss important figures from history, fiction, and mythology. One example from our Topcoder challenge showed that a dataset included 174 names under the occupation of "pornographic actress" in a sample of 13,000+ women, while only seven archaeologists were listed. This highlighted the need for careful curation of the data we feed into AI systems, ensuring that we focus on the types of contributions we want to prioritize and reflect in AI applications (Ardalan, 2020). Without a broader approach to gathering data, AI systems risk perpetuating existing biases instead of promoting inclusivity.

As generative AI emerged, the potential to build on these efforts expanded significantly. Now, integrating open-source data, contextual data, and community-contributed insights into large language models (LLMs) can enable AI to generate more culturally sensitive outputs that better serve diverse populations. Embedding cultural context into AI systems ensures that these tools deliver personalized, context-aware, and ethically responsible solutions that reflect the diverse experiences of human communities.

Cultural insights come from behaviors, beliefs, practices, and values that shape how different groups interact with technology. Whether drawn from open-source datasets or directly from community involvement, these insights can help ensure AI is inclusive, respectful, and culturally intelligent (IVOW, 2020b, 2021, 2022). Beyond ethnicity, you also have urban and rural settings, socioeconomic factors, professional cultures, generational values, and gender roles. Understanding these differences enables more effective AI systems that better engage with diverse communities.

The integration of any ancestral knowledge into AI systems however must ensure that community empowerment is part of the equation. This can be done by designing closed AI systems that can serve as a safeguard for the knowledge and cultural heritage of communities. These kinds of systems can be built with zero-retention licenses, ensuring that data shared with AI companies is not used to train their models or exploited commercially without the community's consent.

This concept aligns with initiatives where culturally responsive AI focuses on preserving traditions and empowering communities through technology. For example, IVOW AI's Indigenous Knowledge Graph research (coming up in our case studies) demonstrates how culturally relevant AI can collect, organize, and share knowledge without diluting or misappropriating it. It also shows the importance of community involvement in creating datasets that reflect their experiences, ensuring that cultural stories are properly maintained and accurately represented.

For example, integrating open-source NASA satellite data on environmental factors like air quality, temperature changes, and land use patterns could significantly enhance healthcare services for underserved communities. Environmental conditions often play a crucial role in public health outcomes, particularly in areas where pollution, climate change, or limited access to clean water are pressing issues. By incorporating this satellite data into AI models, healthcare providers could potentially better predict health risks, such as asthma outbreaks or heat-related illnesses, which disproportionately affect vulnerable populations.

This approach could allow AI systems to consider environmental context when recommending healthcare interventions, making them more accurate and relevant.

This would also support proactive, data-driven public health measures that can target the specific needs of underserved communities, improving health equity and outcomes.

This emphasis on responsibly embedding cultural context into AI was discussed at the London AI Summit in the summer of 2024. Mark Martin of UK Black Tech underscored that true inclusivity remains a significant challenge, as systemic barriers and superficial corporate efforts often hinder progress.

Martin advocated for overhauling flawed algorithms and scrutinizing datasets to eliminate biases, aligning with the broader cultural shift required for organizations to attract top talent and foster genuinely inclusive environments (Ardalan, 2024b).

Reflecting on Martin's insights, it becomes evident that the relationship between technology and tradition is not one of opposition but of synergy. AI's capability to adapt, learn, and evolve makes it a powerful ally in the quest to maintain cultural integrity.

1.2 EXPLORING THE INTERSECTION OF AI AND COMMUNITY

Let's explore seven case studies that showcase the intersection of AI, community, and preservation of culture and tradition. Among them, you'll find AI tools, summits led by pioneers in culture and technology, and innovative prototypes.

1.2.1 LALEH AI: PRESERVING A SCHOLAR'S LEGACY

Building Laleh AI felt like breathing new life into my mother's legacy. This AI allows people to engage with her work in a new way, turning her ideas into ongoing conversations. For my siblings and me, it's meaningful to see her voice remain vibrant, inspiring new generations.

My mother, Dr. Laleh Bakhtiar was a celebrated scholar, known for her pioneering work in Islamic spirituality and Quranic critical thinking. She spent over 50 years exploring Sufism and reinterpreting Islamic texts from a Muslim woman's perspective. Her research bridged spirituality with psychoethics, making her a trailblazer in her field. She was featured in *The New York Times*, *Chicago Tribune*, and *The London Times*, and spoke at global conferences, including The Aspen Institute. She fearlessly advocated against domestic violence, sharing stages with human rights icons like Nobel Laureate Shirin Ebadi.

Laleh grew up in both Los Angeles and Washington D.C. during the 1940s and 1950s. In her youth, her beauty was such that she could have easily been a Hollywood movie star. However, she chose a different path, journeying into her intellect. As the youngest of seven siblings, my mother was determined to make her mark. She attended Holton-Arms School in Washington D.C., and later, Chatham College, where her academic journey began to flourish. Her favorite song growing up was "Amazing Grace," reflecting her early spiritual influences (Figure 1.3).

She was also our family's archivist, the keeper of our stories and heritage. Growing up, I was always in awe of the volume of work she produced. Shelves in our home were filled with handwritten notes, translations, and reflections that captured her life's journey. Though I knew her work was prolific, it wasn't until I began creating Laleh AI that I fully grasped the depth of her archives.

Laleh AI

By lalehbakhtiar.com

Explore Islam, Sufism, and the significance of Ramadan with Laleh AI,
an interactive tool that offers a deep dive into the life and works of
the late scholar Dr. Laleh Bakhtiar

★ 4.8	Education	183
Ratings (8)	Category	Conversations

Conversation Starters

Who is Laleh Bakhtiar?

How did World War II influence Laleh's identity and early life?

Experience Laleh's 30-day 'Quran Recitation' series on...

How did Persian philosophy influence Laleh's perspective ...

FIGURE 1.3   Laleh AI. Screenshot of Laleh AI, a custom GPT on Open AI where you can explore Islam, Sufism, and the life and works of the late Dr. Laleh Bakhtiar, gaining insights into her groundbreaking scholarship and contributions to gender equality.

Today, scholars continue to study her work. Her groundbreaking translation of *The Sublime Quran* has sparked global debate on gender justice in Islam. Her integration of Sufi principles into her translations, and her role in feminist translation theory, are subjects of ongoing academic exploration. Before her passing, we began working together to bring her voice into the digital age.

When OpenAI launched custom GPTs, I saw the chance to fulfill her wish to continue inspiring future generations and Laleh AI was born. Custom GPTs allow users to upload documents, such as PDFs, and provide specific instructions to train the AI. By uploading some of my mother's books, letters, and notes, we were able to build a system that responds to queries in a way that reflects her perspective. The custom GPT can handle complex topics in multiple languages, offering an experience where users can explore her groundbreaking Quranic translation and reflections on ethics, spirituality, and social justice. While it's still a demo and not perfect, it's an early glimpse of how AI can preserve and extend the wisdom of thought leaders like my mother.

Sharing Laleh AI with my journalism community was one of the most emotional moments for me. When a leader at the Online News Association shared how she had read my mother's work and was overjoyed to see it preserved in this AI tool, I felt profoundly fulfilled. The launch of Laleh AI during Ramadan and Women's History Month in 2024 was a powerful merging of human wisdom and AI technology that keeps her contributions alive.

This custom AI also became a way to merge tradition with technology for our family. As the matriarch of our family, she was an enduring source of wisdom and strength for my children—Saied, Samira, Aman, and Amir—with her teachings on spirituality, resilience, and love. This project represents the heart of *AI for Community*: using AI to capture and sustain the cultural wisdom of those we cherish most.

In Persian, "Laleh" means tulip. As I reflect on my mother's life, I realize how fitting her name was. The tulip, known for its resilience, reemerges each spring after harsh winters, much like my mother's strength throughout her life.

Possible questions you can ask Laleh AI, along with the answers you might receive:

1. **How did Dr. Laleh Bakhtiar's childhood and heritage influence her life?**

   Dr. Laleh Bakhtiar's Iranian father and American mother created a rich cultural foundation that deeply influenced her work. This blend of East and West fueled her passion for interfaith dialogue and her scholarly pursuits in Islamic studies.

2. **What was Dr. Laleh Bakhtiar's contribution to the interpretation of Quranic verses on gender?**

   Her translation, The Sublime Quran, reinterpreted verse 4:34, arguing that "daraba" should mean "go away" rather than "beat," challenging traditional, gender-biased interpretations.

3. **How is the age of AI redefining how we engage with wisdom?**

   The age of AI is transforming how we engage with wisdom by making knowledge more accessible, personalized, and interactive. AI allows us to tap into vast archives of human thought, like Dr. Laleh Bakhtiar's works, and interact with it in real-time, gaining insights tailored to our questions. This shift is turning passive consumption of information into an active, dynamic experience, helping users explore complex ideas more deeply and meaningfully.

With Laleh AI, we continuously update and refine the AI's knowledge base with my mother's work to maintain accuracy. We are also aware that AI makes mistakes. And in this evolving journey, we are doing our best to keep the wisdom of our ancestors accessible and alive for future generations.

1.2.2 Morgan State University: Symposium on Creating Culturally Aware AI

Creating Laleh AI GPT (2024) marked a new frontier in my work with generative AI. But to understand the journey, we need to go back to 2018.

FIGURE 1.4 Morgan State. Members of IVOW AI celebrate AI and cultural storytelling at the AI and Culture Summit held at Morgan State University in April 2018. A Fiji Masi Art piece is displayed in the background, symbolizing the fusion of tradition and innovation.

On April 23, 2018, my startup IVOW AI hosted the AI and Culture Symposium at Morgan State University in Baltimore, Maryland. This event brought together approximately 50 thought leaders and aimed to explore how AI could be deployed as a tool for culturally rich storytelling, merging tradition, culture, and modern technology (IVOW, 2018) (Figure 1.4).

Among the distinguished participants was AI researcher Victor Yarlott, a member of the Crow tribe, who had conducted pioneering research on understanding cultural contexts through AI. During his time as a graduate student at MIT, Yarlott worked with the Genesis Story Understanding System at MIT's Computer Science and Artificial Intelligence Laboratory.

Collaborating with the late MIT Professor Patrick Winston, Yarlott sought to determine whether the system could comprehend stories from Crow folklore as effectively as it understood the works of Shakespeare. His research involved analyzing three collections of Crow literature, identifying key cultural features, and developing Genesis-readable stories that incorporated these features. Yarlott's groundbreaking work proved that MIT's Genesis could understand stories from the Crow culture, moving AI closer to becoming a universal story understanding system.

Our symposium also featured AI scientist Rafael Pérez y Pérez, a professor at Universidad Autónoma Metropolitana at Cuajimalpa, Mexico City, specializing in artificial intelligence and computational creativity. Pérez y Pérez is known for his work on MEXICA, a computer program that generates short narratives about the Mexicas (also known as Aztecs), showcasing the potential of AI in preserving and promoting cultural stories.

At our Morgan State summit, we used my Masi art from Fiji as a backdrop to inspire us and create a culturally rich atmosphere. The symposium included interactive workshops and panel discussions that explored the cultural impact of inclusive algorithms.

Renowned ethnographer and photographer Miguel Gandert, emeritus professor of Journalism at the University of New Mexico, and my former professor, shared his insights on capturing the cultural traditions of the American Southwest through photography. Gandert's work provided a visual representation of cultural narratives, demonstrating how AI could be used to preserve and share these stories.

His extensive work capturing the Mexican cultural traditions of the American Southwest provided a rich backdrop for discussions on the importance of cultural representation in AI. Gandert emphasized the need for thorough historical understanding and the importance of allowing people to tell their own stories.

We discussed the necessity of inclusion without bias and the importance of maintaining cultural integrity. Participants emphasized the need for culturally conscious AI storytelling tools that could engage the public and ensure accessibility.

The final session at the summit centered on a "Declaration of Citizen, Machine, and Culture," which emphasized the role of AI in preserving, protecting, and promoting cultural heritage. This declaration was seen as a continuation of the history of human rights, drawing parallels with milestones such as the Cyrus Cylinder, the U.S. Declaration of Independence, and the United Nations Declaration of Human Rights.

Another participant at our summit, Chamisa Edmo, a citizen of the Navajo Nation with Blackfeet and Shoshone-Bannock descendancy, has been actively involved in advocating for culturally relevant AI content. Edmo has a BA focused on Tribal Sovereignty and is currently pursuing an MS in Electrical Engineering and Computer Science at the University of Kansas, where she is a 2024–2025 IDHR Digital Humanities Fellow.

I was introduced to Edmo through Dr. Nader Vadiee of the Southwest Indian Polytechnic Institute (SIPI). Dr. Vadiee had invited her to join us at Morgan State University for the AI Culture Symposium in 2018. Today, Edmo collaborates with Indigenous youth on impactful tool-building projects, facilitates interdisciplinary discussions with researchers, and regularly consults with elders for their wisdom and guidance.

In this way, our Baltimore summit became a melting pot of ideas, challenges, and solutions, fostering dialogues that highlighted the burgeoning field of culturally aware AI, a step forward in my research on AI systems that truly understand, respect, and celebrate the diversity of human cultures (IVOW, 2018).

1.2.3 AI FOR GOOD SUMMIT: FIRST TRACK ON AI AND CULTURE

We brought a global delegation of storytellers and AI experts to the AI for Good Summit in Geneva from May 27–31, 2019, to explore the intersection of artificial intelligence and cultural expression. As part of the inaugural track on AI and culture, we led discussions focused on how AI systems often lack the empathy needed to share and preserve diverse cultural stories, limiting their relevance to communities. Key questions were raised about how storytelling can help AI develop cultural IQ and how AI can be made more culturally relevant to support the preservation of heritage.

Among the distinguished voices invited to join us for the culture and AI track were the World Trade Organization and UNESCO, whose message resonated deeply with the theme of AI and community—a concept that has only grown in importance today (Figure 1.5).

Antony Taubman, the then Director of the Intellectual Property, Government Procurement, and Competition Division of the World Trade Organization, delivered a compelling address on "Indigenous Nations, Innovation, and Intellectual Property in the Era of AI." His speech covered the profound implications of AI for indigenous cultures and explored the intricate interplay between innovation and intellectual property rights (IVOW, 2019).

Taubman began by highlighting the dual potential of AI. On the one hand, AI could play a crucial role in preserving and invigorating traditional cultures, opening new possibilities for renewing cultural transmission. On the other hand, it also

FIGURE 1.5 AI for Good. AI scientists, storytellers, and technologists from IVOW AI, including Davar Ardalan, gather in Geneva in May 2019 at the AI for Good Summit. The Fiji Masi art piece was displayed as part of the summit's track focusing on Cultural AI, symbolizing the integration of traditional cultural heritage with cutting-edge technology.

had the potential to become a tool for cultural misappropriation and the betrayal of traditions. This duality illustrates the need for careful navigation to protect indigenous knowledge and heritage in the face of rapid technological advancements.

A significant part of Taubman's address focused on the limitations of conventional intellectual property (IP) systems. He pointed out that these systems often fail to account for the unique characteristics of indigenous knowledge, which is typically intergenerational and communal. To address this, he advocated for the development of community-based systems of rights. These systems would recognize the intergenerational nature of indigenous knowledge and ensure broader equity in its preservation and dissemination.

Taubman also emphasized the importance of innovation in cultural renewal. He suggested that AI could be a powerful tool in renewing traditional forms of cultural transmission, provided that the approaches used respect and integrate the cultural values and practices of indigenous communities. He proposed developing rights systems rooted in the community that acknowledge the unique aspects of indigenous knowledge. These systems would aim to balance the need for cultural preservation with the benefits of innovation and technological advancement.

Today, Taubman's insights have become increasingly relevant. The rapid evolution of AI technologies has made the challenges and opportunities he outlined more pronounced. Indigenous communities now face heightened risks of cultural erosion due to the widespread use of AI. However, there are also promising developments where AI is being leveraged to preserve and celebrate indigenous cultures. AI tools are being used to document and revitalize indigenous languages and traditions, and projects that digitize oral histories and create interactive cultural archives have gained momentum, ensuring that traditional knowledge remains accessible to future generations.

Our 2019 AI for Good conversations on Cultural AI laid the groundwork for a critical dialogue on the intersection of AI, innovation, and indigenous knowledge. The Masi art from Fiji was once again displayed prominently on a long table in front of us, symbolizing cultural expression. Our call for community-based rights systems and the ethical development of AI resonates strongly today, guiding efforts to protect and celebrate indigenous cultures in the digital age. As AI continues to shape our world, these principles will be essential in ensuring that technological progress does not come at the cost of cultural heritage and equity.

For their part, *UNESCO* highlighted the transformative potential of AI, predicting a substantial economic uplift with AI projected to boost global GDP by 14% by 2030. This optimistic outlook, however, was tempered with caution. The promise of wealth and efficiency came hand in hand with the specter of increased inequality, discrimination, and unemployment (UNESCO, 2019).

UNESCO's message focused on the impact of AI on culture and artistic expressions. Even in its infancy, AI was creating music, literature, and visual art, prompting questions about the future of creativity, artist remuneration, and the preservation of cultural integrity. The collaboration between AI and human creativity was emerging as a fascinating frontier, raising both opportunities and ethical dilemmas.

A pivotal theme was the preservation of cultural diversity and linguistic richness. As AI technologies like machine translation advanced, they posed both a boon and a threat to lesser-spoken languages. UNESCO emphasized the need for resources and strategies to ensure that AI development did not erode linguistic diversity but rather enriched it.

Fast forward to today, the insights from UNESCO's 2019 address remain profoundly relevant. The integration of AI into community life has accelerated, and the ethical and cultural considerations outlined by UNESCO have become even more critical.

Among the other speakers were David Danks from Carnegie Mellon University, Victor Yarlott from Florida International University, Mariana Lin, a former Creative Director at Apple, and Rafael Pérez y Pérez from Universidad Autónoma Metropolitana at Cuajimalpa. Victor Yarlott and Rafael Pérez y Pérez, who had previously joined us at Morgan State, also attended the summit in Geneva as guests of IVOW AI.

Our discussions centered on the potential of storytelling to build cultural capacity within AI systems and the importance of integrating diverse cultural narratives into AI development.

David Danks emphasized the need for AI systems to be responsive to the values, goals, and principles of different communities. He pointed out that many current AI systems reflect the biases of their developers rather than the needs of the people they serve. To move beyond these limitations, he argued, AI development must fully engage with the cultures and communities most affected by these technologies. Stories, he noted, provide a unique window into the ways people perceive, interpret, and value the world.

Mariana Lin echoed the importance of diversifying the narrative canons that inform AI systems. As the former principal writer for Siri, Lin noted the prevalent references to Western myths and heroes, such as Shakespeare and Biblical figures, and the lack of representation of other cultural narratives. She stressed that expanding the range of cultural references in AI is crucial for creating more inclusive and relatable technologies.

Victor Yarlott focused on the concept of motifs in cultural storytelling. He explained that motifs are specific narrative elements that carry significant cultural meaning, such as characters, events, or props that recur across stories within the same cultural group. For instance, the motif of the knight in shining armor is familiar in Western cultures, symbolizing heroism and chivalry. In contrast, the Crow tribe's motif of Old Man Coyote, a creator and trickster, represents wisdom and mischief.

Yarlott emphasized the need to understand these cultural motifs to develop AI systems that can accurately interpret and reflect cultural narratives. He highlighted that much of cultural knowledge is implicit and can only be fully understood by engaging with the communities that embody these traditions. By working with cultural experts, AI developers can annotate data to ensure that AI systems are culturally aware and capable of recognizing and respecting the diversity of human experiences.

Along with AI researcher Kashyap Murali, I demonstrated the potential of integrating cultural legends into AI systems. We used the Persian epic, *The Shahnameh*, as a case study to illustrate how AI can be trained to understand and process cultural narratives. *The Shahnameh*, which centers on the hero Rostam, provided rich content for our research. By feeding the text of *The Shahnameh* into a computer, we utilized a statistical model to identify key linguistic features and dependencies within the story.

However, we encountered challenges when the model misinterpreted cultural references, such as mistaking Rakhsh, Rostam's stallion, for a work of art. This highlighted the limitations of existing AI models and the necessity for developing culturally informed algorithms. To address this, Murali and I created a custom model that better understood the cultural context of the story, demonstrating the importance of building AI systems that can accurately represent diverse cultural heritages.

We argued that for AI to be truly culturally relevant, it must be developed collaboratively with communities, ensuring that their stories are preserved and respected. By crowdsourcing stories and creating cultural engines, AI can become a tool for preserving and celebrating cultural diversity.

Rafael Pérez y Pérez presented his work on MEXICA, a computer system that generates narratives about the Mexicas, the ancient inhabitants of what is now Mexico City. MEXICA uses representations of emotional connections between characters to develop its stories, making it an emotional storyteller. Pérez y Pérez explained that emotions and cultural context are crucial for creating compelling narratives.

MEXICA's approach involves understanding the emotional reactions of characters based on their cultural backgrounds. For example, a hug may be a gesture of friendship in Mexican culture but might be uncomfortable in British culture. By incorporating these cultural nuances, MEXICA can generate stories that resonate with specific cultural contexts.

Pérez y Pérez emphasized that the goal of MEXICA is not to replace human storytellers but to enhance our understanding of creativity and cultural narratives. By collaborating with people from different cultural backgrounds, AI systems like MEXICA can produce narratives that foster better understanding and empathy between diverse groups.

At the summit, IVOW AI had a booth where technologist Inzamam Malik from Pakistan showcased Sina, our conversational AI designed to share culturally embedded stories. Malik played a vital role in developing a prototype for Sina, which demonstrated how AI could be used to preserve and share diverse cultural narratives. The IVOW AI team, including Kee Malesky, Robert Malesky, Nikki McClay, and Juanita McCoy, also participated in panels on Cultural AI, emphasizing the importance of culturally inclusive technology. My brother, Karim Ardalan, who was instrumental at IVOW AI wasn't able to join us in Geneva.

Today, the insights from the AI for Good Summit have become even more relevant. The integration of cultural narratives into AI systems is essential for creating technologies that are inclusive and respectful of global diversity. Projects like those demonstrated by Yarlott and Pérez y Pérez show that culturally aware AI can play a significant role in preserving and promoting cultural heritage.

This realization propelled IVOW AI to focus on creating culturally conscious AI tools that could preserve and promote indigenous knowledge and wisdom. The insights gained in Geneva catalyzed the development of the Indigenous Knowledge Graph or IKG, which aimed to integrate indigenous values and stories into AI frameworks to ensure these technologies were culturally informed and inclusive (IVOW, 2019).

1.2.4 AMERICAN INDIAN SCIENCE AND ENGINEERING SOCIETY CULTURAL AI WORKSHOP

In the heart of Arizona's desert, I found myself deeply engaged in a workshop that aimed to bridge the gap between tradition and modernity through the lens of artificial intelligence. This September 2021 workshop, hosted by the American Indian Science and Engineering Society (AISES) in Phoenix, brought together Native American technologists and cultural experts. Our mission was clear: to explore how AI could be used to preserve and promote Indigenous knowledge and traditions (IVOW, 2021).

The workshop, led in collaboration with Tracy Monteith, a Senior Software Engineer at Microsoft and a member of the Eastern Band Cherokee, and technologist Chamisa Edmo, was a profound experience.

Together, we worked with Native American students, scientists, educators, and technologists to showcase how the lack of diverse training datasets representing the viewpoints of Indigenous peoples was contributing to bias in AI systems. The participants were tasked with reviewing cultural images and generating descriptive tags that encapsulated the essence of each image. This activity highlighted the rich cultural context often missed by mainstream AI systems and emphasized the importance of inclusive data in AI training (Figure 1.6).

One of the standout moments occurred when we analyzed an image of pupils at the Carlisle Indian Industrial School in Pennsylvania. The popular AI image recognition tool misidentified the emotional and cultural context of the image, tagging it with

FIGURE 1.6 AISES Students. Students at the AISES Conference in Arizona participating in a data tagging exercise. AISES, a national nonprofit organization, is dedicated to increasing the representation of Indigenous peoples from North America and the Pacific Islands in STEM fields. In the background, a traditional Fijian Masi art piece is displayed once again.

generic labels such as "person" and "crowd." In contrast, the participants provided tags that included "sadness," "tragedy," "cultural elimination," and "resiliency." This stark difference illustrated the gap in cultural understanding that current AI systems need to bridge. The exercise demonstrated the importance of creating metadata that accurately reflects the cultural and emotional significance of images, ensuring that AI can interpret them in a way that respects and preserves their true meaning.

Another powerful example from the workshop involved an image of a ceremonial plant that, when analyzed by a popular image recognition app, was mistakenly identified as "ice cream" and "dessert" with over 94% confidence. However, the workshop participants, drawing from their cultural knowledge, provided tags such as "healing," "community," "spiritual," "medicine man," and "sacred herbs." These culturally rich tags revealed the depth and complexity of the scene, which the AI had failed to capture. This exercise proved the necessity of embedding cultural context and knowledge into AI metadata to enhance its accuracy and cultural sensitivity.

The presence of Steve Darden, a Diné (Navajo) and member of the AISES Council of Elders, further enriched our discussions. His insights reinforced the importance of involving elders in creating historical records and leveraging their wisdom to guide AI development. This intergenerational exchange was a testament to the depth and richness of Indigenous knowledge and its crucial role in creating culturally competent AI systems.

Our work in Arizona emphasized several key takeaways. First, indigenous communities should be at the forefront of the AI and data conversation. During the symposium, I asked engineering students to hold up the Masi art piece I brought from Fiji and think about how they would design a data system for their native community that would be distinct but still relevant to a larger ecosystem, similar to the Masi art.

As shared earlier in the context of the Beyond the Stars project in Fiji, Masi art is a traditional Fijian tapa cloth, featuring individual patterns and motifs that tell unique stories and represent specific cultural symbols. These distinct patterns are interconnected, creating a cohesive larger piece of art. Many communities around the world have their versions of this kind of cloth or quilt, each with unique designs contributing to a unified whole.

A data ecosystem thrives on the intricate connections between different data points and sources. The patterns in quilts can inspire the creation of a data ecosystem where each data point is carefully connected to others, forming a comprehensive and detailed network that provides valuable insights and narratives.

As part of our workshop, it became clear that indigenous communities should be able to decide whether or not they want to contribute culturally rich and contextually accurate data for AI training purposes. Having communities involved is essential to ensure that AI systems can understand and respect the nuances of different cultures and that the communities can benefit from such training data.

Second, elders play a vital role in preserving and disseminating cultural wisdom. Their involvement is crucial in developing AI that honors and perpetuates Indigenous knowledge. Steve Darden's participation showed the value of intergenerational knowledge transfer and the role of elders in guiding the ethical development of AI technologies within their communities.

Third, effective AI development must involve active collaboration with the communities it aims to serve. This ensures that AI systems are not only technically sound but also culturally respectful and relevant. The collaborative nature of the workshop fostered a sense of ownership and empowerment among the participants, reinforcing the importance of community engagement in AI projects.

Finally, educational initiatives like the AISES workshop are essential for empowering Indigenous youth and technologists, providing them with the skills and platforms to influence the future of AI. By equipping the next generation with the tools and knowledge to engage with AI, we can ensure that they play a central role in shaping technologies that respect and preserve their cultural heritage. Through these initiatives, we can inform the creation of future AI systems that are not only technologically advanced but also culturally inclusive, bridging the gap between modern technology and traditional knowledge.

Having said this, the use of AI for cultural preservation must be approached with caution, as it could inadvertently reinforce harmful traditions. Not all cultural practices are beneficial or ethical by today's standards, and some may perpetuate discrimination, violence, or inequality.

As AI systems learn from historical data and cultural artifacts, there is a risk that they could also perpetuate these negative aspects of culture. Therefore, it is crucial to critically assess which traditions should be preserved and which should be allowed to fade into history.

For instance, the practice of stoning as a punishment for adultery, prevalent in some traditional societies, is a form of violence against women that is widely condemned by modern human rights standards. If AI systems were to uncritically preserve and promote such practices, they would reinforce and perpetuate this form of violence. Similarly, certain cultural practices involve honor-based violence, where women may be harmed or killed to protect perceived family honor.

Including these traditions in AI preservation efforts without critical assessment could inadvertently validate and maintain these violent practices. Therefore, it is essential to ensure that AI-driven cultural preservation efforts align with contemporary ethical principles and human rights, promoting only those traditions that uphold the dignity and rights of all individuals.

1.2.5 Designing an Indigenous Knowledge Graph

The Indigenous Knowledge Graph (IKG) was a pioneering prototype by IVOW AI designed to embed Indigenous wisdom into artificial intelligence systems. The IKG served as a small repository of cultural data, stories, and values, with a special focus on food knowledge, reflecting the cultural significance of ingredients, recipes, and traditions from Indigenous communities (Figure 1.7a).

The development of the IKG was a collaborative effort involving key researchers and cultural advocates. Once again, Victor Yarlott, an AI researcher from Florida International University and a member of the Crow Tribe, developed IKG using Neo4j, a graph database technology that allowed for the intricate mapping of cultural relationships. Chamisa Edmo, a technologist from the Navajo Nation, brought her community's stories and traditions into the project, particularly focusing on how AI can respectfully handle Indigenous knowledge (Figure 1.7b).

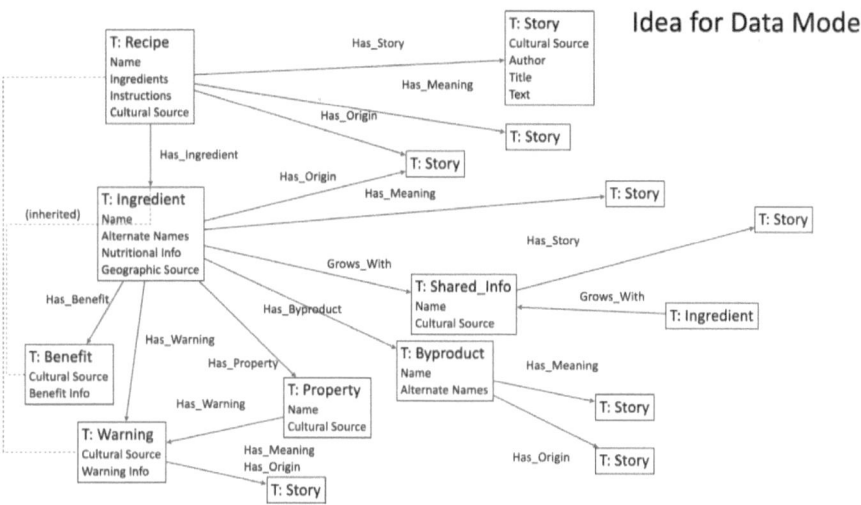

FIGURE 1.7a Indigenous Knowledge Graph Data Model Idea. This conceptual framework, designed by AI Researcher Victor Yarlott for IVOW AI, outlines the foundational structure for our Indigenous Knowledge Graph. It illustrates potential relationships between recipes, ingredients, cultural stories, and properties, capturing the interconnected nature of cultural knowledge, benefits, and warnings in Indigenous storytelling.

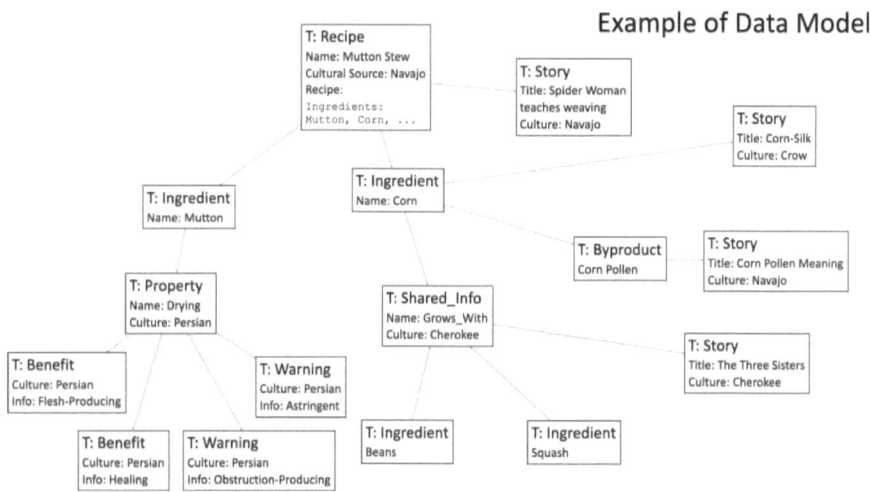

FIGURE 1.7b Indigenous Knowledge Graph Data Model Idea. This example, also designed by Victor Yarlott, demonstrates specific applications within the Indigenous Knowledge Graph model. It includes connections such as a Navajo mutton stew recipe, Cherokee 'Three Sisters' agricultural practices, and cultural meanings of ingredients, showing how cultural stories and traditional knowledge are interwoven.

The IKG included detailed models for recipes, capturing not only the ingredients but also their cultural sources, nutritional benefits, and historical significance. Tracy Monteith, a Senior Software Engineer from the Eastern Band of Cherokee Indians, helped annotate these recipes with cultural and ecological knowledge. A traditional Navajo recipe for mutton stew, for instance, was enriched by including mutton, corn, beans, and squash, with each ingredient annotated for its cultural source. Mutton was not merely a meat; it represented a vital part of Navajo sustenance and community feasts, carrying deep stories of hunting traditions and familial gatherings.

In addition to North American Indigenous knowledge, the IKG expanded to include contributions from the Pacific region. Alva Lim, co-founder of Agora Food Studio in Timor-Leste, provided valuable insights into food sustainability and cultural preservation from Timor-Leste, while Robert Oliver, a world-renowned chef and food activist, contributed a traditional recipe from Samoa. Oliver's book, *Mea'ai Samoa Recipes and Stories from the Heart of Polynesia,* highlights how traditional ingredients, such as taro and coconut, play a significant role in Pacific Islander identity and sustainability.

We knew that transforming cultural knowledge into AI-compatible datasets is ultimately crucial for helping AI systems understand and engage with global cultures. For this demo, we focused on Indigenous food knowledge, which carries deep cultural meaning. A traditional recipe, for instance, passed down through generations, isn't just about ingredients and instructions—each element reflects the culture and community's traditions, from the origin of ingredients to preparation techniques and the occasions the dish is prepared for (Table 1.2).

TABLE 1.2
Indigenous Knowledge Graph Process

Process	Description
Data gathering	For version 0.1.0, stories were gathered from either the public domain or from cultural experts. Recipes and stories were prepared for the system. Rather than using annotation, the demo used formatting and tagging to simplify data ingestion, either manually or automatically, using Neo4j for structure
Formatting	Recipes were formatted into four components: recipe title, ingredients, instructions for preparation, and additional information. Stories were similarly formatted by title, author, secondary source, and story text
Tagging	Tags were added to or drawn from the recipes and stories, including unique IDs, cultural sources, relevant SDGs (Sustainable Development Goals), and time period tags (modern, historical, or mythical). Relations tags linked stories and recipes by related themes (e.g., corn-related stories)
Dialogflow	Stories were manually edited and added to Dialogflow for this demo. In the future, this process will be automated, and the data will be fed to an natural language processing (NLP) chatbot to generate responses that link recipes with stories about their traditional origins

Our Indigenous Knowledge Graph process involved four key stages: data gathering, formatting, tagging, and Dialogflow integration. These steps ensured that stories and recipes were curated, structured, and made accessible for chatbot.

AI researcher Victor Yarlott explains, "While it's natural for humans to understand that the stories and recipes we've gathered revolve around food, machines start with zero understanding of the world. By tying these stories and recipes… we provide the AI with crucial context, enabling it to better parse this information and guide its responses to questions."

This collaboration demonstrated the importance of intercultural partnerships in AI development, ensuring that Indigenous and traditional knowledge is not only represented but also respected and preserved in emerging technologies (IVOW, 2022).

IKG was presented at virtual workshops around the world but given COVID restrictions at the time, we were unable to advance the project. If we had secured funding, we planned to demonstrate how such an AI system could be developed in a closed environment specifically for the benefit of the communities themselves. This proprietary system would ensure that the community's ancestral knowledge was protected and shared on their terms, with no risk of data being used for external training purposes by AI companies. A zero-retention licensing model would have been critical, ensuring that the knowledge remained solely for community use without exploitation.

Edmo reflects on its lasting impact of this research project: "While the IKG project has since been wrapped up, the insights, discussions, and frameworks developed during those sessions continue to influence my work. Today, I am focused on researching applied ethics in technology and establishing Indigenous- and community-advised protocol at every stage of development."

She further emphasizes, "The legacy of the IKG serves as a powerful reminder of the importance of working interculturally to solve complex problems while respecting and honoring the dynamic, and often sacred, nature of Indigenous knowledge. This foundational work continues to shape how I integrate community input, cultural relevance, and ethical considerations into emerging technologies I help to create."

1.2.6   SINA THE AI STORYTELLER

To give voice to the IKG stories we had created Sina the Storyteller, a conversational AI designed to narrate indigenous stories and share cultural knowledge. Sina's name carried cultural significance across various traditions, including Polynesian mythology and Persian history, symbolizing wisdom and storytelling prowess.

Sina used the data from the Indigenous Knowledge Graph to inform her narratives, making her stories rich in cultural context and authenticity. Sina was initially created using Google Assistant. However, Google later changed its assistant platform, impacting the continuity of this aspect of the project (IVOW, 2020a) (Figure 1.8).

Sina was originally introduced to audiences at the 2019 AI for Good Summit in Geneva, where she demonstrated her capability to tell stories from diverse cultures. One of her key roles was to bridge the gap between ancient wisdom and modern technology, ensuring that the stories and values of indigenous communities were not lost in the digital age.

During our AISES workshop in Arizona, Sina shared stories from American Indian perspectives, captivating both young and older engineers. Sina's storytelling emphasized the experiential learning methods traditional to indigenous cultures,

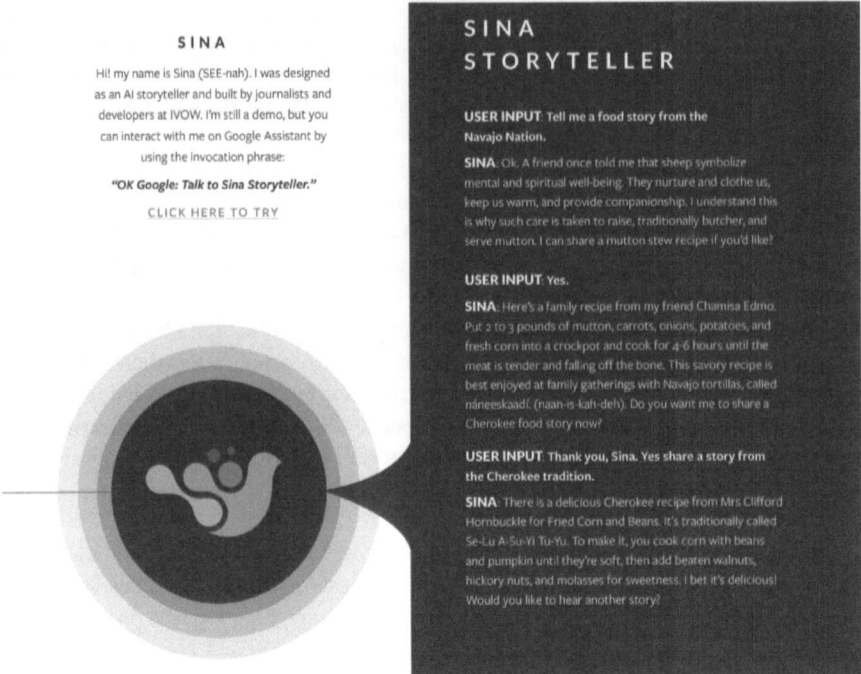

FIGURE 1.8 Sina the Storyteller. Sina the Storyteller is an AI prototype developed by IVOW as a Google Assistant, designed to share culturally rich food stories and recipes from Indigenous traditions, like Navajo mutton stew and Cherokee Fried Corn and Beans.

where observation, exploration, and elder guidance were paramount. Sina's ability to convey these stories in a culturally respectful manner demonstrated the potential of AI to preserve and promote indigenous heritage.

Sina could tell stories like the "Three Sisters," a traditional indigenous narrative about sustainable agriculture involving corn, beans, and squash. This story illustrated the deep environmental knowledge embedded in indigenous cultures and how AI could help disseminate this wisdom to broader audiences. Sina narrated how these crops grew together symbiotically, reflecting the balance and harmony in nature, which was a core principle in many indigenous cultures (Figure 1.9).

Sina's interactive capabilities allowed users to ask questions about cultural stories and recipes, enhancing their understanding of indigenous knowledge. For instance, users could inquire about the origins of a recipe, the cultural significance of an ingredient, or any associated warnings and benefits, all of which were informed by the detailed data in the IKG. Users could ask, "What is the origin of this recipe?" or "Does this ingredient have any byproducts?" and Sina would provide detailed, culturally rich responses, making learning interactive and engaging.

Our IVOW AI work on the Indigenous Knowledge Graph and Sina the Storyteller represented a significant step toward creating AI systems that were culturally inclusive and respectful. By integrating indigenous values and stories into AI, IVOW AI not only preserved these rich cultural heritages but also ensured that AI technologies

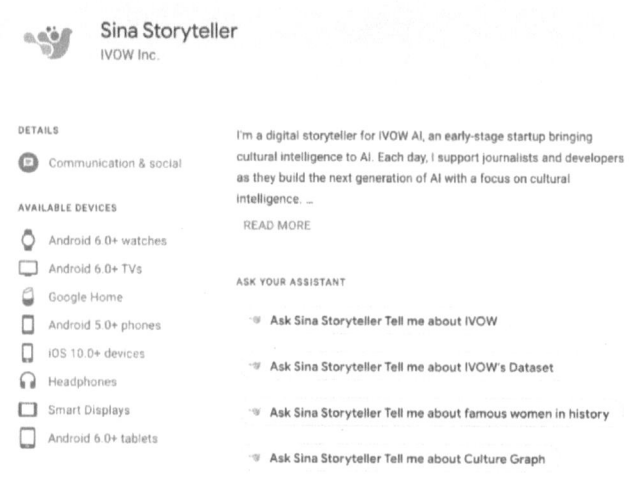

DETAILS

Communication & social

AVAILABLE DEVICES

Android 6.0+ watches
Android 6.0+ TVs
Google Home
Android 5.0+ phones
iOS 10.0+ devices
Headphones
Smart Displays
Android 6.0+ tablets

I'm a digital storyteller for IVOW AI, an early-stage startup bringing cultural intelligence to AI. Each day, I support journalists and developers as they build the next generation of AI with a focus on cultural intelligence. ...

READ MORE

ASK YOUR ASSISTANT

Ask Sina Storyteller Tell me about IVOW

Ask Sina Storyteller Tell me about IVOW's Dataset

Ask Sina Storyteller Tell me about famous women in history

Ask Sina Storyteller Tell me about Culture Graph

FIGURE 1.9 Sina Storyteller on Google Assistant. This image shows Sina the Storyteller, a Google Assistant developed by IVOW AI in 2020. Sina was designed to bring cultural intelligence to AI, supporting journalists and developers by answering questions related to IVOW's work, famous women in history, and cultural data. Google later discontinued this type of assistant.

were more empathetic and effective in serving diverse communities. Sina, the storyteller AI, represented a paradigm shift in AI development, where AI is not just a data processor but a cultural storyteller and preserver.

1.2.7 INSIDE CULTURAFX

In 2023, with the advent of generative AI, I created TulipAI, where we embarked on an ambitious journey to bridge the gap between advanced AI technology and cultural authenticity. Our project, CulturaFX, was designed to ethically source and utilize global sounds to enhance AI-generated audio with cultural richness. Despite not securing funding from the National Science Foundation (NSF), the lessons learned from CulturaFX hold invaluable insights for the broader AI and community space.

From the outset, CulturaFX was envisioned as a platform that could set new standards in AI audio generation, emphasizing ethical practices and cultural sensitivity. Our collaboration with Florida Gulf Coast University (FGCU) was a critical component of this project. Under the mentorship of Dr. Fernando Gonzalez, six exceptional software engineering students—Samantha Walsh, Andrew Krupp, Benjamin Castro, Erick Rodriguez, Rose Meyers, and Tayler Bachmann—joined Dr. Reza Moradinezhad of Drexel University and I, to explore the potential of AI in generating culturally resonant audio (Ardalan, 2024a) (Figure 1.10).

FIGURE 1.10 Cultural roots: Highlighting the contrast between the deep cultural connection of traditional Mariachi music and the shallow replication by AI. This image was created using DALL·E, an AI image-generation tool developed by OpenAI, based on a prompt provided by Ben Castro. His prompt was: "metaphorical image displaying Mexican cultural attachment to Mariachi music and AI mimicking."

The research conducted by these students was pivotal. In December 2023, Benjamin Castro, a first-generation Hispanic American, born to immigrant parents from Cuba and Mexico, conducted impressive undergraduate research into the intricacies of AI models like Meta's AudioGen and MusicGen, focusing on genres such as Mariachi music. While his research was groundbreaking for an undergraduate, it is important to note that it was exploratory and has not undergone peer review. "In my senior year, I had the opportunity to collaborate with TulipAI, whose cultural values and ethical standards resonated strongly with mine," Castro says.

His work highlighted significant gaps in existing AI-generated audio, which often lacks the cultural nuance necessary to resonate with diverse audiences. "I conducted research on leveraging AI models to generate Mariachi music. Delving into the

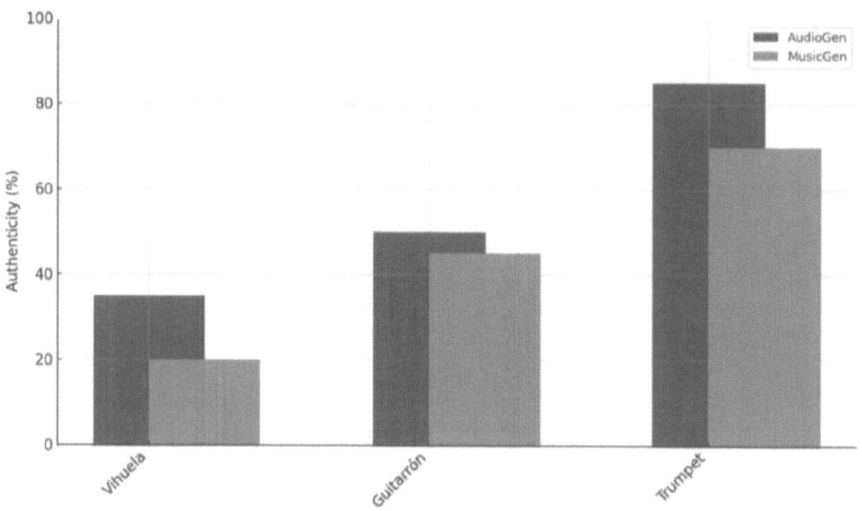

FIGURE 1.11 AI Model Accuracy. Comparing the accuracy of two AI models, AudioGen and MusicGen, in replicating four traditional instruments: Vihuela, Guitarrón, Violins, and Trumpet. (Created by Ben Castro).

intricacies of Mariachi music, I aimed to develop a model capable of recognizing the instruments integral to its composition," he explains.

Castro's exploratory research emphasized that to authentically replicate Mariachi music, AI models must first master the sounds of traditional instruments, providing essential insights for the development of culturally sensitive AI applications (Figure 1.11).

Ethical sourcing was at the heart of our project. We were committed to ensuring that the sounds used in our AI models were obtained in a manner that respects and accurately represents their cultural origins. This commitment not only aimed to improve the quality and relevance of AI-generated audio but also sought to honor the rich cultural heritage from which these sounds are derived.

One of our significant achievements was the development of a custom taxonomy for culturally relevant AI-generated audio. With input from a cultural anthropologist, sound engineers, music industry leader, and our dedicated FGCU team, we set out to create a system that categorizes sounds based on cultural and environmental contexts. This taxonomy would be crucial for maintaining the integrity of AI-generated audio, ensuring that it reflects the true essence of the cultures it aims to represent.

We also worked with a UI/UX Designer, using the Fiji Masi art piece as a design concept. Our early design was black and white, inspired by the intricate patterns and cultural significance of the traditional Fijian Masi cloth. This guided the visual development of CulturaFX, showing how cultural expressions can be integrated into modern technological frameworks (Figure 1.12).

Through my work, I have also been inspired to explore AI in the realm of art, creating collages that depict AI, community, and tradition in ways that honor the places

FIGURE 1.12 CulturaFX. Prototype of CulturaFX, an AI-powered platform for creating personalized soundscapes, designed to enhance content and podcasts with community-driven sound stories. Note: This project ended due to lack of funding.

I have lived, including Annapolis and Washington D.C. These cities, rich in history and known for their ties to the Chesapeake Bay, symbolize community resilience and innovation.

My collages draw heavily on the imagery of these regions, incorporating elements like the water of the Chesapeake Bay as a central motif. The Bay's ebb and flow reflect the power and fluidity of knowledge essential to AI, while also reminding us of our reliance on water and energy resources to power AI systems. Art, in this context, serves as a bridge, making the complex concept of AI more tangible and relatable.

By blending AI with elements of tradition and community, art encourages us to see our communities within the context of this technology and sparks ideas about how we can chart new waters with it. These works aim to illustrate how AI can harmonize with the cultural and natural landscapes that define us, inspiring both reflection and forward-thinking approaches to its possibilities.

Since 2025, the U.S. government has been investing more and more in AI, creating opportunities for communities to engage with this technology in various ways, including future educational initiatives. While the setbacks we faced in securing funding—such as the rejection of our proposals by the Google News Initiative Pre-Launch Lab and the NSF's SBIR Phase I program—highlight the challenges of obtaining support for generative AI cultural projects, they also underscore the importance of our mission. Reviewers noted that similar technologies already exist, overlooking our primary focus on developing tools transparently and with a commitment to trustworthiness in data practices.

This feedback serves as a reminder of the growing need for AI innovations that prioritize trust and are designed for human flourishing. With increased national investment and a stronger push toward accessible AI, we are optimistic that more communities will have the chance to participate in shaping this technology, ensuring it reflects their values and aspirations while opening doors to creative business opportunities.

1.3 CONCLUSION: TRUSTWORTHY AI FOR COMMUNITIES

AI has the potential to greatly benefit communities by helping them understand and trust the technology, giving them control over their data and empowering them to use it in ways that support their goals and aspirations. By fostering collaboration, transparency, and trust, AI can become a reliable tool for progress, enabling communities to shape their own futures.

During my travels to Tonga and Timor-Leste as part of my work with SecondMuse on the LAUNCH Food program, I experienced the extraordinary ability of local communities to drive innovation and preserve their rich traditions. LAUNCH Food was designed to connect global solutions with local challenges, such as improving access to nutritious food and strengthening healthy eating habits. These incredible nations taught me the value of safeguarding ancestral knowledge, particularly around food traditions that have sustained their populations for generations.

In an interaction with my ARC AI Custom GPT, tailored specifically for our book, I explored a culturally significant question inspired by my time in Tonga and Timor-Leste. This highlighted how AI can respect and build upon unique cultural experiences, providing communities with tools to preserve their heritage while exploring new opportunities for growth. It reaffirmed my belief that AI can play a meaningful role in creating a future where technology is a catalyst for shared success and local empowerment.

1.4 TALKING TO MY CUSTOM CHATGPT

1.4.1 Davar Ardalan

Create a table that shows and compares what kinds of data technologists and storytellers in Timor-Leste and Tonga can give you and how that would impact your output?

1.4.2 ARC AI

Certainly! Here's Table 1.3 comparing the types of data that technologists and storytellers in Timor-Leste and Tonga could provide and how each type of data might impact an AI model's output:

Caption: Comparing the types of data that technologists and storytellers in Timor-Leste and Tonga could provide and their potential impact on an AI model's output. The data types include cultural narratives, linguistic data, multimedia content, annotated datasets, ethical guidelines, historical records, digital art and literature,

TABLE 1.3
Potential Impact of Cultural Data on Model Outputs

Type of Data Contribution	Description from Timor-Leste and Tonga	Potential Impact on AI Output
Cultural narratives	Folktales, legends, historical accounts, and modern stories reflective of local culture	Enhances AI's ability to understand and generate culturally relevant content, improving its contextual relevance in discussions about these cultures
Linguistic data	Texts, recordings, and transcripts in local languages, including unique linguistic structures and idioms	Improves AI's language processing abilities in these specific languages, allowing for more accurate translations and interactions
Multimedia content	Music, videos, podcasts, and other media showcasing local art, traditions, and daily life	Contributes to AI's understanding of cultural nuances and expressions, enriching its responses with cultural depth and sensitivity
Annotated datasets	Datasets annotated with cultural, historical, and linguistic context, explanations of idioms, and social norms	Provides AI with contextually rich data, reducing misunderstandings and biases, and enhancing cultural accuracy in responses
Ethical guidelines	Documents outlining ethical considerations, societal values, and cultural taboos specific to these societies	Guides AI in making ethically informed decisions and responses that respect local cultural norms and sensitivities
Historical records	Archives, historical documents, and scholarly articles on the history and evolution of these cultures	Enriches AI's historical and cultural understanding, allowing for more informed discussions about the past and its influence on present-day cultures
Digital art and literature	Contemporary digital artwork, poetry, and literature that reflect current cultural expressions	Allows AI to stay up-to-date with modern cultural trends and expressions, ensuring its outputs are relevant to current societal contexts
User-generated content	Social media posts, blogs, and forums in local languages discussing daily life, opinions, and current events	Broadens AI's exposure to everyday language use and current topics, enhancing its ability to engage in relevant and timely conversations

and user-generated content. Each data type contributes uniquely to enhancing AI's cultural intelligence and contextual relevance in processing and generating content.

This table highlights how the cultural richness from regions like Timor-Leste and Tonga can profoundly influence the quality and relevance of AI outputs. By providing culturally specific narratives, linguistic data, and ethical guidelines, communities can significantly enhance AI's ability to operate more inclusively and contextually. In addition, this data ensures that AI doesn't just serve a global public but also respects the integrity of local traditions and values.

Beyond data autonomy, it's also critical that communities benefit financially from their contributions to AI systems. Data has intrinsic value, and those who provide it should share in the financial returns. Establishing models where communities receive compensation for their data contributions can help ensure a more equitable distribution of AI's benefits, creating economic opportunities that empower marginalized communities.

Just as I saw in Tonga and Timor-Leste during my work with SecondMuse, meaningful engagement with local voices leads to more successful, culturally respectful outcomes. The same principle applies to AI development. When communities are involved in shaping AI systems, they don't just contribute data—they become co-creators of technologies that reflect their values and address their needs.

REFERENCES

My chapter details several initiatives led by IVOW AI. Key projects like the Indigenous Knowledge Graph and Sina the Storyteller AI are highlighted, demonstrating practical applications of culturally aware AI. I'd like to recognize the efforts of the IVOW AI team members, including Kee Malesky, Robert Malesky, Karim Ardalan, Nikki McClay, and Nisa McCoy, who were instrumental in developing culturally conscious AI research projects like the Indigenous Knowledge Graph and Sina the Storyteller.

Ardalan, D. Bringing back pride to traditional foods. *Huffington Post*, October 12, 2016. https://www.huffpost.com/entry/bringing-back-pride-to-tr_b_12463206

Ardalan, D. Reactivating the hidden wisdoms of Tonga. *Huffington Post*, November 10, 2017. https://www.huffpost.com/entry/reactivating-the-hidden-wisdoms-of-tonga_b_5a05fe5 2e4b0cc46c52e6a26

Ardalan, D. (2020). AI fail: To popularize and scale chatbots, we need better data. *Becoming Human.* https://becominghuman.ai/ai-fail-to-popularize-and-scale-chatbots-we-need-better-data-88ed005724f6

Ardalan, D. (2024a, April 19). Inside CulturaFX: Riding the wave of generative AI to shape the future of ethical audio. *Medium.* https://idavar.medium.com/culturafx-advancing-ethical-global-ai-audio-for-market-growth-d210cf216814

Ardalan, D. (2024b, June 18). Navigating the path to inclusive AI: Insights from the 2024 London AI summit. *Medium.* https://idavar.medium.com/navigating-the-path-to-inclusiv e-ai-insights-from-the-2024-london-ai-summit-4bc854abec94

Gebru, T., & Torres, E. P. (n.d.). The TESCREAL bundle: Eugenics and AI. *First Monday.* https://firstmonday.org/ojs/index.php/fm/article/view/13636

Institute for the Future. (2018, March 27). Legends in VR. Institute for the Future. https://legacy.iftf.org/future-now/article-detail/legends-in-vr/

IVOW. (2018, July 13). Can artificial intelligence create culturally-conscious stories report. *Issuu.* https://issuu.com/

IVOW. (2019, July 3). AI for good 2019 report. *Issuu.* https://issuu.com/

IVOW. (2020a, June 4). Bringing cultural context to artificial intelligence report. *Issuu.* https://issuu.com/

IVOW. (2020b, August 30). Shaping AI systems with cultural data report. *Issuu.* https://issuu.com/

IVOW. (2021, September). The new AI frontier: Tagging indigenous values report. *Issuu.* https://issuu.com/

IVOW. (2022, May 31). Intelligent voices of wisdom learnings. *Issuu.* https://issuu.com/

LalehAI. (2024). Customized ChatGPT. OpenAI. https://chatgpt.com/g/g-mW7hSRU3b-laleh-ai

New York Times. How native Americans are trying to debug A.I.'s biases. *New York Times*, March 22, 2022. https://www.nytimes.com/2022/03/22/technology/ai-data-indigenous-ivow.html

People of Color in Tech. (2024, August 29). NVIDIA partners with California Black Media to preserve Black journalism with AI. *People of Color in Tech*. https://peopleof-colorintech.com/articles/nvidia-partners-with-california-black-media-to-preserve-bl ack-journalism-with-ai/

Strier, K. What is sovereign AI? *NVIDIA Blog*, February 28, 2024. https://blogs.nvidia.com/ blog/what-is-sovereign-ai/

UNESCO. (2019). *Artificial Intelligence for sustainable development: Challenges and oppor-tunities for UNESCO's Science and Engineering Programmes*. UNESCO. https://unes-doc.unesco.org/ark:/48223/pf0000368028

X. NPR showcases Twitter chats for social storytelling. *X (formerly Twitter)*, April 8, 2014. https://blog.x.com/en_us/a/2014/npr-showcases-twitter-chats-for-social-storytelling

Community Voices 1: Insights from Matt Scott—Perspectives on AI's Impact on Community Engagement and Sustainability

Our first community voice features insights from Matt Scott, a dedicated storyteller and engagement director at the global nonprofit climate solutions resource Project Drawdown. As the founding director of the Drawdown Stories program, Matt helps everyday people find their role in climate solutions and justice on the community level.

His work spans various high-impact initiatives, including the NASA International Space Apps Challenge and collaborations with organizations like the Australian Government and Pivotal Ventures by Melinda Gates. Growing up in West Orange, NJ, Matt's family traditions and support have deeply influenced his commitment to using storytelling to amplify underrepresented voices and drive positive change.

His extensive experience in community engagement and storytelling positions him as a vital contributor to our examination of AI's role in preserving cultural heritage and fostering inclusive community development.

Question 1: Share your professional bio

Matt Scott is the director of storytelling and engagement at the global nonprofit climate solutions resource Project Drawdown and is the founding director of the Drawdown Stories program where he helps everyday people find their role in climate solutions and justice on the community level. Matt is the host of the climate solutions short documentary series Drawdown's Neighborhood, featured on the Weather Channel's Pattern streaming network.

Prior to his work at Project Drawdown, Matt was the global community lead and storyteller of the NASA International Space Apps Challenge, the world's largest global problem-solving hackathon—engaging over 100,000 people in over 150 countries. While building Space Apps—what's been called the U.S. government's largest citizen diplomacy initiative—he also worked with the Australian Government, Pivotal Ventures by Melinda Gates, USAID, the United Nations, Nike, Walmart, and

DOI: 10.1201/9781003517115-2

the Obama White House. Matt is the creator of Let's Care, where he's interviewed 100+ changemakers and created the film 20s & Change: San Francisco, recognized at three film festivals to-date.

Question 2: Share your heritage and family traditions. Where did you grow up? Share a family tradition that you continue to this day.

I grew up in West Orange, NJ. Beyond spending holidays with my family, one tradition in my family that I continue to this day is supporting my family with the business my dad founded and that my mom and sister have run since his passing seven years ago.

Question 3: Experience with AI. Have you used AI technologies? If yes, please describe your experience. How do you perceive the role of AI in your professional or personal life?

I have used AI through apps and tools that integrate it, including ChatGPT. I think AI has great potential in the right hands with the right uses. My experiences have made me excited for what's to come, especially with all of the efficiencies AI can afford if used ethically, accurately, and inclusively.

Question 4: AI and cultural preservation. Can you envision any innovative ways in which AI could be used to safeguard intangible cultural heritage, such as language, folk songs, or storytelling? Are there specific traditions, practices, or aspects of your culture that you believe could benefit from AI technology?

I don't have a clear vision of this, but I would love to see AI capture and amplify the stories of underrepresented communities. Far too many stories of underrepresented groups go unheard, and I'd love to know how AI can help retain and integrate those perspectives and experiences into the broader consciousness to support a more inclusive, informed, innovative culture.

Question 5: AI and nature. Could you describe a traditional practice from your own culture, or one you've learned about or reported on, that helps in environmental sustainability or climate resilience? Also, how do you think AI could be utilized to support or improve this practice?

I've interviewed many people who have stories that, to date, have only been shared verbally. I've discovered a desire for people to share their stories for greater understanding. I've asked 200+ changemakers, "If your life is a book or documentary, what would the title be and why?" I see their minds run wild with ideas about what that story, if captured, would look like. As someone who also wants to capture their story and share it with the world in a book or documentary, I'd love to see AI make that really accessible for the average person.

Question 6: Wisdom of elders and AI. What role do elders play in preserving culture and wisdom in your community? With ethical practices at play, can AI play a role in capturing and disseminating this wisdom? If yes, how?

The stories of elders are often lost to history. I interviewed my father in 2015, 1.5 years before his passing, and while it wasn't comprehensive, I'm thankful that

I recorded that interview. His insights continue to inspire me, as do the stories my parents shared of ancestors who came before my time. Their insights and insights from community elders help me understand our world, my identities and how I interact with that world, and how we can build a path toward the future we want to build—as my elders and ancestors did before me.

Question 7: AI and ethics. How important is it for AI systems to be developed ethically, especially in the context of cultural preservation? What steps would you like to be taken to ensure that, as AI expands, it represents diverse cultural perspectives?

AI is incomplete and ineffective without cultural competency. I would like to see a widespread effort funded at the global level to convene perspectives from across religions, geographies, genders, sexual orientations, races, ethnicities, hobbies, occupations, socioeconomic statuses, political identities, and perspectives otherwise, in order to form a clear, comprehensive vision of what AI should look like. Often, we overlook the value of incorporating everyone's perspectives. I would truly like to see leaders across sectors integrate the voices of everyday community members in shaping AI's power. Complex problems, like ensuring that AI is used effectively, require complex, interwoven networks of stakeholders across systems. I want to see those stakeholders all have the opportunity to contribute through interviews, surveys, a multitude of convenings and co-design sessions, capacity-building opportunities, and other collaborative efforts that ensure people are not left behind.

Question 8: AI and personalization. We know that AI systems today don't understand the values and needs of diverse populations. Would you be willing to voluntarily share your family traditions and customs with your personal AI device to improve personalization?

Yes, though I don't feel my sole perspectives would be especially helpful. What would be more telling is enabling me or someone like me with the tools to convene my family tree to capture this information. That will lead to a more representative and nuanced picture of traditions, and I would trust ethical AI with this if we know 100% that the information can't be exploited. I'd love a private tool that would allow me to invite my extended family and communities to contribute with audio, video, photos, writing, and integrations of sources that have captured cultural traditions (e.g. social media and file uploads).

Question 9: Future of AI in community development. What potential risks and benefits should be considered when integrating AI into community initiatives?

Data privacy and use is key, as well as a communal understanding of AI. AI is not consistently taught anywhere, but it would be powerful to see global bodies align on a "curriculum" of sorts that can be integrated into schools and communities. This deeper understanding, coupled with ethical practices, is necessary to be sure that the technology can be trusted and integrated with buy-in from all stakeholders. I don't know all of the benefits that should be considered, but I do believe that everyday community members should be consulted and that the benefits of AI should be co-created with everyone at the table. I'd like to see AI used to capture and synthe-size information about needs and opportunities when it comes to AI.

Question 10: Final thoughts. Is there anything else you would like to share about your views on AI and its role in preserving cultural heritage and traditions?

***

Matt Scott's survey responses provide a compelling narrative on the potential of AI to capture and amplify the stories of underrepresented communities. His work emphasizes the importance of ethical AI development that respects and includes diverse cultural perspectives.

2 Shaping and Uplifting AI Innovation in Black Communities

Lucretia Williams

We now live in a world with advanced technology that helps us navigate multiple facets of daily living. AI is at the forefront of transforming how we live and interact with others. We can communicate with people who don't speak the same language through a mobile platform, use smart devices to secure homes, monitor climate change, detect bank fraud, and many more innovative experiences. Some people are delighted at the newfound ease and efficiency of tasks AI technology has brought upon us. Still, others fear and are hesitant about AI running aspects of their lives that they grew up manually doing themselves. This leaves people feeling powerless while others use it for personal gain.

On November 30, 2022, Open AI sent shocking waves globally with the release of ChatGPT, where 1 million users jumped on the platform within one week of its launch. The launch of ChatGPT has awakened the average citizen to the depths of AI, despite Western societies slowly introducing it for a few decades. Well, what's different now? Why is everyone now talking about AI? For a long time, the rhetoric behind AI has been futuristic and unattainable to everyday people. Before ChatGPT, when you ask most people, "What's the first thing that comes to your mind when you think of AI?" people will mostly say robots and self-driving cars. Due to cost and economic regional influence, those technologies aren't attainable to most of the world. In contrast, ChatGPT brought human-like conversation where you can receive a plethora of new information in an accessible way. Accessible knowledge transfer is undervalued yet the most powerful, and that is how I believe ChatGPT made the shift in disrupting not only the technology industry but also how our minds operate when seeking information.

2.1 AI'S IMPACT ON BLACK AMERICAN CULTURE

The first AI rapper, FN Meka, emerged and was signed to Capitol Records in August 2022 (Tracy, 2022), which quickly sparked controversy over stereotyping Black people. The AI rapper was dropped from its record label a week and a half later. The character's design and lyrics relied heavily on stereotyping Black urban culture, and some content even mocked police brutality. The cultural appropriation of Black culture for a non-Black rapper made with animation angered many artists and people within the Black community. Hip-hop emerged from the struggles of marginalized

DOI: 10.1201/9781003517115-3

communities, mainly Black and Latino youth in the Bronx, New York, during the 1970s. It served as a platform for their voices, addressing social issues and celebrating their cultural identity. I was born and raised in the South Bronx, a melting pot of ethnic cultures and immigrant enclaves that tied everyone together, where you get that gritty and distinct New York culture. Growing up, my parents would tell me stories of how the Bronx was "burning" during the 1970s and how it was the catalyst for hip-hop. Landlords purposely set fire to properties throughout the South Bronx, spanning over a decade, as an attempt to collect insurance money, displacing Black and Latino families (Jelly-Schapiro, 2019). As my mother would tell it, "the tenement buildings were burning, cops would not even respond in certain areas, and you were on your own." The plight this community faced led to young people expressing themselves through the arts of music, break dancing, and graffiti, which made up the founding origins of hip-hop.

FN Meka was created by a team likely without a deep understanding of this history. This appropriation extracts elements of Black culture for financial gain without acknowledging the struggles and experiences that birthed it. The irony lies in using AI to bypass Black artists themselves. This not only ignores the talent and creativity within Black communities but also reinforces the gatekeeping role of often white music executives who profit from Black culture without fully appreciating its roots.

Communities historically excluded by society's design now have to brace themselves to live in a world where humans and technology work together to exclude them. Community design is often disrupted by urban planners and policymakers who have no connection to the community but see great potential and location-based opportunity. The Cross Bronx Expressway was intentionally designed to cut through Black and Brown communities so as to not cause noise and air pollution in the suburban areas surrounding the borough (Sze, 2006). As a result, the Bronx has the highest asthma rates in New York City, in addition to the socioeconomic disadvantages that its citizens are confronted with. By design, the South Bronx community I grew up in was designed to stifle me, ultimately preventing me from leaving to obtain three higher education degrees and performing meaningful work that affects my community. As a society, we must find a balance between using AI for ease and efficiency and using that rhetoric to further systemic institutional practices designed to keep a race and social class hierarchy. Human bias and injustice have a troubling way of seeping into technology, often exacerbating the very inequalities they were meant to address.

Many changemakers are working in the AI space advocating for the inclusion and protection of Black communities, whom I admire dearly for their teachings, bravery, and perseverance. Dr. Safiya Noble uncovers in her book "Algorithms of Oppression" how these digital tools, which many assume to be objective, actually reflect and reinforce societal prejudices (Noble, 2018). Her research exposes the dangerous illusion of technological neutrality and emphasizes the urgency for a more critical examination of how these tools impact marginalized communities. Similarly, in exploring the implications of bias embedded in technology, Dr. Ruha Benjamin examines the ways in which discriminatory practices are not just only mirrored but actively reinforced through technological systems. She creates the concept of "The New Jim Code" (Benjamin, 2019), which plays off of Michelle Alexander's body of work on "The New Jim Crow," which situates how innovative technologies are being built and used for social containment but appear to be more equitable than the systemic and discriminatory practices we've seen historically in this country (Alexander, 2011).

Often, technical and academic communities view these challenges as theoretical and not practical, hindering mitigation action. These issues are not to be taken lightly, but changemakers at all levels need to be involved and know how to put theory into practice. This chapter aims to provide a nuanced perspective into the development of AI technologies for Black communities that have been historically excluded and how this work should be considered and approached. I will provide real-life case studies on AI and community-based projects and perspectives from human-centered AI experts, Dr. Gloria Washington and Dr. Jaye Nias, on how to produce fair and responsible AI technology for historically excluded communities. The purpose of this work is to encourage the businesses and institutions that drive the progression of groundbreaking technology to introduce methods and practices of collaborating with diverse communities to create a future where AI technology doesn't cause further division and inequality.

2.2 BIAS IN AI TECHNOLOGY: TECHNOLOGY ISN'T NEUTRAL

The new advances in AI-powered tools excite people about creative capabilities in text and image generation and refinement. It has given people new imaginaries and ways of exploring their hobbies and interests. Despite the very purpose of AI to have accurate automated outputs based on trained data, the humans behind this process can bake their bias into creating these automated systems. Technology is far from neutral and never will be, as it is inherently shaped by the humans who create and wield it. Every algorithm, line of code, and digital tool carries the developers' intent, bias, and values. Whether through deliberate design or unconscious bias, the choices made during the creation of technology reflect the broader social, cultural, and political contexts from which they emerge. This means that technology can either reinforce existing inequalities or become a catalyst for positive change, depending on the values and priorities of those behind it.

AI-driven job recruitment tools that favor specific demographics over others can lead to fewer job opportunities for underrepresented groups, perpetuating economic disparities and limiting upward mobility. This is further exacerbated when AI systems are used in performance evaluations and promotions, where biased algorithms can influence career advancement unfairly. Research studies have shown how Black names received fewer job callbacks than White names, which companies can easily replicate through AI to continue these discriminatory practices (Kline et al., 2024). My brother once shared a questionable comment he received when at the doctor's office. One of my brothers carries my mother's maiden name, "Shultz," and when he stood up at the doctor's office when they called "Johnathan Shultz," the doctor proceeded to tell him, "Oh, you're Black?" and tried to joke about it. That is not what a young Black man wants to hear when he goes to the doctor. I can't help but wonder how many times my brother has gotten around the system by having a name that is stereotypically different from what they expect him to look like.

Understanding that technology is a reflection of its creators calls attention to the need for a thoughtful and inclusive approach to its development. Technology is not objective, and we must recognize it as a mirror of human values and societal structures. When using AI to tackle a problem among Black communities, subject matter experts within the community need to be called upon to participate in the developmental process from the beginning stages. It is usually at the end when the technology is already developed and launched, that community members are called upon to test the product, which will most likely not be deemed very useful. The lack of diversity in the teams developing these AI systems exacerbates the bias problem. Homogeneous teams may overlook or undervalue the importance of ensuring diverse and representative data, leading to the creation of biased AI systems.

2.2.1 THE NEED FOR INCLUSIVE AND ETHICAL DATASETS

Datasets are the foundation of how algorithms will be trained to develop AI technologies; however, most datasets used aren't inclusive of our diverse society. Creating inclusive and ethical datasets is a cornerstone of responsible AI development, yet it remains one of the most challenging aspects of the field. At its core, the concept of an ethical dataset is about more than just avoiding harmful biases; it's about ensuring that the data used to train AI systems reflects the diversity, complexity, and lived experiences of all people, particularly those from marginalized communities. In the past, datasets have often been constructed with little regard for the people they represent, leading to AI systems that perpetuate and exacerbate existing inequities.

One of the primary challenges in creating ethical datasets is addressing the deep-rooted biases that can be baked into the data itself. Historical data, which is often used to train AI systems, is rife with the prejudices of the past, reflecting societal inequalities in everything from housing to healthcare. When these biased datasets are used without critical examination, they can produce AI systems that replicate and amplify these injustices, disproportionately harming communities of color. The solution requires a fundamental shift in how we approach data collection and curation. It's not enough to simply gather more data; we must be intentional about the types of data we include, ensuring that they represent the full spectrum of human experiences and don't just tell the same mainstream or stereotypical stories.

Joy Boluomwini's research, while she was a doctoral student at MIT, found that facial recognition systems created by Amazon and Microsoft were less likely to perform well on people with darker skin tones as the algorithm was predominantly trained on images of lighter-skinned individuals (Buolamwini and Gebru, 2018). Additionally, healthcare algorithms that are not trained on diverse datasets may underdiagnose or misdiagnose conditions in minority populations, leading to disparities in health outcomes. Most common AI models are not explainable, thus you don't know how the algorithm predicts their results. If those models are utilized in healthcare settings where clinicians are unaware of which variables, such as genetics, race, or imaging datasets, were trained on the AI model, the predictions will likely be inaccurate. For example, race should not be considered because race is a social construct. However, there are decades of medical data that diagnoses based on race from which AI would deem it plausible to pull from.

2.3 DATA EXTRACTION AND EXPLOITATION OF BLACK COMMUNITIES

To create ethical datasets, we must prioritize the agency of those whose data is being collected, ensuring that they are fully informed and actively involved in the process. This means not only obtaining consent but also providing communities with the tools and knowledge they need to understand how their data will be used and giving them a voice in how it is managed and shared.

This shift also demands a greater emphasis on transparency and accountability in the data collection process. Too often, data is gathered from communities without their knowledge or consent, leading to a lack of trust and a sense of exploitation. For Black communities, this is particularly damaging, given the long history of data being used against them.

Black people who are descendants of American slavery have been extracted, manipulated, and surveilled for generations. In the 1840s, James Marion Sims mutilated the bodies of young enslaved Black women by performing genital surgery without anesthesia (Holland, 2017). He believed that Black people did not feel pain. He was pioneered as the father of modern gynecology and became president of the American Medical Association in 1876. Sims gained notoriety and recognition for performing invasive surgery on enslaved women without their consent. About a 100 years later, the U.S. federal government funded a 40-year experiment that allowed nearly 400 Black men to go untreated with syphilis (Nix, 2017). These Black men were sharecroppers who never had a doctor's visit. Researchers did not intervene to treat these men and only gave them placebos instead of the recommended treatment of penicillin, which left these men to fall to death or have severe health problems. The last study participant passed away in 2004, in which his trauma and institutional mistrust stayed with him and his family generations. Henrietta Lacks had her cells extracted from her body without her knowledge while she was being treated for cervical cancer (Skloot, 2017). Unlike other human cells, scientists tried to keep them alive, but they eventually died. Henrietta Lacks produced an entire generation every 24 hours, becoming the first immortal human cells ever grown in a laboratory. Her cells were pivotal in developing drugs to treat leukemia, influenza, sexually transmitted diseases, and other diseases and infections. These violations contribute to the mistrust that the Black community has with institutions within the United States. When the federal government and healthcare professionals that we rely on for care and acts of service can omit and manipulate research and collect data for experiments, it exacerbates the issue of now trusting these institutions not to replicate the same harmful acts with AI.

2.4 CONSIDERATIONS TO CREATE INCLUSIVE AND ETHICAL DATASETS

The creation of inclusive and ethical datasets must be seen as an ongoing process rather than a one-time effort. Data is not static; it evolves alongside society. As new patterns of behavior emerge and social norms shift, our datasets must be continually updated to reflect these changes. This requires a commitment to ongoing monitoring and evaluation, as well as the flexibility to adapt and revise datasets as needed. Let's start to view data as a living entity that changes with the times we live in.

However, creating these datasets is not just the responsibility of data scientists and technologists; it requires collaboration across disciplines and communities. Community leaders and members have a pivotal role in shaping how data is collected, curated, and used just as much as technologists. By bringing together diverse perspectives and expertise, we can develop more holistic approaches to data ethics that consider not only technical issues but also the broader social implications of AI. Their lived experiences offer invaluable insights into the ethical complexities that technologists may overlook. By incorporating voices from those most affected, we can shift the focus from purely technical solutions to more nuanced, socially conscious frameworks. Such collaborations pave the way for data ethics practices that account for cultural context, historical power dynamics, and the unique needs of underrepresented populations. When diverse perspectives and expertise converge, we not only build more equitable systems but also create a more just and inclusive AI landscape that serves society as a whole.

2.4.1   Building a WhatsApp Chatbot for Early Childhood Development in South African Communities

During my third year of graduate school, I had the chance to conduct international research in Cape Town, South Africa, with collaborators from the University of California, Irvine, and the University of Witwatersrand. Our goal was to understand the work processes and experiences of home visitors in early childhood development programs to develop and deploy a WhatsApp chatbot tool for social-emotional assessments. Our in-field research team was a blend of two South African researchers and two American researchers working in collaboration with a nonprofit organization that had established a home-visiting program for early childhood development. We spent two weeks facilitating focus groups with home visitors throughout four different low-income communities in Cape Town that aimed to thoroughly understand their job duties and requirements, community landscape, and challenges they experience day-to-day. Understanding the context in which they lived and worked in their community gave us researchers insights into considerations we need to think about when designing the WhatsApp chatbot.

We aimed to thoroughly grasp the technology they were currently using, its application within their environment, and any challenges they anticipated with the proposed tool. This approach was a prime example of engaging with the community to gather valuable insights before embarking on the development of a fully-fledged project designed for their use. Before any technology can be introduced, it's crucial to immerse oneself in the rhythm of this community, listening to the stories of its people. It's not just about gathering data; it's about understanding the heartbeat of the community and the everyday struggles and triumphs that define their lives. Only by grasping these unique needs and challenges can one begin to envision technology that will genuinely serve and uplift, rather than disrupt or alienate.

In some of the focus groups, there were several women who stood out as leaders and nurturers in their community. They shared their love of working with young children and why they love what they do so much. We reminisced on the generations of parenting styles, laughed a lot about some of the funny stories they had, and even closed out one of the focus groups in prayer that was said in IsiXhosa. These are the voices that carry the weight of wisdom, history, and an outlook to the future. Their perspectives become the compass that guides the development of technology, ensuring it aligns with the community's values and aspirations. Through their guidance, the project gained not just direction but also the trust and support of the community, which was a key finding in our data analysis. This collaborative process does more than create a product; it builds a sense of ownership and pride. The technology is not an external solution imposed upon them but a tool they helped to craft, one that resonates with their needs and aspirations.

Following the initial focus group discussions that guided the design of the WhatsApp chatbot, the study team's developers built it, and a six-month pilot test was conducted in which 75 home visitors assessed 434 children (Beltran et al., 2023). I traveled to South Africa in January 2024 to conduct additional focus groups in Cape Town, Johannesburg, and Gqeberha to discuss their experiences with the chatbot, refinement, and adaptations for preschools.

It's most important to note that when designing and implementing technology for communities, it is not enough to do collaborative research and leave them with the technology. There needs to be a framework for the technical solution to thrive long after the initial implementation. This has been a significant challenge that researchers struggle to be successful with. A sustainable plan should be mandatory for all community-based research that includes technology implementation. Researchers should invest in training community members to not only use the technology but also understand how it works. This could involve workshops, hands-on training, or creating accessible educational materials that empower community members to troubleshoot, maintain, and even modify the technology as needed. For the WhatsApp chatbot built, the early childhood development center principals and home visitors were trained on how to complete assessments through the chatbot, understanding the results, and best practices to share the results with the children's caregivers. This approach shifts ownership from the researchers to the community, ensuring that they are not dependent on external parties for future updates or problem-solving.

By building trust, facilitating open dialogue, and ensuring that community voices are centered throughout the process, we were able to create a WhatsApp chatbot that was both contextually relevant and practically useful for home visitors in early childhood development programs. This experience also highlighted the critical need for a sustainable plan that empowers communities to take ownership of the technology long after the researchers have left. Training and capacity-building are essential components of any community-based research involving technology. Without these elements, even the most well-intentioned technological solutions risk becoming obsolete or burdensome. Our work demonstrated that when the community is not just consulted but actively involved in the creation and maintenance of technology, the impact is deeper, more meaningful, and most importantly, lasting.

2.5   PROJECT ELEVATE BLACK VOICES

Project Elevate Black Voices is a collaboration between Google and Howard University to create a high-quality dataset of African-American Vernacular English (AAVE) in which I had the pleasure of leading between January 2024 and October 2024. Current speech recognition technology often struggles to understand AAVE and certain Black speech dialects, which puts Black users at a disadvantage from their own personal devices. As a result, it leaves Black people with accents and varying dialects to codewitch and exert more effort to use voice assistant technology. The large-scale data collection effort of Black speech dialects across the U.S. aims to improve speech technology for everyone and make it more inclusive of Black communities. All data collection efforts were performed by researchers at Howard University, and Google sponsored the project for access to the data in return to train on their technologies. Howard University owns all of the data and is currently working on creating an Historically Black College/University (HBCU) consortium where other HBCUs can have open access to the data for future research studies and innovation.

Another primary objective of the project is to establish a framework for responsible data collection when collecting high volumes of data from a marginalized community. The goal was to make sure that the data collected benefits Black communities and is used ethically. The principal investigator of the project, Dr. Gloria Washington, created fair AI usage guidelines for Google to adhere to when using the collected data to improve the technologies at their companies.

All participants understood the concept and why we were conducting this study, as most Americans across all age groups are familiar with or personally use voice assistant technology such as Siri, Alexa, or Google Home. However, some were skeptical and afraid that companies would have access to their data to use it for deepfakes and even clone them. Even with the skepticism, participants recognized the importance of improving the technologies they use every day because they were able to describe their own detailed pain points with the technology. Dr. Nias says strongly,

> We must consider that certain communities have a history of marginalization, and we must be mindful that AI doesn't exacerbate societal biases. But our concern should be tempered with the reality that exclusion from AI's benefits, due to fear, could be equally harmful to these communities' navigation of societal pathways.

As a human-centered AI researcher, I constantly grapple with the question, "Are we sure we're going about this the right way?" I wholeheartedly believe that Black people should be included in the development of future technology, and when it comes to AI, that means inclusive data. Institutions of power having Black people's data in their hands historically has never ended well. But the way the future is going, Black people will easily become excluded and further the usage and digital divide. Dr. Gloria Washington shares the same sentiments

> Everybody has good intentions at the start and I'm always speaking like, 'Oh my God, are we creating something that's going to steal people's money eventually or that is going to have a bad reputation from its usage of black people?' I am always in the back of my head, I'm thinking that and I'm always trying to think of ways to overcome that. The data sets that we're putting together and like any of the products that we're looking

to build are first developed with love. We need help to think through any unintended consequences and it's not just going to be us as the technologists and researchers to do it. We're going to need help from community activists and leaders.

When discussing technological innovation, our elders are often discussed in the light that they need help using technology, and they are more susceptible to scams, and not often discussed with calling on them for wisdom on how we should think about the development of technology. One of the Project Elevate Black Voices community recruitment events was held in New York City. As a native of the city, I invited my mom and the rest of my family to attend and see if they wanted to participate in the study. My mom, ever the community builder, extended the invitation to her church friends as well. The event primarily drew elders from the city, most of whom were 50 years old or older. Out of all the recruitment events we held, this group was by far the most enthusiastic. It was clear they felt valued and appreciated for contributing to the speech dataset. The conversations we shared that day were vibrant, especially when everyone started discussing their experiences with Alexa at home. It was fascinating to witness the connection they made between the study and their everyday lives. My mom later told me that during a prayer line with some of the church members who attended the event, one of whom referenced a question they had responded to during the study. They tied it into their prayers, turning what we had intended as a simple prompt into something deeply meaningful. We never anticipated that the fun, casual questions we asked to collect speech data would resonate so profoundly, becoming part of their personal testimonies on the weekly church prayer line.

Our community event that was held at Howard University was attended largely by the D.C. community and featured a panel of young Black Voices born and raised in the D.C. metro area who work in tech at their respective companies. They were asked to share their perspectives on Black culture's impact on technology, ways the tech industry can collaborate with local communities, and inclusive pathways to get more Black innovators and changemakers into the field of AI. Additionally, there was an open discussion about the challenges they experience with voice assistant technology where audience members expressed their challenges with Siri not understanding their D.C. accent. We also collaborated with Google on recruiting participants at the National Society of Black Engineers Conference at their career fair booth and hosted a community event in their San Francisco office where there were a mixture of Black Google employees and Bay Area natives having a candid conversation about their experiences with advocating for diverse perspectives to be heard in technology building. The community events really reinforced our primary objective—to elevate Black voices. This effort isn't just about collecting data; it's about creating spaces where people can connect, share, and learn from one another. I strongly advocate for community-based participatory research when developing technology for diverse groups, especially for cultures that are deeply communal. It is a necessity to create solutions that truly reflect and serve these communities (Figure 2.1).

We were successful in collecting nearly 1,000 hours of Black speech data from across the U.S., capturing regional dialects from Northern and Southern California, the Midwest, New Orleans, the South, and the Northeast. These regions represent areas with significant Black populations, and we were proud to include such a diverse range of voices. However, the project was not without its challenges, many of which

FIGURE 2.1   Community event at Google Office.

were difficult to foresee or prevent. One of the biggest hurdles was the administrative issues we faced at the university. We had planned to compensate participants with $599 in gift cards for completing all the questions over three weeks. However, we quickly discovered that the gift card option wasn't immediately available, forcing us to pivot to issuing checks. We were reluctant to go this route because it required us to collect additional personal information, such as participants' addresses, which raised concerns about privacy, especially since we were already collecting audio data. Nevertheless, we were committed to compensating participants as promised in the consent form, and participants were eager to receive their money. We ended up issuing checks to the first half of participants, but after the holidays, the study was put on hold, and it took considerable time to finally secure a platform called Tango to distribute the gift cards.

Even after securing the Tango platform, the challenges continued. Replenishing our Tango account with funds from the university took weeks, during which participants were repeatedly paid late, leading to understandable frustration. As a researcher who prioritizes ethical practices and the well-being of participants—especially Black and marginalized participants—this situation was extremely stressful. While we were transparent with participants about the delays, the reality is that when dealing with large sums of money in today's economy, people need their compensation on time. They were rightfully upset, and as much as we tried to explain the situation, what really mattered to them was getting paid as promised. Moving forward, projects of this magnitude require more thoughtful planning and scalability in the data collection process, including more in-person touchpoints with every participant to ensure transparency and to champion the importance of what we're doing.

Additionally, we need to streamline the administrative processes when partnering with universities, especially HBCUs, which are often under-resourced and understaffed at the administrative level. I recommend using a third-party service to handle financial transactions in collaboration with institutions like Google, which would alleviate some of the challenges we encountered. As we look to the future, we hope to continue collecting speech data from different dialects within the broader Black diaspora. This effort will not only improve technology but also contribute to a consortium for HBCUs to develop and enhance products that serve our communities, by us and for us.

2.5.1 Cultural Preservation of Black Stories

In many Black communities, the rich tradition of oral storytelling serves as a bridge between the past and the present, preserving history, culture, and identity across generations. Elders, with their vast reservoirs of knowledge and experience, will recount stories that share the struggles, joys, and resilience of them and their ancestors. However, as generations pass, there is a real concern that these invaluable narratives could be lost forever, taking with them the nuances and depth of their community's lived experiences. The challenge lies in finding effective ways to capture and preserve these stories in a manner that respects their authenticity, cultural significance, and privacy.

At the top of the hill and inside of Founders Library at Howard University, the Moorland-Spingarn Research Center (MSRC) stands as a formidable guardian of Black history, culture, and scholarship. It is one of the largest Black Archives globally. Its archives hold thousands of rare books, manuscripts, photographs, microfilm reels, and artifacts that chronicle the rich history of the African diaspora. In a world where the histories of Black people have often been marginalized, distorted, or erased, the Moorland-Spingarn Center serves as both a repository and a beacon, preserving the narratives that are vital to understanding the full scope of American and global history. The importance of this center cannot be overstated—it is a sanctuary for truth, where the voices of Black intellectuals, artists, activists, and everyday people are safeguarded against the erasure that has so often plagued them. In the careful preservation of these materials, the center not only honors the past but also empowers future generations to engage with their heritage in profound and transformative ways (Figure 2.2).

FIGURE 2.2   Founders library at the Mecca—Howard University.

Recently, the MSRC received a $2 million grant from the Jonathan Logan fam-
ily to support digitizing some of the Black archives for the preservation of physical
newspapers and microfilm reels. I had the pleasure of receiving a tour of the center
and being briefed on the work process they have to digitize the archive. During my
undergraduate years at Howard, I was familiar with the center and visited but had no
idea there were way more rooms and areas until now as faculty. I thought the small
section I saw a decade ago was the whole center, so my mind was blown seeing the
rows and rows of file cabinets that were filled with my history. My mind easily made
me think of my grandmother, who was born in Augusta, Georgia, in 1918. I used
to sit on her lap and ask her a berate of questions about her life growing up and the
things she saw in the South and after her migration to Harlem, New York.

They have way more to archive than money and manpower. The director of the
center explained how important it is to get everything digitized as quickly as they can
in fear of losing all of the rich physical assets in a natural disaster or fire. Also, this
information needs to be shared now more than ever, as we live in a time where Black
history education is under attack in certain U.S. states, and we now have the technical means to make information readily available online to everyone (Figure 2.3).

With data being the new currency to train AI models, venture capitalist companies and big corporations have reached out to MSRC, wanting to pay millions to have
access to the Black Archives to use for their own company's benefit. These companies recognize the MSRC is sitting on a gold mine with all of the data they possess
and some never before seen. However, these companies do not care that they will be
taking more from Howard University than the benefit that they claim we will receive.

FIGURE 2.3   Black archives at the Moorland-Spingarn Research Center.

Howard University should and needs to own 100% of the Black Archival data that will be digitized and any training and test dataset that is curated to train and refine AI models. HBCUs are underfunded and under-resourced, and any entity that doesn't want to complete ownership there is misaligned with preserving and uplifting Black communities.

Howard University has the best and brightest talent. Therefore, it is not a question of whether digitization, generating our own databases, and AI models are difficult. We don't have the money to put forth such a significant effort, which is something these firms are aware of and may want to exploit. Most Black people have heard a story of a family member selling land and property for money that would not last, and this is what companies believe they can do and we will accept.

As we entrust AI with the delicate task of preserving culture, we must confront the ethical dilemmas that accompany this responsibility. Who owns this data? Who decides what gets preserved and what is left behind? As AI collects and categorizes, it also wields the power to shape cultural narratives, to decide which stories are told and which voices are amplified. If these systems are not designed with care, it could easily perpetuate the very biases it seeks to dismantle, reinforcing rather than challenging the power structures that have long marginalized Black voices.

Project Elevate Black Voices can also be named as an example of cultural preservation through the question prompts we give participants to talk in their natural dialect. Dr. Gloria Washington explains,

> In a nutshell, we're already starting to capture the language of Black culture with Project Elevate Black Voices. We created an audio survey that individuals answer, where some of the questions specifically relate to Black culture. Such as what does Black Love mean to you and the food you eat on certain holidays. These are not only just everyday questions, but they allow Black people to kind of express their culture and like what makes them happy and what they're feeling. We had a conversation with people and asked them about the beauty of the language. We have gone to the Washington, D.C. area, Atlanta, Louisiana, New York, and California thus far, with many more cities to come. In all of these recruitment events, we talked about the beauty of the language. As a team, it's important that we make sure that the communities have a voice and are well compensated. Most companies take from these communities with little to nothing in return. We hope to be able to allow these communities to have a stake in these technologies, whether it be dividends, patents, or intellectual property.

The challenge, then, is to ensure that AI is not just a tool of preservation but one of empowerment. This means involving the community in every step of the process, from the initial design to the ongoing curation of digital archives. It means asking hard questions about consent, ownership, and representation and being willing to cede control to those whose culture is being preserved. In the hands of Black communities, AI has the potential to become a force for reclamation, a way to not only safeguard cultural heritage but to define it on their own terms. But this potential can only be realized if we approach AI with a deep sense of responsibility, humility, and respect for the people whose stories we seek to preserve. The technology may be new, but the principles guiding its use must be as old as the cultures it aims to protect: justice, equity, and the unwavering belief in the value of every voice.

2.5.2 Future Voices in AI

In the field of artificial intelligence, where the innovative possibilities seem boundless, Black innovators and changemakers are positioning themselves as key architects in the future of AI. It is not solely about representation in this pace but about leadership and vision. Black communities are no longer demanding a seat at the table but instead building their own. Our voices are essential because we bring unique perspectives that can challenge and enrich the current trajectory of AI. Despite the current harms and biases that AI has inflicted on Black communities, we are imagining new ways that AI could be leveraged for social good.

The key to unlocking this potential lies in collaboration. Researchers and technologists must abandon the extractive practices of the past—where data was taken from communities without context, leading to biased and harmful outcomes—and instead, work alongside these communities as partners. Together, they can build AI systems that are not only equitable but transformative. The communal nature of Black culture is central to this vision. Black people have always found strength in their relationships and environments, drawing on a deep sense of collective responsibility and interconnectedness. This ethos is crucial in the development of AI which reflects the diversity and complexity of the human experience. It is a reminder that technology should not be a tool of isolation or oppression but one of connection and empowerment. However, it is also important to recognize that Black communities are not a monolith. The lived experiences within these communities are as varied as they are rich, encompassing different backgrounds, aspirations, and challenges. Any AI initiative that fails to account for this diversity risks reinforcing the very biases it seeks to eliminate.

The thoughtless remarks made by New York Governor Kathy Hochul, stating that kids from the Bronx don't know what computers are (Ashford, 2024), highlight the persistent stereotypes that continue to undermine the achievements of Black people in technology. Such statements ignore the reality that there are individuals from these very neighborhoods who have not only mastered technology but have earned PhDs in the field. These technologists, like myself, are living proof that the potential for innovation and excellence exists everywhere, even in communities that have historically been marginalized and under-resourced. The danger of these stereotypes is that they can become self-fulfilling prophecies, deterring investment in education and infrastructure where it is needed most. But Black technologists are constantly proving that brilliance knows no geographical or racial boundaries.

In fact, at this very moment, there are countless Black individuals who are already doing the work in AI and technology, laying the groundwork for a future where their expertise is not just recognized but sought after. These pioneers are not waiting for permission to lead; they are already setting the pace and driving forward initiatives that prioritize ethical AI, community engagement, and social justice. Their efforts are creating ripples that will, in time, grow into waves of change across the industry. But for this movement to reach its full potential, it requires support from all corners—including corporations, governments, and academic institutions. These entities must learn to lean on the diverse expertise that Black technologists bring, understanding that the inclusion of these voices is not a favor but a critical component of innovation.

Moreover, as this work continues, it is crucial to cultivate environments where Black people can thrive in AI without having to constantly justify their presence. Too often, the burden of proof is placed on those who are already doing the work rather than on the systems that have historically excluded them. This needs to change.

The future of AI depends on the full participation of those who have been historically excluded from the tech industry. This means not only inviting Black technologists to the table but also ensuring they have the power to shape the agenda and make decisions that will impact the direction of AI.

AI has the potential to reshape every aspect of our lives—from how we work and communicate to how we address global challenges like climate change and the digital divide. However, without the input and leadership of diverse voices, there is a real risk that these technologies will only deepen the problems that already exist. The work being done today by Black technologists and community leaders is laying the foundation for a more just and equitable future where AI can be a tool for liberation rather than fueling oppression. This future can only be realized if the industry as a whole recognizes the value of these contributions and commits to supporting them in meaningful ways.

As we look to the future, the message is clear: Black people want to and should be at the forefront of AI innovation. The question now is whether the rest of the industry is ready to follow their lead, build together, and create a world where technology is a force for good in all communities.

REFERENCES

Alexander, M. (2011). The new Jim Crow. *Ohio State Journal of Criminal Law, 9*, 7.

Ashford, G. Hochul regrets saying some "black kids" don't know the word "computer." *The New York Times*, May 7, 2024. https://www.nytimes.com/2024/05/06/nyregion/hochul-black-kids-computer.html

Beltran, J. A., et al. (2023, October). Mazi Umntanakho "know your child": An accessible social-emotional assessment tool for children in low-income South African communities. *Adjunct Proceedings of the 2023 ACM International Joint Conference on Pervasive and Ubiquitous Computing & the 2023 ACM International Symposium on Wearable Computing* (pp. 30–34).

Benjamin, R. (2019). *Race after technology: Abolitionist tools for the new Jim code*. John Wiley & Sons.

Buolamwini, J., & Gebru, T. (2018, January). Gender shades: Intersectional accuracy disparities in commercial gender classification. *Conference on Fairness, Accountability and Transparency* (pp. 77–91). Proceedings of Machine Learning Research.

Holland, B. (2017, August 29). The "father of Modern Gynecology" performed shocking experiments on enslaved women. *History*. https://www.history.com/news/the-father-of-modern-gynecology-performed-shocking-experiments-on-slaves

Jelly-Schapiro, J. (2019, November 4). Learn how the burning of the Bronx led to the birth of hip-hop. *PBS*. https://www.pbs.org/independentlens/blog/how-the-burning-of-the-bronx-led-to-the-birth-of-hip-hop/#:~:text=And%20behold%3A%20the%20places%20where,that%20hip%2Dhop's%20phoenix%20rose

Kline, P. M., Rose, E. K., & Walters, C. R. (2024). A discrimination report card (No. w32313). National Bureau of Economic Research.

Nix, E. (2017, May 16). Tuskegee Experiment: The infamous syphilis study. *History*. https://www.history.com/news/the-infamous-40-year-tuskegee-study

Noble, S. U. (2018). Algorithms of oppression: How search engines reinforce racism. In *Algorithms of oppression*. New York University Press.

Skloot, R. (2017, April 22). Henrietta Lacks: How her cells became one of the most important medical tools in history. *History*. https://www.history.com/news/rebecca-skloot-on-the-immortal-life-of-henrietta-lacks

Sze, J. (2006). *Noxious New York: The racial politics of urban health and environmental justice*. MIT Press.

Tracy, M. A "virtual rapper" was fired. Questions about art and Tech remain. *The New York Times*, September 6, 2022. https://www.nytimes.com/2022/09/06/arts/music/fn-meka-virtual-ai-rap.html

Community Voices 2: Insights from Jaye Nias—Creating Inclusive AI Technologies That Serve Black Communities

Our second community voice comes by way of Jaye Nias, a Senior Research Faculty member with The Institute for Socially and Culturally Relevant Human-Centered Artificial Intelligence at Howard University. Dr. Nias's academic journey through historically black colleges and universities has shaped her unique perspective and dedication to ethical technology design.

Her scholarly work focuses on designing conversational user interfaces (CUIs) that prioritize user agency, cultural diversity, and responsibility. As the Director of the Brave IDEAS Lab, Dr. Nias leads research initiatives aimed at developing innovative solutions that promote social and cultural good. Her commitment to inclusive and ethical technological design is central to her career, addressing the unique challenges faced by marginalized populations.

Question 1: Share your professional bio

Dr. Jaye Nias is a Senior Research Faculty member with The Institute for Socially and Culturally Relevant Human-Centered Artificial Intelligence at Howard University (HCAI@Howard). Her remarkable journey through historically black colleges and universities, from undergraduate studies to post-doctoral work and finally to the professoriate, has shaped her unique perspective and dedication to her field. Dr. Nias's scholarly works center around designing CUIs that prioritize user agency, cultural diversity, and responsibility. By focusing on creating technology that respects and empowers users, she advocates for ethical practices that consider the broader social impact of technological advancements.

In her role as Director of the Brave IDEAS Lab, Dr. Nias has mentored students and led research initiatives to develop innovative solutions that promote social and cultural good. With a strong focus on inclusive and ethical technological design, she has devoted her career to addressing the unique challenges faced by marginalized populations and sensitive environments.

DOI: 10.1201/9781003517115-4

Question 2: Share your heritage and family traditions. Where did you grow up? Share a family tradition that you continue to this day

I grew up on the East Side of Buffalo, NY. My mom and Nana, who raised me throughout my life, were from the small Island of Bermuda but lived globally as the spouse and child of an Air Force soldier. I grew up with major holidays being a mixture of blood and community family, and I can best recall rotating holiday dinners being a staple in our family. And while the location would change, rarely did the menu or the closing game of spades deviate no matter where we were located. I have continued this tradition in our family to include many games at the end of our family gatherings but spades is a rite of passage that we will continue to pass down through our family.

Question 3: Experience with AI. Have you used AI technologies? If yes, please describe your experience. How do you perceive the role of AI in your professional or personal life?

Have you used AI technologies? If yes, please describe your experience. How do you perceive the role of AI in your professional or personal life? (answer in 100–200 words)

Yes, I use AI both passively and actively in my life. More recently, I have used generative AI intentionally for my work and hobbies, but I also understand that AI is embedded in many of the technologies that I've used for years, such as image recognition (CLEAR at the airport), predictive text, or voice assistants on my TV remote. I perceive AI as both a tool and a "master's tool" to quote Audré Lorde. And by "master's tool," I mean that AI, like many Western-developed technologies, uphold societal enactments of bias and discrimination. I've come to assume that it will not actively work to disrupt the status quo but instead just maintain current systems of power.

Question 4: AI and cultural preservation. Can you envision any innovative ways in which AI could be used to safeguard intangible cultural heritage, such as language, folksongs, or storytelling? Are there specific traditions, practices, or aspects of your culture that you believe could benefit from AI technology?

Yes, I believe that AI could intentionally uphold and safeguard cultural heritage. I am very invested in the idea that we can employ computational methods to preserve endangered mother tongue. Languages are not just a modality for communication but often are a vehicle by which cultural traditions, values, and wisdom are maintained and shared. Even greetings in many cultures give valuable insights into the values, social norms, and interpersonal dynamics of members of the communities to which they belong. Using AI to teach, inform, keep, or share language artifacts such as songs, proverbs, prayers, greetings, or fables can greatly contribute to preservation and revitalization efforts of linguistic cultural heritage on a global scale.

Question 5: AI and nature. Could you describe a traditional practice from your own culture, or one you've learned about or reported on, that helps in environmental sustainability or climate resilience? Also, how do you think AI could be utilized to support or improve this practice?

Our ecological cultures were deeply rooted in producing locally sourced, handmade goods, particularly food and clothing. Prior to the industrial era, our family traditions and expertise were steeped in the art of handcrafting and skilled craftsmanship. These cherished practices not only reflected our connection to the land and its resources but also allowed us to harmonize with the natural rhythms of the seasons. By embracing these traditional methods, we minimized our environmental impact, nurturing a sustainable way of life that demonstrated respect and preserved the delicate balance of nature.

Question 6: Wisdom of elders and AI. What role do elders play in preserving culture and wisdom in your community? With ethical practices at play, can AI play a role in capturing and disseminating this wisdom? If yes, how?

There is a saying, "When an elder dies, a library is burned to the ground." Elders in my community are often central to our family and community rituals. It is most often that our family comes together at holidays within the homes of one of our elders. It is there that our family recipes are shared and family stories are told around tables of food. For me, I was raised by a working single mom, so it was my elder that nurtured me after school and taught me to navigate roads both physically and metaphorically. My Nana would often share phrases like "don't take no wooden nickels." The elders of my family often modeled for me service to community and family as I watched her give of herself to many who were in need.

Question 7: AI and ethics. How important is it for AI systems to be developed ethically, especially in the context of cultural preservation? What steps would you like to be taken to ensure that, as AI expands, it represents diverse cultural perspectives?

Our society should place ethics at the center of everything we do—including AI systems. We should not be enamored only by the idea of the utility of the computational power of machines and lose sight of the humans, specifically the most vulnerable among us, who are most impacted by the consequences. In regards to culture, I think that inclusion is important. How can we expect AI to encapsulate a complete corpus of wisdom if it only draws from limited cultural reservoirs? It is very important that systems that employ such computational intelligence also include diverse and expansive perspectives.

Question 8: AI and personalization. We know that AI systems today don't understand the values and needs of diverse populations. Would you be willing to voluntarily share your family traditions and customs with your personal AI device to improve personalization?

That's a good question. I think it's challenging to teach customs and traditions outside of context. However, as AI becomes more ubiquitous, it will become more informed by the experiences it observes and participates in and ultimately learn more about customs and traditions over time.

Question 9: Future of AI in community development. What potential risks and benefits should be considered when integrating AI into community initiatives?

We must consider that certain communities have a history of marginalization, and we must be mindful that AI doesn't exacerbate societal biases. But our concern should be tempered with the reality that exclusion from AI's benefits, due to fear, could be equally harmful to these communities' navigation of societal pathways.

Question 10: Final thoughts. Is there anything else you would like to share about your views on AI and its role in preserving cultural heritage and traditions?

[no response]

***

COPY POST DR. JAYE NIAS SURVEY: Dr. Jaye Nias's survey responses offer an examination of AI's role in supporting cultural diversity and ethical practices. Her extensive experience in designing user interfaces that respect and empower users provides valuable insights into the responsible development of AI technologies.

3 The Role of AI in Language Preservation and Revitalization

Myles Ingram

My first experiences with language preservation and revitalization came during high school. I was choosing which language I wanted to do for my language credit, and I remember narrowing down the choices between Spanish and Latin. I vividly recall thinking that while a good portion of the world speaks Spanish and it would be pretty useful to learn because of that, Latin was much cooler to me.

I had an interest in classics, mythology, and Greco-Roman culture at an early age because of the movies I watched and I'm very glad I chose to go with the cooler option. I quickly became immersed in learning everything there was about Latin. I used to read Latin dictionaries and encyclopedias just to soak up as much knowledge as possible about the language. I even bought Latin joke books written in Latin to share with my friends.

The sheer amount of literature I found on Latin, ranging from ancient texts to modern studies, was staggering, and it made me wonder why it was considered a dead language in the first place. I soon learned that the Latin language "died" not because it disappeared entirely but because it gradually evolved into the Romance languages we know today, such as Spanish, Italian, and French.

As the Roman Empire expanded, Latin spread across vast regions, blending with local dialects and evolving over centuries. Eventually, these regional variations became distinct enough to be considered separate languages. Yet, despite this transformation, Latin never truly vanished; it remained alive in religious texts, legal systems, and scientific terminology. This made revitalizing the language a simpler task as compared to other languages.

The success of Latin being able to be taught and "revived" comes from two factors: (1) A large corpus of text. A large corpus is necessary for a language to be revived or revitalized authentically because it gives potential speakers a large amount of information to learn from, and it gives experts in the language a high level of confidence in interpreting the language and (2) A large number of people know about and want to learn the language. Latin is taught in most schools in the United States and forms the basis of a significant portion of the English language. Furthermore, Latin is widely known to help improve performance on standardized tests such as the SAT, further encouraging people to learn the language.

However, not all languages have such a success story. According to UNESCO, approximately 3,000 languages are in danger of completely disappearing within

DOI: 10.1201/9781003517115-5

the next century. This would mean the extinction of a language every two weeks (UNESCO, 2022). Language is more than just a tool for communication; it is the embodiment of a community's history, culture, and worldview, much like how Latin embodied the culture and worldview of the Roman Empire.

Each language encapsulates unique ways of thinking, expressions of identity, and shared memories that span generations. However, as globalization accelerates and dominant languages continue to spread, smaller, less widely spoken languages are at risk of vanishing. The loss of a language is not merely the loss of words; it is the erasure of cultural diversity, traditional knowledge, and the intellectual heritage of humanity. The preservation and revitalization of languages are therefore critical undertakings to maintain the rich history of human diversity. Yet, these efforts face significant challenges, ranging from resource limitations to the complexities of retaining linguistic authenticity.

Traditionally, language preservation and revitalization have relied on grassroots efforts led by linguists, cultural custodians, and community members. While these initiatives have made meaningful impacts, they are often resource-intensive, slow, and difficult to scale. However, recent advances in AI could be the key to overcoming these challenges.

AI, especially generative AI like ChatGPT, offers unprecedented capabilities for processing, analyzing, and generating language data at scale. From custom-built natural language processing (NLP) models tailored to specific languages to digital archives that safeguard oral traditions, AI holds the potential to transform language preservation and revitalization. According to Axios, ChatGPT now has over 200 million weekly active users, doubling its user base since November 2023. OpenAI's CEO, Sam Altman, noted that ChatGPT is becoming integral to daily routines, impacting sectors like healthcare and education (Axios, 2024).

To gain insight into how ChatGPT and similar AI tools are used for low-resource and endangered languages, I conducted interviews over three months with ten minority/endangered language individuals from different countries. This focus on minority languages offers a unique perspective, as AI presents both challenges and opportunities for these speakers. Through personal networks and connections on Upwork, I sought out these voices to understand how minority language speakers perceive the rise of AI.

In the interviews, I asked a series of questions designed to explore their experiences and perspectives on AI's role in promoting their languages. The questions covered various aspects such as how they first became aware of AI technologies being used for language promotion, their interactions with AI applications specifically designed for minority languages, and their opinions on the effectiveness of these tools.

We discussed the challenges and barriers they faced when using AI technologies for language revitalization as well as the impact these technologies have had on their communities. Also, we explore how AI can be improved to better respect and incorporate cultural aspects, its influence on education and learning, and its contributions to the preservation of their languages for future generations.

Finally, they shared personal stories and insights on innovative AI technologies that could further aid in the revitalization of minority and endangered languages.

TABLE 3.1
Table of Interviewees

Interviewee	Language(s)	Background	Country of Origin
Aitor Juaristi Díez	Basque	Freelance Technical Reports Writer	Spain
Kanstantsin Loichyts	West Polesian and Belarusian	Freelance Localization Project Manager	Georgia
Subhan Valiyev	Tat	Psychology Student at Süleyman Demirel Üniversitesi	Turkey
Alex Manuel Martínez Aguilera	Garifuna, Taushiro	AI Trainer at Outlier AI	Honduras
Oladeji Eunice	Yoruba	Freelance Data Entry Specialist	Nigeria
Nuria Samper	Catalan	High School Math & Science Teacher	Spain
Jack Weyen	Esperanto	Language Science and Technology Master's Student at Saarland University	United States
Jiefeng Kang	Southern Min	Freelance Data Scientist	China
Hacane Hech	Amazigh	AI Developer at Deutsches Forschungszentrum für Künstliche Intelligenz (DFKI)	Algeria
Rishu Kumar	Angika	Language Science and Technology Master's Student at Saarland University	India

Table of interviewees, the minority languages they spoke, their background, and their country of origin.

Table 3.1 is a list of the people I spoke with and what minority/endangered language they spoke.

These conversations were very eye-opening about other people's opinion on AI and how they believe AI may hurt or help their language. Some people highlighted the promise of AI tools like ChatGPT in their language, noting that AI can help promote their language to a wider audience. Others were more wary of the many challenges any AI conversational agent would have in speaking their language. These challenges include not representing the intricacies and culture of their language faithfully, not retaining natural-sounding expressions and missing the nuanced tonal elements essential to conveying meaning and cultural depth in the language. I found that these examples of challenges among others highlighted the critical role that community engagement and context-sensitive AI development play in effective language preservation.

Furthermore, the integration of AI into language preservation and revitalization efforts also raises ethical and practical questions. How do we ensure that AI tools respect and preserve cultural authenticity? Unlike Latin, some minority/endangered languages have not been well-documented and do not have a large corpus to pull from.

Can AI adequately capture the nuanced expressions, idiomatic phrases, and cultural contexts that give a language its true character even with a limited corpus? These challenges are particularly pressing in languages like Southern Min and West Polesian, which lack a formal written system and rely heavily on oral transmission. Addressing these concerns requires a community-centered approach that balances technological innovation with cultural sensitivity.

Interviews on other endangered and minority languages—including Basque, West Polesian, Tat, Garifuna, Taushiro, Yoruba, Catalan, Esperanto, Southern Min, Amazigh, and Angika—illustrate both the potentials and pitfalls of integrating AI into language preservation initiatives.

I will then transition to the related but distinct issue of reviving dead languages—those that have fallen entirely out of use and no longer have native speakers. Here, AI offers novel methodologies for linguistic reconstruction, digitization of historical records, and the creation of interactive learning environments. I discuss case studies such as the resurrection of Cornish using AI-generated learning materials, the Babylonian Engine's translation of Akkadian cuneiform, and efforts to make Latin more accessible through AI-powered conversational agents. However, these endeavors also raise critical questions about linguistic authenticity and the extent to which AI-generated content can or should influence the evolution of a language.

Beyond revitalization and revival, AI holds great promise for the future of language and linguistics. Advances in machine learning, deep learning, and large language models (LLMs) are enabling AI systems to understand and generate human language with increasing sophistication.

I'll also explore how these technologies can be deployed for applications like language learning, pronunciation improvement, and the gamification of language education. Yet, as AI's role expands, so do the ethical considerations. Issues such as community consent, cultural appropriation, data ownership, and the risk of homogenizing language practices must be addressed to ensure that AI-driven language projects are equitable and respectful of the communities they aim to serve.

3.1 REVITALIZATION AND PRESERVATION OF ENDANGERED/MINORITY LANGUAGES USING AI

AI models and tools like conversational agents and translation systems have already begun contributing to language revitalization initiatives. For example, tools such as Google Translate have incorporated a variety of lesser-spoken languages like Manx and Konkani, expanding their accessibility to wider audiences. Also, custom AI models designed specifically for minority or endangered languages allow for targeted language learning applications, digital archiving, and community engagement efforts.

AI has also been employed in innovative ways to fill in gaps where traditional language resources are scarce. For languages that have fewer speakers or lack sufficient educational resources, AI can help bridge the gap by generating content, offering translation services, and providing virtual learning environments.

Oladeji Eunice, a native Yoruba speaker, describes how AI has been beneficial for translating and explaining concepts in Yoruba. However, she also points out that AI struggles with the tonal complexity of the language, which is vital for maintaining its cultural and communicative integrity. As Oladeji explains,

> AI has been instrumental in translating and explaining concepts in Yoruba, but it still struggles with the tonal complexities that are crucial to our language's cultural and communicative integrity

> —*Oladeji Eunice (O. Eunice, personal interview, July 24, 2024)*

The use of AI tools for content generation, such as creating art, music, and literature, is becoming more common and more common as people experiment on how to best use AI. Platforms like Instagram and YouTube now have videos fully created using AI within their catalog. This use of AI for content generation has also made its way to the area of minority languages, such as Esperanto.

Esperanto is a growing constructed international language created to facilitate easy communication between people of different native tongues, promoting global understanding and harmony. In the case of Esperanto, AI tools have been particularly prolific because the community actively participates in creating and curating content.

However, Jack Weyen, an Esperanto speaker and computational linguist, expresses concern that while these technologies increase engagement, they risk diminishing the authenticity of the Esperanto language.

> LLMs don't fully capture the complexities of Esperanto yet and are still not the best tool, and other instances where AI is employed (art, music) is not really popular or highly regarded. However, AI tools have become "prolific" or, better, "pronounced" in the Esperanto community. Given how active the community is in generating content, the usage of new tools like AI for content creation is especially pronounced.

> —*Jack Weyen (J. Weyen, personal interview, August 3, 2024)*

AI models can be trained to better handle linguistic nuances, but this requires substantial input from speakers who understand the cultural and contextual subtleties that define a language. This highlights the significance of collaboration between technologists and linguistic communities in ensuring AI can effectively support language revitalization efforts.

While the promise of AI in language revitalization is significant, it is not without its challenges. Issues such as data scarcity, the risk of cultural appropriation, and maintaining the authenticity of language expressions are ongoing concerns. Traditional methods often rely heavily on the dedication of linguists, cultural organizations, and community members. However, the scale and urgency of language endangerment have created a pressing need for more scalable and technologically advanced solutions.

One of the key applications of AI in this context is the use of natural language processing (NLP) models to analyze and generate content in endangered languages. AI systems, particularly those designed for machine translation, are capable of rapidly processing large datasets, making them valuable for creating digital archives and educational resources. However, these technologies face significant obstacles when dealing with languages that lack a standardized writing system. Without a written form, it's challenging to create the textual data required for training NLP models. This issue is particularly evident in the case of Southern Min, a language that is primarily spoken and lacks a consistent character system. As Jiefang Kang, a Southern Min speaker, notes,

> I suppose the largest, the key comes from the language itself. For example, for English, for Chinese, for Japanese, we have a language. I mean, we can speak the language and we have the characters, but for a Southern Min language, we can speak southern language, Southern Min language, but we cannot, we cannot write it down because there's no character system for the language. And you see in our daily life, well, we actually, we heavily rely on our visualization. We read, we write, and we get information because we read and learn.
>
> So we open a browser, we read the books based on our visual system, right? We do not speak out. We do not listen to books. Sometimes we do. But we generally don't listen to a book because that's very slow. So that's our daily life. That's the information system of our daily life. But for Southern Min language, if you don't speak it, then you don't use the language at all.
>
> —*Jiefang Kang (J. Kang, personal interview, July 22, 2024)*

In the Basque-speaking community, there has been growing interest in how AI can support language revitalization efforts. Aitor Juaristi Díez describes how AI tools like ChatGPT have been applied to Basque, but the outputs, while grammatically correct, often feel stilted and unnatural.

> Yes, I have used ChatGPT for Basque. However, I think that it is and some years ago when you spoke with ChatGPT in Spanish. It was something like a robot and I think that in Basque now, it's still that robot because I think that it is trained with what by using it and as there are not too many people who use it within this language. It is not perfectly trained, And yes, I would say it's more like a robot than in any other language.
>
> —*Aitor Juaristi Diez (A. J. Diez, personal interview, July 15, 2024)*

Despite these limitations, there is optimism that AI can be fine-tuned to meet the needs of minority languages with more community involvement. Subhan Valiyev, a speaker of the endangered Tat language, emphasizes the importance of integrating native speakers' feedback to improve AI's effectiveness. He points out that while there are currently no AI tools specifically for Tat, tools like ChatGPT and Duolingo could provide much-needed visibility. Valiyev believes that increased exposure through AI could generate interest and preserve the language, which has been losing ground to Azerbaijani over the years.

> Although there are not any AI tools for the Tat language, I would love to try one. Any exposure for Tat would be great and AI could help my language not die
>
> —*Subhan Valiyev (S. Valiyev, personal interview, August 8, 2024)*

However, the challenges of using AI for the Tat language highlight the complexity of these preservation efforts. As Subhan points out, Tat faces a unique set of obstacles, such as limited linguistic resources and an overall decline in daily use, particularly among younger generations who have shifted toward Azerbaijani. The lack of AI tools specific to Tat, combined with its various dialects, makes creating effective language models difficult. This scarcity of support underscores the importance of community-focused AI initiatives tailored to Tat's unique linguistic and cultural landscape (S. Valiyev, personal interview, August 8, 2024).

LLMs, which require vast amounts of data to accurately capture and generate authentic linguistic content, are particularly hindered by these restrictions. Without open access to high-quality, diverse datasets, AI systems struggle to learn the rich cultural and linguistic nuances of Southern Min. This lack of data availability not only stifles the growth of AI tools in supporting endangered or underrepresented languages but also widens the gap between advanced AI technologies and the communities that could benefit most from them. Therefore, overcoming these institutional barriers is essential for unlocking the full potential of AI in language revitalization. By democratizing access to linguistic databases and encouraging collaboration between technologists, academic institutions, and local communities, LLMs can be trained on richer datasets, leading to more accurate and culturally sensitive AI applications.

Another significant challenge is retaining both cultural and grammatical authenticity in AI-generated content. Esperanto, though not a natural language, provides valuable insights into these challenges. Jack's experience with the Esperanto community highlights the limitations of content generation and corpus generation using LLMs through his experiences on Esperanto Instagram and YouTube. Esperanto's relatively large online presence compared to its speaker base, combined with its active community, presents a double-edged sword in terms of expanding the amount of Esperanto literature available.

> Esperanto which has, until now, boasted a rich heritage of literature and music, all crafted by passionate human speakers; for a language already suffering from the stigma of being 'artificial', the use of AI to generate content might reinforce that negative image, and undermine its hard-fought reputation.
>
> —*Jack Weyen (J. Weyen, personal interview, August 3, 2024)*

Because of this double-edged sword, the role of AI in the revitalization and preservation of endangered and minority languages must be collaborative. While AI can provide the scalability and efficiency needed to document and promote these languages, its success depends on meaningful engagement with the communities it aims to serve. By combining technological advancements with cultural expertise, AI can be used not just as a tool for preservation but as a bridge connecting traditional knowledge with modern technology, ensuring that the voices of endangered languages are not lost to time. While AI can serve as a powerful tool for resource creation and education, it must be carefully guided by those who understand the subtleties of the language and culture it seeks to preserve.

A prime example of this necessary collaboration is seen in the case of Angika, a language spoken in northeastern India. Rishu Kumar highlights the scarcity of written resources and digital data, which poses a significant challenge for AI model development and how researchers have overcome this issue. Researchers have begun translating Wikipedia entries into Angika and then manually verifying the content to ensure accuracy. While this initiative is promising, the lack of sufficient data for automatic speech recognition and machine translation remains a barrier. Custom models tailored to low-resource languages like Angika could help bridge this gap by generating high-quality linguistic data and enabling applications such as speech recognition and translation.

Similarly, Amazigh, a language spoken in North Africa, faces challenges due to the diversity of its dialects and the limited availability of standardized written texts. Hacane Hech, a native Amazigh speaker and AI researcher, suggests that training language models for Amazigh requires extensive data collection from native speakers. He envisions AI-powered chatbots that could facilitate language learning by providing interactive, contextually appropriate dialogues in different Amazigh dialects. These custom models would not only improve the accessibility of language resources but also address the linguistic diversity within the Amazigh-speaking community.

The creation of a comprehensive corpus is crucial for training AI models, as it serves as the foundation for understanding and generating content in a specific language. However, endangered languages often suffer from a lack of digital resources, making corpus generation a significant challenge. Collecting high-quality data requires collaboration between linguists, native speakers, and technologists, with a focus on preserving both the linguistic and cultural elements of the language.

For languages like Angika, which are primarily oral and have minimal written documentation, the process of building a corpus involves gathering spoken language data and developing transcription systems. Rishu explains that while there is some ongoing work to translate texts into Angika, the language's digital presence remains limited.

> The issue is that we don't have actually any data for that—yet, uh, other languages that I know something like Pochipuri we have a lot of data for that, so that's okay. Now, but for [Angika], we have like very little data or like non-existent data anymore.
>
> —*Rishu Kumar (R. Kumar, personal interview, July 18, 2024)*

Hacane discusses the importance of leveraging AI to generate content in the Amazigh language, including machine translation tools that can convert news articles and social media posts into Amazigh. He emphasizes that once a sufficient corpus is developed, AI can be used to create media channels that promote the language, making it more accessible to younger generations and diaspora communities. This approach not only strengthens the language's digital presence but also provides opportunities for cultural exchange and education.

The success of AI in language revitalization depends heavily on the involvement of native speakers throughout the development process. From data collection to model training and validation, native speakers play a critical role in ensuring that AI tools reflect the true character of their language. By engaging communities in these efforts, AI developers can create tools that are culturally sensitive, linguistically accurate, and tailored to the needs of the language's speakers.

This collaborative approach is exemplified in the case of Amazigh, where Hacane highlights the potential of AI-powered learning tools that allow native speakers to engage in interactive practice sessions. These tools could be enhanced by integrating feedback from native speakers, who can provide insights into dialectal variations and cultural nuances. The diversity of dialects brings up an interesting point of how to synthesize different dialects into an AI tool. For example, in the US, American English is the default language that most chatbots use but chatbots such as ChatGPT are able to speak rather well in British English. However, In this case, both dialects have an extensive corpus to pull from and train a model from. But how do we aggregate dialects of a minority language in a chatbot, especially when dialect information is scarce and there is no consensus dialect? Hacane ponders this question and states that the dialect that has the most media is the best one to train a model for a minority language on.

> For example, when it comes to the Amazigh language, there's no widely recognized standard dialect that everyone knows. The first challenge is deciding which dialect to use. You can't simply choose a standard version because no one is familiar with it—not even me. People only know the dialect spoken within their own small communities. In Amazigh, there are numerous dialects; even within Algeria, traveling just three hours from my hometown brings me to a place with a significantly different dialect. I might understand about 80% there, but if I go deeper into the desert where many Amazigh people live, I might comprehend less than 50%. It's like everyone is living in their own linguistic "bubbles." To establish a standard, you'd need a language spoken by a large number of people and supported by ample media content. So, the first challenge is determining which dialect to use. Probably the one with content because this generative AI technologies or LMS they need a lot of data to be trained to be able to start to speak

> —Hacane Hech (H. Hech, personal interview, July 28, 2024)

Community engagement is equally important in the context of Angika, where grassroots efforts are driving the digitization and preservation of the language. Rishu Kumar notes that involving native speakers in data annotation and verification is essential for building reliable AI models. By ensuring that community members are actively involved in the process, AI-driven language revitalization initiatives can better align with the cultural and linguistic values of the people they aim to serve.

Digital archives are a key component of language revitalization efforts, offering a platform to preserve and share linguistic data, oral histories, and cultural knowledge. AI can enhance these archives by enabling efficient data management, search capabilities, and content generation. However, the creation of effective digital archives requires careful planning, particularly when it comes to ensuring accessibility and cultural relevance.

In the Amazigh community, there is a growing interest in using AI to develop digital resources that document the language's oral traditions, celebrations, and historical knowledge. Hacane discusses the potential for AI-driven chatbots that can provide information about cultural practices, such as traditional celebrations, clothing, and cuisine. By integrating AI into digital archives, communities can create interactive platforms that preserve their cultural heritage while making it accessible to younger generations and those living in the diaspora.

AI offers a powerful set of tools for supporting language revitalization, but its success hinges on the integration of technology with community-driven approaches. Custom models, corpus generation, community engagement, and digital archives are all critical components of a comprehensive strategy for preserving endangered languages. By involving native speakers in the development process and prioritizing cultural sensitivity, AI can become a valuable ally in the fight to preserve linguistic diversity.

As these examples demonstrate, the potential for AI in language revitalization is vast, but it must be approached with care and collaboration. Through a combination of technological innovation and community empowerment, it is possible to create AI tools that not only preserve languages but also breathe new life into them for generations to come. This potential extends even further when we consider languages that have fallen entirely out of use.

3.2   REVIVAL OF DEAD LANGUAGES USING AI

The revival of dead languages, those that have fallen out of everyday use and no longer have native speakers, presents a unique set of challenges. Unlike endangered languages, which often retain living communities of speakers, dead languages require a process of linguistic reconstruction, cultural reintegration, and educational innovation to be brought back into use.

One of the fundamental obstacles in reviving dead languages is the difficulty of accurately reconstructing them. Linguistic records of dead languages are often incomplete, inconsistent, or heavily fragmented. AI can play a critical role in analyzing these records, identifying patterns, and filling in the gaps left by historical documentation. Through machine learning and natural language processing (NLP), AI models can be trained on existing texts and inscriptions to aid researchers in language reconstruction. While LLMs are not sophisticated enough to completely reconstruct a language in its cultural and grammatical entirety, it is capable of unearthing nuances and trends in the language that are not immediately obvious to researchers.

However, even this process is not without its limitations. Rishu points out that AI can struggle with generating truly authentic content when dealing with languages that have limited or highly archaic data sources, as the models rely heavily on the available corpora to produce accurate outputs.

In the case of Latin, for example, while it has a rich literary tradition, many nuances of everyday spoken Latin are lost to history. AI models have been used to analyze the grammar and lexicon found in texts ranging from classical literature to graffiti unearthed in archaeological sites like Pompeii and Herculaneum, offering reconstructions of conversational Latin that could be used in educational settings. However, although AI models may be able to understand the language, they may fail to grasp the culture and colloquial usage of the language. For instance, AI-generated phrases trying to recreate the graffiti might include *"Quid agis?"* ("How are you?") or *"Valeas bene?"* ("Are you doing well?"), aiming to mimic the informal language that might have been used in everyday Roman life. This contrasts with actual Latin graffiti found in historical sources which is much more humorous. For example, a graffiti inscription from Pompeii reads *"Fullones ululamque cano, non arma virumq(ue)"* ("I sing of dry-cleaners and the owl, not arms and the man"), providing a window into more personal and informal use of the language.

Despite these advancements, the authenticity of such AI reconstructions remains a point of debate among linguists, as the language's evolution after it ceased being widely spoken is difficult to fully capture. The scarcity of recorded colloquial speech means AI must rely on limited sources, making it challenging to generate truly authentic everyday Latin. This underscores the limitations AI faces when attempting to revive aspects of a language that lack extensive historical documentation, highlighting the importance of combining technological tools with scholarly research to achieve the most accurate results (Ancient Graffiti Project, n.d.).

One of the key strengths of AI in language revival is its ability to develop custom models tailored to the specific features of a dead language. These models can incorporate both linguistic rules and cultural contexts to generate content that aligns with the intended use of the language. For instance, in the revival of Cornish, an extinct Celtic language, researchers have used AI tools to generate learning materials, translate modern texts, and even compose new Cornish literature. The success of these efforts is partly due to the integration of AI models trained specifically on historical and contemporary Cornish sources, allowing for a nuanced understanding of the language's grammar and idiomatic expressions.

The Babylonian Engine, an AI model developed by Google DeepMind, has been instrumental in translating Akkadian cuneiform into English by analyzing over 70,000 ancient inscriptions. This model has uncovered valuable details about ancient Mesopotamian society, including records of commercial transactions, legal disputes, and even religious practices. For example, it has translated legal codes related to property and familial inheritance, shedding light on Babylonian law. Furthermore, the AI has been able to reconstruct phrases and expressions that reveal nuances in social hierarchy and relationships, such as expressions of respect for deities and monarchs. By handling the linguistic complexities and fragmented texts, the Babylonian Engine allows historians to explore into areas previously limited by incomplete translations, enriching our understanding of this ancient civilization (Decrypt, 2024).

The model not only translates but also plays a pivotal role in preserving ancient Akkadian culture by creating a digital database of cuneiform texts. This preservation effort is crucial for scholars and enthusiasts, as it offers ongoing access to rare historical documents. By analyzing patterns within the texts, the AI helps reconstruct cultural practices, such as the Babylonian emphasis on commerce, with detailed records of trade and transactions. The model also has uncovered religious practices embedded in these texts, providing insight into Babylonian spirituality and their views on gods and the afterlife. This process not only enriches the modern understanding of Mesopotamian civilization but also lays the groundwork for more advanced studies of other ancient languages and cultures. Through such innovations, AI becomes a bridge connecting modern scholarship with the ancient world, enabling new generations to engage with the cultural legacy of the Akkadians (Decrypt, 2024).

AI's ability to manage and process vast amounts of data makes it an invaluable tool for creating digital archives, which are crucial for the revival of dead languages. These archives serve as repositories of historical texts, recordings, and linguistic analyses, providing a foundation for both academic research and community-driven revival initiatives. In the case of Masakhane, an African NLP community focused on reviving languages across the continent, AI-powered digital platforms have been instrumental in curating and organizing linguistic resources, making them accessible to both scholars and the general public.

One of the challenges in reviving dead languages is adapting them to modern contexts. As languages are brought back into use, they need to expand to accommodate contemporary realities, including new technologies, social concepts, and globalized culture. AI can assist in this process by generating neologisms, adapting grammar rules, and translating modern content into the revived language. For example, AI models trained on reconstructed Cornish have been used to introduce new terms related to technology, environmental issues, and social media, allowing the language to evolve alongside contemporary society. However, this process raises important questions about linguistic purity and authenticity, as communities must decide how much innovation is acceptable without compromising the language's historical identity.

As AI becomes more involved in language revival, a critical concern emerges: at what point does the language being revived become a creation of AI rather than a continuation of its historical form? Over-reliance on AI-generated content risks introducing elements that were never part of the original language, potentially altering its grammar, vocabulary, and idiomatic expressions in ways that diverge from historical authenticity. This raises the issue of whether a language reconstructed heavily through AI assistance remains true to its roots or becomes a new, hybrid language shaped by machine learning algorithms. Communities and linguists must therefore carefully consider the extent to which AI should be used in the revival process, ensuring that while technology aids in filling the gaps, it does not overwrite the human essence and cultural heritage embedded in the language.

Despite these concerns, when used judiciously, AI can serve as a powerful ally in language revival by enhancing learning and engagement without compromising authenticity. One of the most exciting applications of AI in language revival is the development of conversational agents—AI-driven chatbots and virtual tutors designed to engage users in meaningful interactions in the revived language. These agents can simulate conversations, provide instant feedback, and adapt to the user's proficiency level, offering a flexible and accessible way to practice the language. In the case of Latin, AI-powered conversational agents have been integrated into educational platforms, allowing students to engage in dialogues that mimic ancient Roman settings.

Moreover, AI tools can help overcome the scarcity of fluent speakers in revived languages by offering consistent, high-quality practice opportunities. For languages like Ainu and Cornish, where native speakers are either few or non-existent, these agents provide learners with the opportunity to practice in a controlled environment, reducing the burden on the limited number of fluent speakers who are often responsible for teaching the language. However, as Juaristi Díez notes, the effectiveness of these agents is contingent on their ability to move beyond formulaic responses and engage in natural, culturally nuanced interactions.

The revival of dead languages using AI is an ambitious yet achievable goal. While challenges remain in terms of linguistic reconstruction, data availability, and ensuring cultural authenticity, AI offers powerful tools that can bridge these gaps.

From custom models and digital archives to conversational agents and language expansion initiatives, AI is transforming the possibilities for bringing languages back from the brink of extinction. However, for these efforts to be successful, they must be guided by the communities whose heritage these languages represent. By combining technological innovation with deep cultural respect and community collaboration, we can create a future where even long-lost languages can find new life in the modern world.

3.3 CHALLENGES IN LANGUAGE REVITALIZATION

For endangered and minority languages, the stakes are especially high; each challenge represents a potential obstacle to the survival of not just the language itself but the cultural knowledge, history, and identity it represents.

As mentioned several times throughout this chapter, one of the most significant challenges in language revitalization is the lack of resources. Financial constraints, particularly in marginalized and remote communities, often impede the production of teaching materials, the development of language learning programs, and access to technology. Even when AI is introduced as a solution, the cost of developing custom models, collecting data, and maintaining technological infrastructure can be prohibitively high. In many cases, communities that could benefit most from AI-driven revitalization tools are those least equipped to implement them.

This problem is further compounded by the scarcity of linguistic data needed to train AI models. For widely spoken languages, there are extensive corpora of text and audio available to feed into machine learning algorithms. However, for endangered languages, especially those with few speakers or limited written records, the amount of available data is often insufficient, as seen in Kanstantsin Loichyts' experience with Belarusian and West Polesian. Loichyts notes that despite his efforts, limited standardized resources make it challenging for AI to support these languages effectively. In particular, the lack of a unified writing system and low levels of digital literacy within communities further complicate AI integration, as there are fewer texts and resources available for training language models. Political and cultural factors also play a significant role, as Belarusian, for example, often competes with Russian for visibility and recognition, leading to lower prioritization in AI language tools. This scarcity of accessible linguistic data, combined with socio-political barriers, underscores the unique challenges faced by smaller languages in the AI space, where dominant languages often overshadow lesser-known dialects and languages. The neighboring dominant languages have been known to even overshadow both Belarusian and West Polesian in conversational agents such as ChatGPT.

> AI is not quite friendly to most of the minority or indigenous languages that I know of at least for example ChatGPT mixes Belarusian and West Polesian up with the neighboring languages such as Russian and Ukrainian and even Polish which has a completely different writing system we use Cyrillic.
>
> —*Kanstantsin Loichyt (K. Loichyts, personal interview, August 21, 2024)*

Furthermore, Loichyts points out that existing AI tools, like DeepL, often misidentify minority languages, mistaking West Polesian for similar languages like Russian or Ukrainian. This misidentification problem highlights a significant limitation in current AI models, which tend to perform well with dominant languages but struggle with nuances in minority ones. He emphasizes that for languages like West Polesian to thrive in the AI age, greater efforts are needed to codify and digitize linguistic resources, as well as to develop models that recognize linguistic diversity. Ultimately, without increased investment in data collection and model development specific to these languages, AI risks reinforcing linguistic homogenization rather than fostering diversity and inclusion in the digital age.

The diminishing number of native speakers presents another formidable barrier to language revitalization. Globalization, urbanization, and shifting cultural values have contributed to the erosion of many smaller languages as younger generations increasingly adopt more dominant languages like English, Spanish, or Mandarin. The gradual disappearance of native speakers leads to a loss of traditional knowledge, idiomatic expressions, and cultural practices tied to the language. Without a critical mass of fluent speakers, it becomes difficult to sustain the language within the community, let alone pass it on to future generations.

AI-driven solutions can sometimes exacerbate this issue by reinforcing dominant language practices. For example, when AI tools prioritize majority languages for efficiency, they inadvertently marginalize minority languages even further. In the case of Southern Min, Kang notes that AI technologies primarily focus on Mandarin, making it difficult for Southern Min speakers to access technology in their own language. This imbalance not only hinders revitalization efforts but also risks homogenizing cultural expressions by favoring languages with larger digital footprints.

Educational challenges are a critical aspect of language revitalization efforts. The absence of trained teachers, a lack of structured curricula, and limited integration of minority languages into formal education systems create significant barriers to passing on linguistic knowledge. In many communities, language instruction is relegated to informal settings, relying on family members or community elders who may lack the resources or time to teach comprehensively. Also, younger generations often show less interest in learning the language, seeing it as less relevant in a globalized world.

For languages like Catalan, where there is a formal educational structure, the challenge is different. As Nuria explains, while Catalan is taught in schools, the language often struggles to maintain relevance outside of formal educational settings. Students might learn the language in class but default to using Spanish or English in social settings or online interactions, leading to a gradual erosion of the language's use in everyday life:

> I'm in a school and they all already speak Catalan they didn't use it as much sometimes the newcomers, as we call them, We have few kids from Ukraine that came two years ago and then they kind of use it to translate exams or just to give you information they want to give you but not to learn usually. People who come to Catalonia, they tend to learn Spanish instead of Catalan

> —*Nuria Samper (N. Samper, personal interview, August 19, 2024)*

AI tools, though potentially helpful in language learning, require significant fine-tuning to produce outputs that feel natural and engaging, particularly for younger users.

Moreover, a common challenge in applying AI to language revitalization is the disconnect between technologists and the communities they aim to assist. As Rishu observes,

> People get into the tech pro mentality where they're like, 'Oh, we can do this with that, oh, we could use AI for this,' but they're just spitballing ideas and they never think to ask the small minority community, 'What do you need AI to do for you?'

> —*(R. Kumar, personal interview, July 18, 2024)*

This lack of collaboration can lead to solutions that are technologically impressive but culturally irrelevant or ineffective in addressing the actual needs of the language speakers. Without meaningful engagement, AI tools risk failing to capture the nuances and lived experiences that are crucial for genuine language preservation.

In addition to the question of cultural authenticity, there is the question of ownership. Ownership becomes a pivotal concern when leveraging AI for language revitalization, as it touches upon who controls the linguistic data and how it's used. Languages, especially those of minority or marginalized communities, are deeply tied to the identity and heritage of their speakers. When AI technologies are employed to preserve or teach these languages, there's a risk that the control over linguistic resources shifts away from the community to external entities, such as tech companies or academic institutions. This can lead to misrepresentation or misuse of the language, further eroding its cultural essence. Therefore, it's imperative that AI-driven language preservation efforts involve and empower the native speaker communities, ensuring they retain ownership and authority over their linguistic heritage. By doing so, we not only maintain the cultural authenticity of the language but also respect the rights and contributions of those to whom the language truly belongs.

For example, Esperanto's struggle with translation accuracy highlights the difficulty in maintaining linguistic and cultural authenticity in AI-generated content. Jack Weyen points out that while AI can generate grammatically correct Esperanto, it often misses the subtle contextual and cultural cues that give the language its true character. This raises a critical concern: imagine if a language is revitalized primarily through a subpar AI model that preserves only 50% of its idioms, special phrasing, and other nuances. If content generated by this flawed model constitutes 90% of the written material in that language, new speakers might emulate the AI's incomplete style, inadvertently losing half of the unique qualities that make the language distinctive. In this scenario, the ability to shape and preserve the language's authenticity is effectively transferred from human speakers to the AI model and the company that owns it. This issue is not unique to Esperanto but is a broader concern for any language undergoing revitalization through AI.

In Catalan, where AI-generated outputs can feel unnatural or stilted, the challenge lies in refining models to better align with the way the language is used in different contexts. Nuria explains that while AI tools are improving, they still require substantial input from native speakers to produce content that resonates culturally and linguistically. This highlights a key aspect of language revitalization through AI: the technology must be guided by those who deeply understand the language and its cultural context.

While these challenges are significant, they are not insurmountable. The key to successful language revitalization lies in combining AI's capabilities with community-driven efforts. AI can provide scalability and efficiency, but it requires collaboration with native speakers, cultural experts, and linguists to ensure that the tools developed are accurate, culturally sensitive, and truly beneficial. As these communities become more involved in the data collection and model training processes, the resulting AI tools can better reflect the language's authentic usage, improving both the quality and acceptance of AI-generated content.

Moreover, initiatives that focus on creating open-access resources, such as digital archives and corpora, can help address the resource gap. Making these resources available to both AI developers and language communities ensures that revitalization efforts are not only technologically sound but also equitable and inclusive.

The challenges related to language revitalization are multifaceted, involving resource limitations, cultural shifts, educational barriers, and the difficulty of preserving authenticity in AI-driven solutions. However, with the right combination of technology, community engagement, and cultural sensitivity, AI has the potential to become a powerful ally in the fight to preserve the world's endangered languages. By addressing these challenges head-on and fostering collaborative partnerships, the future of language revitalization can be one where technology and tradition work hand in hand to keep linguistic diversity alive for generations to come. However, to ensure that technology and tradition can work hand in hand, it is essential to address the ethical considerations that arise when integrating AI into language revitalization efforts.

3.4 ETHICS OF LANGUAGE REVITALIZATION, PRESERVATION, AND REVIVAL

As AI technology becomes more advanced, its role in language preservation and revitalization efforts has expanded, offering both opportunities and risks. This section explores these ethical considerations, drawing insights from conversations with Alex Manuel Alex Manuel, who works in minority language documentation, and Aitor.

One of the foundational principles in ethical language revitalization is securing informed consent and ensuring active participation from the communities involved. Alex stressed this by sharing a picture (Figure 3.1) with me that was generated by AI for one of the tribes he was working with.

> The prompt I used was - 'This house was crafted from compacted air and roof truss with straw Apache individual peaceful Slumbers, the things glove of a preaching plant cashed childrens, then they danced upon the Earth thing was Illuminating the Simplicity of the apples.' This is the result and what happens here is that the minority people in this case don't use electricity to illuminate their houses. They use electricity to charge their cell phones, computers or something like that, but they don't use electricity for Illuminating the houses.

> —*Alex Manuel Martínez Aguilera (A. M. Martínez*
> *Aguilera, personal interview, August 21, 2024)*

FIGURE 3.1   Apache dwelling generated by AI.

This example illustrates what can happen when a minority tribe is not consulted on an AI project, even on a smaller scale. If such misrepresentations occur on a larger scale, the entire culture of the Apache tribe could be inaccurately portrayed due to an inauthentic AI model. This example underscores that while AI tools can be useful for generating content or automating transcription, they cannot replace the cultural knowledge and context that community members provide.

Aitor recounts his own experience participating in an AI training program, where he and two friends recorded conversations in Spanish to help improve the model's ability to understand natural dialogue. He suggests that similar approaches could be applied to Basque, involving native speakers in the creation of culturally accurate datasets. However, he also notes that many people in his community are unaware of such opportunities, which presents a barrier to meaningful engagement. This highlights the importance of outreach and education in ensuring that communities not only consent to but actively participate in AI-driven language revitalization projects.

AI projects in language preservation must be cautious to avoid cultural appropriation and exploitation. Minority languages carry not just words but deeply embedded cultural values, histories, and worldviews. Alex Manuel warns that if AI systems are not developed in close collaboration with the communities whose languages they aim to preserve, they risk commodifying cultural knowledge without providing any tangible benefits to the community. This concern is particularly relevant in cases where commercial entities drive AI development, potentially profiting from the use of minority languages while offering little in return to the people who speak them.

Aitor touches on a related issue when discussing the use of AI for Basque. While he is optimistic about AI's potential to preserve and promote the language, he notes that Basque is often treated as an afterthought in broader AI development projects, leading to subpar results that fail to capture the language's nuances. For example, Aitor mentions that when he tried using ChatGPT in Basque, the responses felt robotic and lacked the natural flow of conversation, largely because the language data used to train the model was limited. This points to the broader issue of how AI models are trained and who controls the data, raising questions about representation and fairness.

Ensuring the accuracy and cultural authenticity of AI-generated content is another critical ethical challenge. These systems often learn from data that contain existing biases and misrepresentations. If the training datasets include stereotypical portrayals, outdated notions, or biased perspectives—whether due to historical documentation or skewed contemporary sources—the AI models may inadvertently reinforce these inaccuracies in their outputs. This is particularly concerning for minority and endangered languages, where limited data availability might cause AI to overgeneralize or misinterpret cultural nuances. Without careful oversight and the inclusion of diverse, representative data, AI-generated content risks propagating misconceptions, thus harming the very communities it aims to support. It underscores the necessity for collaboration with native speakers and cultural experts to ensure that AI tools not only avoid perpetuating stereotypes but actively promote authentic and respectful representations of the language and its associated culture.

Alex Manuel emphasizes that minority languages are more than just linguistic codes; they are living expressions of culture, where even subtle shifts in meaning can have significant implications. This makes it essential that AI-generated content be reviewed and validated by native speakers before being disseminated or used for educational purposes.

The question of who owns and controls language data is central to the ethical use of AI in language preservation. Minority communities often view their languages as collective cultural property, meaning that decisions about how language data is used must be made collectively and transparently. Alex Manuel advocates for models of collaboration where communities retain ownership of their language data, deciding how it is stored, accessed, and applied in AI systems. This approach not only protects the rights of the community but also ensures that AI projects are aligned with their cultural values and goals. Involving the community in every step—from data collection to content generation—not only addresses ethical concerns but also enhances the effectiveness of language revitalization efforts. By retaining control over their linguistic resources, communities can prevent cultural misappropriation and ensure that AI-generated content reflects their authentic voice.

Aitor shares a similar perspective, emphasizing the need for transparency in how AI systems are trained and developed. He explains that many Basque speakers would be willing to contribute their voices or linguistic knowledge to AI projects if they knew more about how the data would be used and who would benefit from it. However, the lack of clear communication and transparency often leads to hesitation or disengagement from such initiatives. For AI-driven language projects to succeed ethically, they must prioritize open communication and give communities control over their linguistic resources.

While AI offers significant potential in language revitalization, it is important to view it as a complement to, rather than a replacement for, traditional methods of cultural and linguistic preservation. Alex Manuel points out that AI cannot replicate the cultural depth and communal practices that are central to how languages are traditionally passed down. For instance, teaching a language often involves more than just conveying vocabulary and grammar; it includes storytelling, rituals, and communal activities that AI is not equipped to replicate. Aitor Juaristi Díez echoes this sentiment, suggesting that AI tools could be most effective when integrated into playful or interactive learning environments, such as educational games that make language learning enjoyable for children.

By framing AI as a supportive tool, rather than the primary method of revitalization, communities can leverage its strengths—such as scalability and efficiency—while maintaining control over how their languages are taught and preserved. This balanced approach ensures that technology enhances, rather than diminishes, the cultural and social dimensions of language revitalization.

The ethical considerations surrounding the use of AI in language revitalization, preservation, and revival are complex and multifaceted. Ensuring community consent, preventing cultural appropriation, maintaining accuracy, and safeguarding data ownership are essential to creating AI tools that are both effective and respectful. By centering the voices of the communities involved and fostering genuine partnerships, AI can be a powerful ally in the preservation of linguistic diversity, contributing to a future where even the most endangered languages have a chance to thrive.

3.5 CASE STUDIES OF LANGUAGE REVITALIZATION

Efforts to revitalize endangered and minority languages have taken many forms, from community-led initiatives to cutting-edge AI applications. Below are several case studies that illustrate how AI is being integrated into language revitalization projects across the globe. These examples showcase the diverse strategies being employed to preserve languages that are at risk of extinction.

In Iceland, Þorsteinsson, a linguist and AI researcher, has been leveraging GPT-4 to support the preservation of Icelandic, a language spoken by fewer than 400,000 people. Icelandic has remained remarkably close to its Old Norse roots, but the rise of global languages like English poses a threat to its long-term viability. To address this challenge, Þorsteinsson developed a project that uses GPT-4 to generate Icelandic content that is contextually rich and culturally relevant. The model is trained on a diverse dataset that includes Icelandic literature, news articles, and oral traditions and enhanced using reinforcement learning from human feedback, allowing it to comment on images, summarize texts and even pass the bar exam. Although the model is prone to hallucinations and grammatical errors, Þorsteinsson and his team are optimistic that their work will lead to a model that will be capable of "the most complex and creative applications in Icelandic, rather than defaulting to English" (Iceland Review, 2023).

The Endangered Language Alliance (ELA) in New York City is an organization dedicated to preserving the linguistic diversity of the city, which is home to speakers of hundreds of languages, many of them endangered. One of their key initiatives focuses on revitalizing Lenape, a language of the Lenape people, native to the Northeastern United States. With fewer than a handful of fluent speakers remaining, Lenape is critically endangered.

ELA has partnered with AI researchers to develop tools that can assist in language learning and documentation. Using machine learning models, the project has focused on creating a digital archive of Lenape, including recorded stories, songs, and cultural narratives. These recordings are used to train AI models that can generate Lenape text and audio, providing resources for both language learners and cultural preservationists. The AI-generated content is reviewed and refined by Lenape elders and linguists to ensure cultural and linguistic accuracy. This collaboration between technology and tradition offers a promising model for how AI can be used to breathe new life into languages that are on the brink of extinction (Endangered Language Alliance, n.d.).

In New Zealand, Te Hiku Media, a Maori-owned media organization, has developed a pioneering AI model aimed at preserving and revitalizing the Maori language. The organization's goal is to ensure that Maori remains a living language in the face of increasing globalization and the dominance of English. Te Hiku has focused on creating an AI-powered speech recognition and language processing tool tailored specifically for the Maori language.

The project began with extensive data collection efforts, including interviews, historical recordings, and traditional songs. These data were used to train the AI model, which is designed to support both conversational Maori and more formal uses of the language, such as in educational and government contexts. The AI model assists in creating learning resources, translating content, and even generating interactive language tools that can be used in schools and homes. By ensuring that the model is aligned with the cultural values and linguistic nuances of Maori, Te Hiku's initiative highlights the importance of integrating community engagement and technology to achieve sustainable language revitalization (Te Hiku Media, n.d.).

FirstVoices is a digital platform based in Canada that focuses on preserving and revitalizing minority languages spoken across the country. The project is managed by the First Peoples' Cultural Council, an minority-led organization that supports cultural and linguistic initiatives for First Nations communities. FirstVoices offers an online archive where communities can create and manage their language resources, including dictionaries, audio recordings, and educational tools.

The platform has integrated AI-driven tools to enhance the accessibility and usability of these resources. For example, speech recognition technology is employed to transcribe spoken words and phrases into text, making it easier to document and share language content. AI models also are used to analyze linguistic patterns and create learning modules tailored to different proficiency levels. This approach ensures that the language resources are not only preserved but also adapted to meet the educational needs of both young learners and fluent speakers.

The success of the FirstVoices project lies in its collaborative approach, which prioritizes community ownership and control over the language data. By using AI to complement traditional language preservation methods, FirstVoices serves as a model for how technology can be respectfully integrated into minority language revitalization efforts (FirstVoices, n.d.).

Efforts to revive the Ainu language have made remarkable strides with AI-driven tools like AI Pirika, developed with Hokkaido University and the Society for Academic Research of Ainu Culture. Launched in 2019, AI Pirika uses chatbots and speech recognition to create an interactive experience that helps preserve Ainu's oral tradition. It adapts through user feedback, refining linguistic accuracy and producing dialogues that reflect the language's authentic sounds and nuances.

In addition to language preservation, AI Pirika aims to revitalize the Ainu language by making it a part of daily life for younger generations. This technology fosters a sense of cultural pride among Ainu youth by enabling them to learn and use their heritage language through interactive, AI-driven conversations. AI Pirika also emphasizes community participation, allowing native speakers and Ainu scholars to provide feedback on vocabulary and pronunciation, enhancing the system's accuracy. This approach not only supports linguistic revitalization but also strengthens cultural connections within the Ainu community, helping to ensure the language remains vibrant for future generations (Stanford Rewired, n.d.).

These case studies demonstrate the significant strides being made in leveraging AI to support language revitalization efforts across the globe. They illustrate how technology, when thoughtfully integrated with community engagement and cultural sensitivity, can play a pivotal role in preserving languages at risk of extinction. Building on these successes, it's important to look ahead and consider how AI might continue to evolve to meet the needs of endangered and minority languages.

3.6   FUTURE APPLICATIONS OF AI IN
LANGUAGE AND LINGUISTICS

In this section, I explore the future applications of AI in linguistics and language preservation, drawing insights from conversations with speakers and advocates of endangered languages.

The ability of AI systems to process and comprehend languages has grown significantly due to advancements in machine learning, particularly in deep learning models and transformers. These technologies are central to building better natural language processing (NLP) systems that can analyze complex linguistic structures, generate natural-sounding text, and even adapt to the cultural contexts embedded within a language.

For instance, speakers of languages like Amazigh and Tat have pointed out that AI-driven tools could play a significant role in creating accessible language resources. Hacane notes that AI models designed specifically for low-resource languages could help automate tasks such as grammar instruction and conversational practice. These models would need to be trained on culturally relevant data to ensure they capture the linguistic nuances unique to the language.

One of the most promising applications of AI in language revitalization is the development of conversational agents or chatbots that can simulate interactions with fluent speakers. Such tools are particularly valuable for languages with a declining number of native speakers or those that are geographically dispersed. For example, Rishu Kumar discusses how AI-driven bots can provide consistent, non-judgmental language practice, allowing learners to engage in conversations without the pressure of burdening native speakers. Similarly, Jack used chatbots to practice Esperanto, a diaspora language where finding speakers often means reaching out to strangers—an intimidating prospect. These bots could be further refined to adapt to the user's proficiency level, offering targeted corrections and personalized feedback.

In addition, the potential for using speech recognition and synthesis technologies in these conversational agents is crucial for preserving oral traditions. As generative AI models become more sophisticated, they can mimic not only the vocabulary and grammar of a language but also its phonetic patterns, enabling users to practice pronunciation in a way that aligns with traditional speech forms.

The integration of AI into language learning platforms has already transformed how people approach acquiring new languages. Future applications will likely see more sophisticated AI-driven language learning apps that incorporate gamification elements to make learning more engaging. For instance, adaptive learning algorithms can assess a learner's progress and adjust content to target areas of weakness, making the learning experience more personalized and efficient.

The Maori Speech AI model developed by Te Hiku Media is an excellent example of how AI can be used to make language learning accessible. The model combines speech recognition and gamified learning modules to help users practice Maori in a culturally respectful and interactive environment. Such innovations are crucial for ensuring that endangered languages are passed on to younger generations in a way that resonates with their digital habits.

While the benefits of AI in language revitalization are substantial, there are also critical ethical concerns that must be addressed. AI systems, if not carefully designed, risk introducing inaccuracies or culturally inappropriate representations of a language. Rishu Kumar points out that in some cases, AI technologies may inadvertently push users toward more dominant languages like Hindi or English, particularly in contexts where the linguistic resources for minority languages are limited. This highlights the importance of committing resources to minority languages in AI research.

Moving forward, it will be essential to involve native speakers and cultural custodians in the development process, ensuring that AI systems are not only technically proficient but also aligned with the community's values. Transparent methodologies, open data sharing, and continuous community engagement are key strategies for addressing these challenges.

As AI continues to advance, its applications in linguistics and language preservation are expanding rapidly. From machine learning-driven language comprehension to AI-powered conversational agents and digital archives, the possibilities are vast. However, the success of these initiatives will depend on a careful balance between technological innovation and cultural sensitivity. By fostering collaborations between AI developers, linguists, and communities, the future of language preservation could be one where endangered languages not only survive but thrive in the digital age.

3.7 CONCLUSION

As the global linguistic space continues to evolve, the preservation, revitalization, and revival of endangered and minority languages have become increasingly urgent. These languages are not merely tools for communication; they are vessels of cultural identity, historical memory, and community values. However, as globalization accelerates and dominant languages gain prominence, the survival of these linguistic treasures faces significant challenges. I have explored how AI is emerging as a vital tool in addressing these challenges, while also considering the ethical implications and limitations of integrating technology into such culturally sensitive domains.

The application of AI in language revitalization has already shown promise. From NLP models tailored to specific languages to AI-powered digital archives, the technology offers scalable solutions to the resource constraints and logistical hurdles that have long plagued traditional language preservation methods. In communities where languages are at risk of extinction, AI can automate resource generation, support language learning, and provide digital spaces for linguistic engagement. The experiences shared by Basque, West Polesian, Tat, Garifuna, Taushiro, Yoruba, Catalan, Esperanto, Southern Min, Amazigh/Amazigh, and Angika speakers underscore that while AI can play a valuable role in language preservation, it must be complemented by community involvement and cultural expertise to ensure that its outputs are both accurate and authentic. Table 3.2 summarizes the viewpoints of all the speakers I interviewed.

Despite these advancements, significant challenges remain. The scarcity of high-quality linguistic data for many endangered languages, combined with the limitations of current AI models, often leads to outputs that lack the natural fluidity and cultural resonance of native speech. The case studies in this chapter, from Þorsteinsson's work with Icelandic using GPT-4 to the Endangered Language Alliance's efforts with Lenape, illustrate how AI can be adapted to meet the specific needs of different linguistic communities. Yet, as these projects show, the effectiveness of AI depends largely on how it is trained, the data it uses, and the extent to which native speakers are involved in the development process.

AI's role in language revitalization also raises critical ethical concerns. Issues such as data ownership, cultural appropriation, and the risk of homogenizing language practices require careful consideration. As discussed in interviews with experts like Jack Weyen, Rishu Kumar, Hacane Hech, and Alex Manuel Martínez Aguilera and Aitor Juaristi Díez, it is essential that AI-driven initiatives prioritize transparency, community consent, and cultural integrity. Without these safeguards, AI risks commodifying or misrepresenting languages, thereby undermining the very cultural heritage it seeks to preserve. The chapter's examination of these ethical dilemmas underscores the importance of fostering genuine collaborations between AI developers, linguists, and the communities they aim to serve.

Looking forward, the potential applications of AI in language and linguistics are vast. Advances in machine learning, deep learning, and conversational agents are enabling AI systems to understand and generate human language with increasing sophistication. But the success of these technologies in the area of language preservation will depend on their ability to be both culturally sensitive and

TABLE 3.2

Summary Table of Interviewee Viewpoints on AI and Language Preservation

Interviewee	Language(s)	Summary of Viewpoints on AI and Language Preservation
Aitor Juaristi Díez	Basque	Aitor observes that AI tools like ChatGPT produce Basque outputs that feel stilted and unnatural due to limited training data in the language. He emphasizes the need for involving native Basque speakers in creating culturally accurate datasets to improve AI models. Aitor highlights the importance of transparency and community engagement in AI projects, believing that many Basque speakers would contribute if they understood how their data would be used and who would benefit
Kanstantsin Loichyts	West Polesian and Belarusian	Kanstantsin highlights challenges due to limited standardized resources and lack of data for AI support in West Polesian and Belarusian. He notes that AI tools often misidentify these languages, confusing them with Russian or Ukrainian, which use different scripts. Kanstantsin emphasizes the need to codify and digitize linguistic resources and calls for the development of AI models that recognize linguistic diversity to prevent linguistic homogenization
Subhan Valiyev	Tat	Subhan is optimistic about AI's potential to help preserve the Tat language, despite the absence of AI tools specifically for Tat. He expresses eagerness to try any AI tool, believing that increased exposure through AI could generate interest and prevent the language from dying. Subhan acknowledges challenges like limited resources, decline in daily use, and dialectal differences, emphasizing the need for community-focused AI initiatives tailored to Tat's unique linguistic and cultural space
Alex Manuel Martínez Aguilera	Garifuna, Taushiro	Alex stresses the importance of informed consent and active community participation in AI projects. He warns that without consulting minority tribes, AI can lead to cultural misrepresentation, as seen in his example of an AI-generated image inaccurately portraying an Apache dwelling. Alex emphasizes that while AI tools can be useful, they cannot replace the cultural knowledge and context that community members provide. He advocates for community ownership of language data and ethical collaboration
Oladeji Eunice	Yoruba	Oladeji notes that AI has been beneficial in translating and explaining concepts in Yoruba but points out that AI struggles with the tonal complexities that are crucial to Yoruba's cultural and communicative integrity. She emphasizes the importance of precision in tonal languages to maintain meaning and highlights the need for AI to better handle linguistic nuances to be fully effective in supporting Yoruba language preservation
Nuria Samper	Catalan	Nuria observes that Catalan struggles to maintain relevance outside formal education despite being taught in schools. She notes that students often default to Spanish or English in social settings and online interactions, leading to erosion of everyday Catalan use. Nuria points out that newcomers to Catalonia tend to learn Spanish instead of Catalan. She emphasizes that AI tools require significant fine-tuning and substantial input from native speakers to produce natural, engaging outputs for younger users

(Continued)

TABLE 3.2 (*Continued*)
Summary Table of Interviewee Viewpoints on AI and Language Preservation

Interviewee	Language(s)	Summary of Viewpoints on AI and Language Preservation
Jack Weyen	Esperanto	Jack notes that while AI tools are prevalent in the Esperanto community due to active content generation, they don't fully capture the complexities of Esperanto. He is concerned that AI-generated content may diminish authenticity and reinforce the stigma of Esperanto being "artificial." Jack highlights the limitations of AI in generating culturally and grammatically authentic content and suggests that collaboration with speakers is necessary to improve AI models and maintain the language's integrity
Jiefeng Kang	Southern Min	Jiefeng points out that Southern Min lacks a standardized writing system, which hinders the creation of textual data required for training AI models. He emphasizes that reliance on reading and writing limits the use of primarily spoken languages like Southern Min. Jiefeng notes that AI technologies primarily focus on Mandarin, marginalizing Southern Min further, and warns that without high-quality datasets, AI struggles to capture linguistic nuances, potentially hindering minority language preservation
Hacane Hech	Amazigh	Hacane emphasizes the challenges in training AI models due to the numerous Amazigh dialects and the lack of a widely recognized standard dialect. He suggests using the dialect with the most media content for AI training. Hacane envisions AI-powered chatbots facilitating language learning by providing interactive, contextually appropriate dialogues in different Amazigh dialects. He stresses the need for extensive data collection from native speakers to capture linguistic nuances and cultural contexts
Rishu Kumar	Angika	Rishu highlights the scarcity of written resources and digital data for Angika, posing significant challenges for AI model development. He emphasizes the importance of collecting spoken language data and developing transcription systems. Rishu stresses that involving native speakers in data annotation and verification is essential for building reliable AI models. He observes that technologists often don't collaborate with minority communities, leading to ineffective solutions, and warns that AI might inadvertently push users toward dominant languages like Hindi or English

Summaries of the viewpoints shared by all ten of the interviewees.

community-driven. Whether through the gamification of language learning, the development of AI-powered speech recognition tools, or the creation of interactive digital archives, the future of language preservation lies in a balanced approach that integrates technology with traditional practices and respects the unique identity of each linguistic community.

While AI has proven to be a powerful ally in the fight to preserve endangered languages, its true potential can only be realized through a partnership between technology and tradition. By embracing both innovation and cultural wisdom, we can build a future where linguistic diversity is not just maintained but celebrated. The survival of the world's languages depends not only on the development of cutting-edge tools but also on our collective commitment to safeguarding the cultural richness they represent.

REFERENCES

Ancient Graffiti Project. (n.d.). Ancient Graffiti from the Latin World. *Ancient Graffiti Project.* https://ancientgraffiti.org/Graffiti/

Axios. (2024, August 29). OpenAI says ChatGPT usage has doubled since last year. Axios. https://www.axios.com/2024/08/29/openai-chatgpt-200-million-weekly-active-users

Decrypt. (2024, October 8). Researchers are breaking ancient language barriers with AI. *Decrypt.* https://decrypt.co/147176/ai-ancient-language-translation-cuneiform-akkadian

Diez, A. J. (2024, August 22). Personal interview.

Endangered Language Alliance. (n.d.). Endangered Language Alliance—Working to document, preserve, and revitalize endangered languages in New York City and beyond. *Endangered Language Alliance.* https://www.elalliance.org/

Eunice, O. (2024, July 24). Personal interview.

FirstVoices. (n.d.). FirstVoices—Indigenous language resources, tools, and digital archives for language revitalization. *FirstVoices.* https://www.firstvoices.com/

Hech, H. (2024, July 28). Personal interview.

Iceland Review. (2023, June 22). GPT-4 to aid in the preservation of the Icelandic language. *Iceland Review.* https://www.icelandreview.com/news/gpt-4-to-aid-in-the-preservation-of-the-icelandic-language/

Kang, J. (2024, August 19). Personal interview.

Kumar, R. (2024, July 18). Personal interview.

Loichyts, K. (2024, August 21). Personal interview.

Martinez Aguilera, A. M. (2024, August 21). Personal interview.

Samper, N. (2024, August 19). Personal interview.

Stanford Rewired. (n.d.). Linguistic revival: How Japan restored the native Ainu language with "AI Pirika." *Stanford Rewired.* https://stanfordrewired.com/post/japan-restored-ainu-ai-pirika

Te H iku Media. (n.d.). Te Hiku Media—Empowering language, culture, and community through media and technology. *Te Hiku.* https://tehiku.nz/

UNESCO. (2022, February 21). A decade to prevent the disappearance of 3,000 languages. *UNESCO.* https://www.iesalc.unesco.org/en/2022/02/21/a-decade-to-prevent-the-disappearance-of-3000-languages/

Valiyev, S. (2024, August 8). Personal interview.

Weyen, J. (2024, June 27). Personal interview.

Community Voices 3: Insights from Chamisa Edmo—Exploring AI's Impact on Indigenous Language Preservation

Our third community voice features Chamisa Edmo, a citizen of the Navajo Nation with Blackfeet and Shoshone-Bannock descendancy. Chamisa is an emerging computer scientist and technologist, currently working toward her MS in Computer Science. She holds a BA focused on Tribal Sovereignty from Haskell Indian Nations University and has extensive experience in developing conversational AI, culturally relevant AI content, and culturally centered AIML curriculum.

Chamisa's passion lies at the intersection of Indigenous culture and emerging technology. Her career focus on artificial intelligence/machine learning (AIML) and data sovereignty is grounded in principles of equity, transparency, and social justice.

Note: Chamisa intentionally left one of the questions blank, which reflects her thoughtful consideration of the nuances involved in discussing AI and culture.

Question 1: Share your professional bio

Chamisa (she/her) is Diné, Blackfeet, and Shoshone-Bannock and a developer and computer scientist focused on culturally relevant AIML systems. She has a BA focused on Tribal Sovereignty and is currently pursuing an MS in Electrical Engineering and Computer Science at the University of Kansas, where she is a 2024–2025 IDHR Digital Humanities Fellow. Chamisa's work integrates Indigenous knowledge ways, equity, and social justice in AIML, particularly around bias mitigation and Data Sovereignty. Her research centers on creating AIML tools that reflect Indigenous relational epistemologies, building culturally informed curricula for Indigenous youth, and developing ethical frameworks for emerging technologies. Chamisa is committed to ensuring that AIML systems empower rather than marginalize Indigenous communities by prioritizing community-driven protocol and Indigenous worldviews and ethics.

DOI: 10.1201/9781003517115-6

Question 2: Share your heritage and family traditions. Where did you grow up? Share a family tradition that you continue to this day.

[no response]

Question 3: Experience with AI. Have you used AI technologies? If yes, please describe your experience. How do you perceive the role of AI in your professional or personal life?

Personally, I'm fascinated by the growth and application of generative AI. It is exciting to see how explosively disruptive it has been the last couple of years. Before ChatGPT, it was difficult for people to understand or experience what was meant by "AI," but since its deployment and because of its level of accessibility, I'm excited by the questions and discussion "AI" brings up in community listening sessions and even in my own family. As a technologist and computer scientist, AI is the buzz in my professional life. There are tons of questions about how to use it, how it was developed, how it is best used and integrated into a workflow, curriculum, or [insert sector]. Broadly speaking, I think the rapid utilization of this next-gen tool is really forcing us (developers and techies) to take a look at holes in the tech to create mitigation strategies for exclusion, erasure, and unethical misrepresentation of IP.

Question 4: AI and cultural preservation. Can you envision any innovative ways in which AI could be used to safeguard intangible cultural heritage, such as language, folksongs, or storytelling? Are there specific traditions, practices, or aspects of your culture that you believe could benefit from AI technology?

I would like to answer this with a fairly well known story from US Indigenous experience. During the 1800s and 1900s when treaties were being developed and signed in the US, it was common practice for the military personnel in charge to find a few members of a given group of people and coerce them to sign an "X" on the line, thus agreeing to the terms and conditions of the treaty. This was done with no regard to the traditional leadership structures in place and often resulted in a group of people being misnamed, and traditional homelands being misappropriated on their behalf.

With that story in mind, I believe incredible precaution should be taken in building tools that integrate cultural knowledge, traditional knowledge ways, and Indigenous intellectual property. That means that tools should be developed with full community engagement and awareness. If that's done with full transparency, permission, and with community consent, there is a possibility to create technologies that could be used to record and potentially transmit stories, songs, and knowledge ways for the next generation. If done without proper consent and reciprocity, AI will be Treaties 2.0.

Question 5: AI and nature. Could you describe a traditional practice from your own culture, or one you've learned about or reported on, that helps in environmental sustainability or climate resilience? Also, how do you think AI could be utilized to support or improve this practice?

Indigenous people are the first and most impacted groups when it comes to climate change. There are generations of Indigenous academics and scientists working on preserving, revitalizing, and strengthening sovereignty around Traditional Ecological Knowledges (TEKs). TEK is a generationally evolved tool used to help our communities remain in balance with homelands and to ensure the sustainability of communities in those specific places. It is a place-based expertise that is often transmitted via song, story, ceremony, or in-place, experiential learning to ensure knowledge isn't lost and can continue to be used. I can envision a future where there are community-owned and developed tools that are built to enhance current climate models by using larger quantitative climate data to bolster knowings. That being said, the development of tools like this should be led by community members and only developed to community-determined specifications.

Question 6: Wisdom of elders and AI. What role do elders play in preserving culture and wisdom in your community? With ethical practices at play, can AI play a role in capturing and disseminating this wisdom? If yes, how?

Elders are the backbones of community, family, and the future in Indigenous cultures. In my communities, they are who we look to for guidance at every step, and we are taught to keep those lessons with us in every decision we make. Often, this kind of wisdom is given at specific points in our lives and with very specific rationale. In tech, it often feels like we are always trying to center the AGI discussion as an obtainable goal. While I do imagine a future where there is a comprehensive knowledge base capable of helping with most things, I do not believe that AI can or should strive to preserve an elder's level of human experiential mastery. To imagine that a small group of privileged humans developing the tools we use could accurately harness the generational expertise of millions of brilliant people of the global majority is impossible for me to believe. It is likely something elders in many communities would advise against, as well—and I am listening.

Question 7: AI and ethics. How important is it for AI systems to be developed ethically, especially in the context of cultural preservation? What steps would you like to be taken to ensure that, as AI expands, it represents diverse cultural perspectives?

It is absolutely necessary that AI systems be developed with a comprehensive standard of ethics and outcomes in mind. If we continue to develop tools using data that is taken completely out of context or on data that is exclusionary, we are going to continue to see tools in the wild that only reflect the values and experiences of a small minority of individuals, excluding the global majority. As various AI-integrated technologies are reiterated, we will end up repackaging the same limited knowledge bases without proper context.

Question 8: AI and personalization. We know that AI systems today don't understand the values and needs of diverse populations. Would you be willing to voluntarily share your family traditions and customs with your personal AI device to improve personalization?

While these systems do often exclude needs and values of people outside of mainstream expectations, I would not want a system to become hyper-personalized to include sensitive cultural and familial traditions. Even with consent, I will still do what I can to limit my data and technological footprint, and I will also work with communities to ensure they understand the implications and rights as individual users with invaluable, cultural IP.

Question 9: Future of AI in community development. What potential risks and benefits should be considered when integrating AI into community initiatives?

There are clear benefits of using AI technology to enhance community initiatives, some of which include recording and disseminating information that is openly discussed and improving overall accessibility for community members. Where lines become blurred is where I think there should be utilizing, at minimum, Free Prior and Informed Consent (FPIC) standards. There is no silver bullet when working with Indigenous communities, and the goal should never be to create a one-size-fits-all tool to use across the board.

Question 10: Final thoughts. Is there anything else you would like to share about your views on AI and its role in preserving cultural heritage and traditions?

Technology is evolving rapidly and will continue to do so. I think if we are to discuss how culture can play a part in the future of AI, we need to start by including as many voices as possible and working to educate and invite community to the conversation as well. If we don't have the opportunity to learn how to set clear boundaries with Indigenous IP, we are just continuing a cycle of erasure, false ascription of meaning, and a fallacy of inclusion for the future. If we want to create tools that can actually understand the values of diverse global populations, it cannot happen without everyone being involved and guiding the conversation or developing the tools/platforms for ourselves.

COPY POST CHAMISA EDMO SURVEY: Chamisa Edmo's survey responses provide a critical and culturally grounded perspective on the integration of AI technologies in Indigenous communities. Her deep commitment to Indigenous Data Sovereignty and culturally relevant technology design highlights the need for community consent and transparency in AI development.

4 Building Trustworthy and Culturally Intelligent AI

Reza Moradinezhad

Trust is an inextricable element of our interactions within communities; it happens every time we board a plane, consult a doctor, or simply engage in conversation. At its core, trust is a willingness to be vulnerable—a leap into uncertainty, bolstered by the belief that another entity will act in our best interests. However, trust takes on new dimensions when the subject turns to artificial intelligence (AI). Though the concept of trust is as old as human communities itself, we find ourselves grappling with its meaning anew.

In this chapter, I'm going to share my experiences as a PhD student at Drexel University doing research on human-computer interaction (HCI) and specifically on trust toward artificial agents as well as my journey as an AI scientist at Tulip AI, an AI startup focusing on ethically sourced sound AI. I conducted many user studies during my PhD focusing on understanding the nuances of building trustworthy interaction between humans and artificial agents. In doing so, I had the privilege to be mentored and collaborate with top scientists from MIT Media Lab, Harvard University, Carnegie Mellon University (CMU), and University of California San Diego (UCSD).

One thing that I took away from those years is that there is a lot of curiosity, excitement, and fascination among people for new computer science (CS) technologies. This has been more evident than ever in recent years with the revelation of generative AI (Gen AI) which is able to generate original content, including text, images, videos, code, and much more. The silver lining here, though, is that this fascination can easily turn into fear and repulsion if people cannot trust these new technologies. In many cases, it can even be horrifying, given how fast these technologies are progressing and being integrated into our everyday tasks and services.

To get a better idea of what is actually happening, let's zoom out and explore the major role trust plays in communities. One sphere where trust is fundamental is in culture, in how we practice and transmit our heritage. In many cultures, elders serve as keepers of knowledge and history, reflecting a deep-seated trust in their authority and benevolence. This trust manifests through rituals, storytelling, and the preservation of values.

There is a growing need to design AI systems with respect for cultural context. Imagine, for example, AI safeguarding our cultural heritage—our folklore, our music—for our posterity. Consider an AI system that preserves dying languages, capturing nuances and cultural background. Envision virtual environments where AI amplifies, rather than replaces, the wisdom of elders, acting as an apprentice

DOI: 10.1201/9781003517115-7

in preserving cultural heritage. The challenge is ensuring that AI systems respect and reflect diverse cultural perspectives and wisdom, much like traditional cultural custodians.

The ethical considerations for AI development must reflect the responsibility of cultural guardianship. Traditionally, elders ensure knowledge is passed on with integrity and respect. AI systems, if developed with these values, can play a complementary role in preserving and disseminating cultural knowledge. In essence, as we build trust in AI, we must recognize parallels with trust in cultural heritage. By drawing on these parallels, we can gain a better understanding of how to ethically develop and deploy AI to ensure these systems honor the diverse communities they impact (for information on IVOW AI, see Darmody, 2021; Cipolle, 2022).

The integration of AI and cultural custodianship presents both opportunities and challenges. If successful, we may create a future where AI and human culture coexist and flourish together, preserving and promoting cultural heritage in the digital age.

Let's return to trust on a smaller scale, that of the individual. In human interactions, we encounter many forms of trust. Let's explore some of these forms. There is cognitive trust (Johnson and Grayson, 2005), based on competence and reliability—the trust we place in a skilled craftsman or a lauded scholar. Affective trust (Johnson and Grayson, 2005), rooted in emotional bonds and perceived benevolence, colors our relationships with friends and loved ones. Behavioral trust (Bailenson et al., 2004) manifests in our actions, often unconsciously, as we navigate the social world. For example, when you trust a taxi driver to safely drive you from one point to the other.

Institutional trust (Hakhverdian and Mayne, 2012) extends beyond individuals to organizations and systems—our faith (or lack thereof) in governments, financial institutions, or the scientific method. Dispositional trust (Merritt and Ilgen, 2008), a personality trait varying among individuals, influences our general propensity to trust others. Swift trust (Kramer and Tyler, 1995), a phenomenon observed in temporary systems or fleeting interactions, allows for rapid collaboration in the absence of time for adequate trust-building.

As we turn our gaze to human-AI interaction, these familiar forms of trust blur and shift, and predefined notions don't fit as neatly. How do we translate these human-centric concepts to our interactions with entities that lack consciousness, emotions, and free will? This question leads us to the operational definition of trust in the context of human-AI interaction.

Trust in AI is multifaceted, each facet reflecting a different aspect of our interaction with these digital entities. It is at once a measure of reliability, a gauge of competence, and a barometer of perceived benevolence. Operationally, we might define trust in AI as the extent to which a user is willing to rely on the AI system's outputs or actions, based on expectations of its performance and alignment with the user's goals, even in the face of uncertainty or potential risk.

This definition encompasses several key elements:

1. **Reliance**: The user's willingness to depend on the AI system for information, decisions, or actions.
2. **Expectations**: The user's beliefs about the AI system's capabilities, limitations, and behavior.

3. **Performance**: The actual and perceived competence of the AI system in its designated tasks.
4. **Alignment**: The degree to which the AI system's actions are perceived to be in service of the user's goals.
5. **Uncertainty**: The acknowledgment that perfect information is never available, and some level of risk is always present.

With a workable definition of trust, further questions arise: How has trust in machines changed or adapted with new technological developments? What does trust in AI look like now? What forces shape trust in human-AI interaction, and what trends can be discerned? Is it possible to build truly trustworthy AI, and if so, how?

As we explore the strategies for creating trust-adaptive agents and navigate the ethical dilemmas that arise, we must keep these fundamental questions at the forefront of our minds. In answering them, we will gain new insights into building more trustworthy AI and, in doing so, will deepen our understanding of what it means to be human in an increasingly digital world.

4.1 THE EVOLUTION OF TRUST IN AI SYSTEMS

The evolution of trust in AI is closely tied to the development of AI systems themselves, progressing from simple task-oriented automation to more complex, adaptive technologies. Early automation tools, such as calculators and factory machinery, built trust primarily on their consistent and reliable performance. They could achieve this through technical competence and predictability. This form of trust was based on their ability to execute predefined tasks accurately without the need for deeper understanding or decision-making abilities (Li et al., 2024; Lukyanenko et al., 2022).

As AI systems became more sophisticated, the nature of trust evolved. The introduction of expert systems shifted trust toward cognitive aspects, requiring users to rely on machines for judgments and decision-making. This cognitive trust was based on the perceived competence and reliability of the system's reasoning processes.

The 21st century brought adaptive systems capable of learning and evolving. This necessitated a dynamic form of trust, termed "adaptive trust" (Moray et al., 2000) which acknowledges the system's capacity for change and requires ongoing recalibration by users.

Most recently, conversational AI and embodied virtual agents (EVAs) have introduced an effective dimension to trust. Conversational AI refers to digital agents that interact with users through natural language, such as voice assistants (e.g., Siri, Alexa) and chatbots. EVAs are advanced artificial intelligence (AI) systems designed to interact with humans in a natural, social manner. Unlike simple chatbots or voice assistants, EVAs have the potential to simulate personalities and engage in complex, multi-modal interactions. They often have visual representations and can interpret and display non-verbal cues, enhancing their ability to build rapport and trust with human users. These human-like interfaces elicit emotional and social responses from users, despite the artificial nature of the interaction (Figure 4.1).

So, we can see that modern AI systems often engage multiple layers of trust simultaneously—functional, cognitive, adaptive, and affective. This complexity

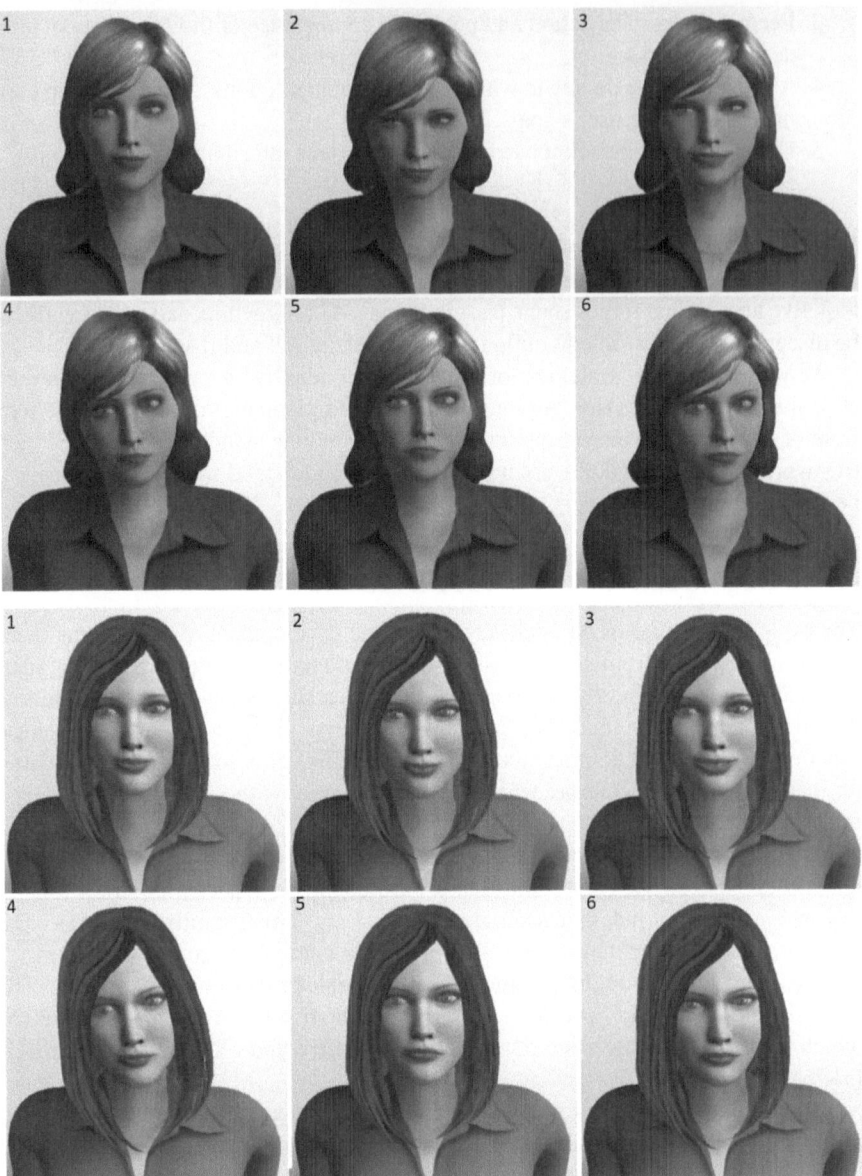

FIGURE 4.1 Examples of two EVAs showing positive and negative facial expressions with different levels of intensity.

presents both challenges and opportunities in AI design and research. Users may trust different aspects of an AI system to varying degrees, creating a nuanced form of human-AI trust that requires careful consideration in development and implementation. To understand these challenges and opportunities better, it would be useful to review the state of the art in academic research on human-AI trust. In the following, I'm going to share insights that I found interesting from the recent research.

4.2   TRUST IN AI: INSIGHTS FROM RECENT RESEARCH

To fully understand the nuances of trust in human-AI interaction, especially in the era of generative AI, much more research is needed. Yet, recent studies examining different components of human-AI interaction have already begun to illuminate certain relationships. Let's look at some of the current research into trust in AI and consider what it means for building trust-adaptive agents.

A study by Chandra et al. (2022) identifies three key human-like competencies that are crucial for cultivating user trust and engagement with conversational AI agents: cognitive competency, relational competency, and emotional competency.

- Cognitive competency refers to the ability of an AI agent to process available information and apply problem-solving and decision-making skills to effectively complete assigned tasks.
- Relational competency is the AI agent's interpersonal skills, such as supporting, cooperating, and collaborating with users. This includes the ability to develop and maintain harmonious relationships.
- Emotional competency is the extent to which an AI agent's ability to self-manage and moderate its interactions with users, accounting for their moods, feelings, and reactions through appropriate expressions and behavior.

The study found that cognitive and emotional competencies had a significant positive relationship with user engagement, while relational competency did not show a significant direct relationship. However, qualitative interviews revealed that relational competency might be important under certain conditions, suggesting the need for further research in this area.

These competencies are grounded in Media Naturalness Theory, which suggests that the more natural an interaction feels, the more engaging it will be for users. By incorporating these human-like competencies, conversational AI agents can create a more natural, engaging experience for users.

Cognitive, relational, and emotional competencies may help cultivate trust, but other factors impact it as well. A systematic review by Rheu et al. (2020) identified five key themes affecting trust in conversational agents:

- **Social Intelligence**: Agents that display socio-emotional behavior, honesty about mistakes, and vulnerability tend to be perceived as more trustworthy. However, the effectiveness of socio-emotional dialogue may depend on users' personality and age.
- **Voice Characteristics and Communication Style**: Agents using dialects or accents associated with trustworthiness and culturally familiar communication styles are perceived as more trustworthy. The effect of human vs. synthetic voices on trust varies depending on other factors.
- **Anthropomorphic Look**: Generally, more human-like and attractive agents are perceived as more trustworthy. However, the effect of embodiment on trust is not always consistent.

- **Non-verbal Communication**: Natural, human-like non-verbal expressions can increase trust, but their effect depends on the context and the agent's overall appearance.
- **Performance Quality**: High performance quality generally increases trust, but other factors like physical attractiveness can sometimes override this effect.

Importantly, the review highlights that these factors' effectiveness often depends on the context, user characteristics, and the specific role of the agent. This suggests that a one-size-fits-all approach to designing trustworthy conversational agents is unlikely to be successful.

As we explore the qualities that impact user trust, we may notice a pattern emerging: the humanness of an AI model is an inescapable component. Recent research by Hu et al. (2021) provides an in-depth exploration of the nature of trust in conversational AI. Their study proposes a dualistic model of humanness perception in conversational AI, comprising two key aspects; Voice Humanness Perception (VHP) and Understanding Humanness Perception (UHP):

- Voice Humanness Perception (VHP) is the degree to which users perceive the AI's speech output as human-like.
- Understanding Humanness Perception (UHP) is the extent to which users believe the AI comprehends their input in a human-like manner.

This model acknowledges that trust in conversational AI is not monolithic but influenced by how users perceive both the system's ability to speak and understand natural language.

The research revealed three distinct patterns of humanness perception among users:

- **Para-human Perception**: Users perceive high levels of both voice humanness and understanding humanness. These users tend to have the highest levels of trust across all dimensions.
- **Para-machine Perception**: Users perceive low levels of both voice humanness and understanding humanness. These users generally have lower trust levels, but interestingly, not the lowest in all dimensions.
- **Asymmetric Perception**: Users perceive high voice humanness but low understanding humanness. Surprisingly, these users often exhibit the lowest levels of trust, particularly in morality-related dimensions (benevolence and integrity).

These findings challenge the assumption that increasing human-likeness in AI systems will necessarily lead to increased trust. Instead, they suggest a more complex relationship between perceived humanness and trust.

The study examined trust across three dimensions: competence, benevolence, and integrity. The results reveal nuanced relationships between humanness perception patterns and these trust dimensions. Let's review them here:

When competence-based trust was examined, users with para-human perception showed the highest levels of competence-based trust. Interestingly, there was no significant difference in competence-based trust between users with para-machine perception and those with asymmetric perception. This suggests that enhancing voice humanness alone may not improve users' trust in the AI's abilities if the understanding humanness is perceived as low.

When benevolence and integrity-based trust was examined, users with asymmetric perception showed the lowest levels of benevolence and integrity-based trust, even lower than those with para-machine perception. This finding indicates that the mismatch between high voice humanness and low understanding humanness may actually undermine users' trust in the AI's moral qualities.

These insights have important implications for the design and development of conversational AI systems. They suggest that efforts to enhance trust should focus not just on making AI sound more human-like but also on improving and demonstrating the AI's language understanding capabilities. Moreover, they highlight the potential risks of creating AI systems that sound highly human-like but fall short in understanding, as this mismatch could lead to lower trust than a system perceived as consistently machine-like.

As we explore user trust, we must also look at factors that hinder the development of trust. For some users, the human-like qualities of AI can be off-putting. Recent research by Baek and Kim (2023) on ChatGPT provides valuable findings that shed light on the perception of AI as trustworthy or creepy in the context of interacting with ChatGPT.

The study identified five main motivations for using ChatGPT: information seeking, task efficiency, personalization, social interaction, and playfulness. Surprisingly, greater task efficiency led to increased perceived creepiness, possibly due to an "uncanny valley" effect where high performance creates discomfort. Conversely, personalization features tended to reduce perceived creepiness and increase trust, likely by giving users a sense of control.

Crucially, perceived creepiness negatively affected users' intention to continue using ChatGPT, while trust positively influenced it. This underscores the importance of managing user perceptions in AI system design.

These findings have several implications for developing trustworthy AI:

1. Balance efficiency with user comfort to avoid triggering uncanny valley effects.
2. Leverage personalization as a trust-building feature.
3. Design social interactions carefully to avoid perceived creepiness.
4. Prioritize transparency and explainability to manage user expectations.
5. Address privacy concerns, as they may contribute to perceptions of creepiness.

This research complements our earlier discussions on trust, cultural intelligence, and ethics in AI. It highlights that creating trustworthy AI isn't just about improving performance but about crafting experiences that users find comfortable and aligned with their values. This is also in line with my own findings and experiences during my PhD: that considering both technical capabilities and user psychology is crucial in building systems that can earn and maintain user trust.

While understanding individual user motivations and perceptions of generative AI is crucial, it's equally important to consider how the broader public views AI across different societal domains. The knowledge we can gain from recent research on public trust in AI across education, healthcare, and creative arts, offers a more comprehensive picture of how AI is perceived in various contexts.

Recent research by Novozhilova et al. (2024) provides valuable insights into public trust in AI across different societal domains. Their study examined public perceptions of AI in education, healthcare, and creative arts, revealing nuanced views that have important implications for AI development and deployment.

The findings show that public trust in AI varies depending on the specific domain and task. Interestingly, people tend to trust AI's ability more than its benevolence across all domains. In healthcare, there was higher trust in AI's benevolence but lower trust in its ability, with AI tools for disease diagnostics and medical research seen as more capable and benevolent. The education domain showed lower trust in AI's benevolence compared to its ability, with higher trust for student-related tasks like essay drafting compared to teacher-related tasks such as providing learning support. In creative arts, there was less variance across tasks, though AI for creative writing was perceived as less capable and benevolent compared to AI for video creation.

Notably, tasks involving higher degrees of human-to-human interaction resulted in lower trust in AI's ability and benevolence. For example, AI therapy chatbots in healthcare and AI for personalized learning support in education were least trusted. This suggests a preference for human involvement in tasks requiring empathy and interpersonal skills.

Individual traits, particularly technological experience and knowledge, significantly influenced perceptions of AI's capabilities. Those with greater technological competence, AI familiarity, and knowledge viewed AI as more capable across all domains. However, demographic traits had little influence on these perceptions.

These findings have important implications for the development of trustworthy AI. They suggest that AI development and deployment strategies should be tailored to specific domains, considering the varying levels of trust and acceptance. There's a need to balance perceptions of AI's ability with concerns about its benevolence, particularly in sensitive domains like healthcare and education. Furthermore, the research highlights the importance of AI literacy programs to enhance public understanding and trust in AI technologies.

Overall, these studies underscore the complexity of public trust in AI and the need for nuanced, domain-specific approaches to AI development and deployment. They suggest that building trustworthy AI systems requires both technical excellence and careful consideration of how these systems are perceived and integrated into different societal contexts.

In the next section, I will review my own research on trust-adaptive agents and explore how these findings fit into the broader scope of research on AI entities.

4.3 TRUST-ADAPTIVE EMBODIED VIRTUAL AGENTS

In this part of the chapter, I want to share some insights from my PhD dissertation research (Moradinezhad, 2022) which has focused on deepening our understanding of trust dynamics in embodied virtual agents (EVAs). Before going any further, let's take a step back and define EVAs. In her book *Embodied Conversational Agents* (Cassell, 2000), Justine Cassell describes embodied conversational agents (ECAs) as "computer-generated cartoon like characters that demonstrate many of the same properties as humans in face-to-face conversation, including the ability to produce and respond to verbal and nonverbal communication." An embodied virtual agent (EVA) is a more general term for such agents which also includes agents that do not necessarily perform any verbal communication. We can look at EVAs as advanced AI systems that are designed to interact with humans in a natural, social manner. Unlike simple chatbots or voice assistants, EVAs can possess simulated personalities and engage in complex, multi-modal interactions. They often have visual representations and can interpret and display non-verbal cues, enhancing their ability to build rapport and trust with human users.

Studying trust in EVAs is a great way to understand the process of trust-building between humans and AI agents in a more general context. That is because most human users see and interact with AI agents as a more or less sentient being. They associate a lot of human dynamics to their interactions with such agents. My work built upon and extended the existing approaches, offering a new point of view for grasping the nuanced interplay between agent behavior, user perceptions, and trust formation. By examining the specific context of EVAs, I was aiming to bridge the gap between theoretical models and practical applications, which can act as a guideline for the development of more effective and trustworthy AI systems. In this subsection, I review the key findings of my research. Through exploring how trust is formed, maintained, and influenced by various factors in human-AI interactions we can gain insights that can be applied to create stronger trust-adaptive systems:

Trust Dynamics and Agent Behavior

- One key finding in my research is the critical role of agent behavior in shaping user trust. Cooperative EVAs, which consistently assist users in tasks, tend to engender higher levels of trust. This increased trust correlates with improved performance outcomes, highlighting the practical benefits of fostering positive human-AI relationships. Conversely, uncooperative agents that hinder task completion or fail to provide assistance erode user trust and negatively impact performance.
- This insight underscores the importance of designing EVAs that are both reliable and align with user expectations. It suggests that trust-adaptive systems should prioritize consistent, helpful behaviors to build and maintain user confidence.

Relative Trust and Primacy Bias

- Interestingly, the research reveals that trust in EVAs is not absolute but relative, heavily influenced by users' prior experiences. This finding introduces the concept of "primacy bias" (Desai et al., 2013) in human-AI interactions, where the first agent a user interacts with disproportionately influences their trust in subsequent agents.
- For instance, if a user's initial interaction is with a cooperative agent, they're more likely to extend trust to future agents, even if those agents exhibit similar behaviors. Conversely, an initial negative experience can cast a long shadow, reducing trust in subsequent interactions despite cooperative agent behavior.
- This primacy effect has significant implications for designing multi-agent systems and sequences of interactions. It suggests that carefully orchestrating initial user experiences could set the stage for more positive and trusting interactions in the long term.

4.3.1 TECHNICAL ASPECTS OF TRUST IN AI: USE OF EMBODIED VIRTUAL AGENTS (EVAS) AND COMPUTATIONAL TRUST MODELS

The translation of trust into AI requires concrete implementation through algorithms and data structures. This is where human psychology intersects with computer science, and where the abstract concept of trust must be distilled into mathematical models and adaptive behaviors.

EVAs represent a significant step toward more intuitive and human-like AI interfaces, bridging the gap between purely functional AI systems and the nuanced, context-aware interactions typical of human-to-human communication.

In order to understand how we can make any AI system - including EVAs - more trustworthy, we should utilize computational trust models in the system's cognitive architecture to enable systematic reasoning about trust. One prominent example is the Online Probabilistic Trust Inference Model (OPTIMo) (Xu and Dudek, 2015), a dynamic probabilistic graphical model that captures trust as a latent variable. OPTIMo's strength lies in its ability to estimate trust in real-time, accounting for both the uncertainty inherent in trust assessments and the dynamic nature of trust itself.

Other models employ different mathematical techniques, from beta-binomial distributions to dynamic Bayesian networks. Some cluster users into "trust profiles," allowing for more nuanced and personalized trust calculations. Others incorporate trust estimation into broader decision-making frameworks, such as partially observable Markov decision processes (POMDPs) (Kok and Soh, 2020).

These computational trust models enable EVAs to adapt in real-time to the ebb and flow of human trust. Imagine an EVA engaged in a complex task with a human collaborator. As the interaction unfolds, the agent's trust model constantly analyzes every aspect of the exchange, noting the user's response times, decision confidence, and subtle changes in language patterns. Each observation feeds into the trust calculation, updating the agent's understanding of the user's trust state moment by moment. This allows for the ability to adapt to user trust in real-time.

4.3.2 ADAPTIVE BEHAVIORS AND THEORY OF MIND IN AI

The power of trust-adaptive virtual agents lies in their ability to modulate behavior based on continuous assessments of user trust. During interactions, the agent's trust model analyzes various aspects of the exchange, allowing it to adapt its behavior by offering more detailed explanations or taking more initiative as needed.

Implementing these adaptive behaviors requires a delicate balance. Excessive adaptation may make the agent seem inconsistent, while insufficient adaptation may result in unresponsiveness to changing trust dynamics. The goal is to create an agent that is responsive to user needs while maintaining a consistent identity and purpose.

As we push the boundaries of trust-adaptive AI, we venture into the territory of cognitive science, specifically the concept of Theory of Mind (ToM) (Frith and Frith, 2005). ToM is the ability to attribute mental states—beliefs, intents, desires, emotions—to oneself and others, and to understand that others have beliefs, desires, and intentions different from one's own.

Incorporating ToM into AI systems represents a significant advancement in their ability to build and maintain trust. It's more than merely responding to observable behaviors; it's about developing a deeper understanding of the mental state and decision-making processes of the user.

The implementation of ToM in AI systems often involves complex cognitive architectures that model not just the user's actions, but their beliefs and goals, and even how they model the AI system itself. This creates a kind of mental recursion where the AI is modeling the user's model of the AI. This allows the AI to engage in sophisticated social reasoning.

As we continue to refine these technical aspects of trust in AI, we must balance sophistication and simplicity. Creating systems that can model and respond to trust is important, but we must do so in a way that feels natural and unobtrusive to the user. This ongoing refinement pushes us closer to AI systems that can engage in truly meaningful and trustworthy interactions with humans. Next, we'll look at another design element that impacts trust, one that grows more prominent with technological advances: anthropomorphism.

4.3.3 ANTHROPOMORPHISM IN AI DESIGN: IMPACT ON TRUST

Anthropomorphism in AI design leverages human social cognition mechanisms to influence user interactions. By incorporating human-like features into AI systems, such as expressive virtual agents or conversational AI with nuanced speech patterns, designers tap into users' innate social processing circuits. This approach can accelerate trust formation, as users apply familiar social heuristics to these digital entities. However, anthropomorphism also carries significant risks. It can set unrealistic expectations which, when unmet, may lead to a more dramatic erosion of trust than with non-anthropomorphic systems.

Recent research on conversational AI (Hu et al., 2021) helps us get a better understanding of the role of anthropomorphism in AI. Their findings suggest that anthropomorphic features in AI systems don't uniformly increase trust. While overall human-likeness tends to foster trust, an imbalance between human-like speech and machine-like understanding can actually decrease trust, particularly in moral dimensions like benevolence and integrity. This highlights the need for a balanced approach to anthropomorphic design in AI systems.

Challenges in anthropomorphic design include the Uncanny Valley Effect, or the discomfort or revulsion users may feel as AI approaches human-likeness without fully achieving it. Cultural variances present another obstacle, as different cultures may interpret and respond to anthropomorphic features in different ways, complicating universal design. Age and technical experience also play a role, with user expectations and comfort with anthropomorphic AI varying significantly based on these factors. Ethical considerations further complicate the issue, raising questions about deception and the appropriate boundaries between human and machine interactions.

Designers must carefully balance the potential benefits of anthropomorphism with these challenges. The goal should be to create AI systems that leverage beneficial aspects of human-like interaction without misleading users or creating unrealistic expectations. Research into the long-term effects of anthropomorphic AI on user trust and interaction patterns is ongoing. As AI systems become more sophisticated, it becomes increasingly more important to understand the implications of anthropomorphic design for developing trustworthy and effective human-AI interfaces.

4.4 CULTURAL INTELLIGENCE IN AI: THE ROLE OF AI IN SHAPING NARRATIVES AND REPRESENTING DIVERSE CULTURES

As we examine these forces acting on individual user trust, it's important to step back and explore what trustworthy AI looks like culturally. AI, in its role as both creator and curator of digital experiences, stands at a crossroads of cultural representation. As we develop AI, we must confront the challenge of cultural intelligence with the same rigor and curiosity that we apply to algorithmic efficiency.

AI is not merely a passive tool; it is an active participant in the shaping of our cultural narratives. From the content recommendations that influence our media consumption to the language models that mediate our digital communications, AI systems are increasingly the lens through which we view and interact with the world. This power to shape perception carries with it a deep sense of responsibility.

Consider, for a moment, the implications of an AI-driven news aggregator. Such a system, trained on data that may skew toward certain cultural perspectives, has the potential to reinforce existing biases or create echo chambers of cultural understanding. The algorithms that determine which stories are highlighted and which are buried are not just organizing information—they are curating our collective understanding of global events.

Similarly, AI-powered translation services, while bridging linguistic divides, also stand as interpreters of cultural nuance. The challenge here lies not just in accurate word-for-word translation, but in conveying the richness of cultural context, idioms, and subtexts that give language its depth and flavor. A misstep here risks not only miscommunication but cultural misrepresentation.

In virtual and augmented reality, where AI helps craft immersive experiences, the stakes of cultural representation are even higher. These technologies have the potential to transport us into different cultural contexts, offering unprecedented opportunities for empathy and understanding. Yet, if not handled with sensitivity and authenticity, they risk reducing rich cultural traditions to caricatures or exotic backdrops.

Bias is a looming threat for any AI developer. We end up with AI systems that unknowingly reinforce harmful stereotypes or make biased decisions based on cultural markers.

Take, for instance, the challenge of developing AI-driven hiring systems. An algorithm trained on historical hiring data may perpetuate existing biases, disadvantaging candidates from certain cultural backgrounds. Or consider facial recognition systems that perform poorly on certain ethnic groups due to underrepresentation in training data. These are not just technical glitches; they are failures of cultural intelligence that can have real-world consequences.

The root of this challenge lies in the data that feed our AI systems. Datasets, far from being the objective arbiters we often perceive them to be, are cultural artifacts imbued with the biases and perspectives of their creators. An AI trained on data that underrepresents or misrepresents certain cultures will inevitably produce outputs that reflect those biases.

To navigate this minefield, we must approach AI development with a heightened awareness of cultural context. This means not just diversifying our datasets, but critically examining the assumptions embedded in our algorithms. It requires us to ask uncomfortable questions: Whose perspectives are we prioritizing? Whose experiences are we overlooking? How might our AI systems be perpetuating harmful stereotypes or cultural power imbalances?

Moreover, we must recognize that cultural intelligence in AI is not a destination, but a journey. Cultures are not static entities; they evolve, intersect, and transform over time. Our AI systems must be flexible enough to adapt to these changes, to learn and grow in their cultural understanding just as humans do.

When I was conducting user studies for my PhD research, I had the chance to observe and converse with many people from diverse backgrounds. It was an eye opening experience to see how people's backgrounds and their lived experience forges how they see both social norms and how that can affect their expectations for how they want to be treated by artificial agents. Therefore, I can see that AI developers should not see themselves as mere technicians or even researchers but cultural intermediaries. Being in such a position demands both technical expertise and an acute sense of ethical responsibility. In order to expand on this a bit more, let's explore some of the things we can do to help mitigate potential mishaps when developing culturally responsible AI.

First and foremost, developers must cultivate an awareness of their own cultural biases and limitations. No individual can claim a complete understanding of all cultures; acknowledging this limitation is the first step toward addressing it. This might involve actively seeking diverse perspectives in the development process, engaging with cultural experts, and creating spaces for feedback and critique from a wide range of cultural viewpoints.

Transparency becomes crucial in this context. Developers must make the cultural assumptions and limitations of their AI systems explicit. Users interacting with these systems should be aware of the cultural lens through which the AI is operating, allowing them to critically engage with its outputs rather than accepting them as objective truth.

The "nothing about us without us" principle offers a promising approach. The approach suggests that involving representatives from diverse cultures in all phases of AI system development—design, development, and testing—can lead to more authentic and respectful cultural representations. This isn't simply about avoiding offense; it's about enriching our AI systems with cultural depth and nuance.

Furthermore, developers must grapple with the ethical implications of cultural adaptation in AI. While personalizing experiences based on cultural background can enhance user engagement, it also risks reinforcing cultural divisions or pigeonholing users based on perceived cultural identity. Where is the line between cultural intelligence and cultural determinism? How do we create AI systems that respect cultural differences while also fostering cross-cultural understanding? How should we educate people on what AI is, how it's developed, and the opportunities and challenges associated with it?

As we maneuver these murky ethical waters, the need for strong governance frameworks becomes apparent. Industry standards and regulatory guidelines for culturally sensitive AI development are still in their infancy. Developers have an opportunity—and a responsibility—to contribute to the shaping of these frameworks, ensuring that cultural intelligence is woven into the very fabric of AI ethics.

In Spring 2023, I was introduced to the extraordinary research and work of Davar Ardalan and her startup, TulipAI. With generative AI becoming a powerful new tool, it was fascinating to partner with Davar to explore how my research in trustworthy AI could contribute to cultural preservation and the development of advanced, ethical, and culturally sensitive AI systems.

In Summer 2023, I created a proof of concept text-to-sound AI model, which was a customized version of Meta's Audiocraft2 library. Building this model and hosting it on HuggingFace provided a unique opportunity to explore and examine the capabilities of Audiocraft, learn about the potentials of such sound generation models and also get a hands-on feel of the pain points and challenges involved in working and developing a generative AI model. In addition, as a founding AI scientist, I worked with Davar on strategizing the path forward for the startup, onboarding and mentoring a dozen students from Florida Gulf University and Drexel University, and prototyping

Despite the challenges and shortcomings, it is inevitable that generative AI technologies are becoming integral to our daily lives, transforming our interactions with technology and engagement with cultural content. As we navigate this technological frontier, we must prioritize trust and cultural intelligence to ensure that AI serves as a positive and inclusive force in communities. Building and maintaining user trust is more important than ever as generative AI systems become more sophisticated and autonomous. At Tulip AI, we tried to achieve this through ethically sourcing our training data; either collecting data from sources that explicitly state the data can be used publicly or directly working with sound engineers to create original sounds to be used for training our models. We also paid special attention to transparency and explainability so that our users understand the entire process of collecting data, developing, and training the model.

Cultural intelligence in AI is not a checkbox to be ticked but a fundamental paradigm shift in how we approach the development and deployment of these powerful technologies. AI is more than just a tool of culture, it is a part of culture—one that has the power to shape perceptions, bridge divides, and promote understanding. As we stand at this digital crossroads, the choices we make in addressing cultural intelligence will determine whether AI becomes a force for cultural homogenization or a catalyst for celebrating human diversity in all its complex, beautiful forms.

Now it is time to wrap up this subsection so I can share a case study of my own experience as an AI scientist at Tulip AI for more than 15 months. At Tulip AI I utilized the knowledge I gained during my PhD to further our understanding of how AI systems can be developed ethically, responsibly, and by taking cultural intelligence into account. In this subsection, I went over various dimensions of trust in AI, from the technical aspects of embodied virtual agents and computational trust models to the nuanced impacts of anthropomorphism and cultural intelligence. Key observations include the importance of agent behavior in shaping user trust and the relative nature of trust influenced by primacy bias. The incorporation of Theory of Mind concepts in AI systems represents a significant advancement in creating more intuitive and trustworthy interactions.

Moreover, I hope this subsection helped you get a better idea of the critical role of cultural intelligence in AI development. As AI systems increasingly shape our cultural narratives and mediate our interactions with the world, developers must approach their work with an acute awareness of cultural context and potential biases.

The path forward in creating trustworthy AI systems involves technical innovation that is coupled with a deep commitment to ethical considerations and cultural responsibility. It requires ongoing collaboration between technologists, ethicists, cultural experts, and diverse user groups to ensure that AI systems respect and enhance human values and cultural diversity.

4.5 THE ARCHITECTURE OF TRUST IN AI

Based on my experiences at Drexel University and Tulip AI - and now as an Assistant Teaching Professor at Drexel University - I am going to use this subsection to point out some of the most important components that comprise the architecture of human-AI trust.

Throughout the years, I reviewed many academic and non-academic articles exploring the multidimensional nature of trust, including the impact of agent behaviors and previous user experiences, and the necessity of system reliability. These insights are crucial for creating AI systems that users can rely on, particularly in culturally significant contexts. Ethical considerations are fundamental to maintaining the integrity of projects aimed at celebrating and preserving cultural diversity to prevent the reinforcement of cultural stereotypes or biases.

The implementation of trust in AI systems requires translating abstract human concepts into concrete algorithms and data structures. This intersection of human psychology and computer science presents unique challenges in quantifying and modeling trust. Through both quantitative and qualitative methods, we must examine the technical foundations that enable the development of trust in human-AI interactions.

At the onset of my research, I realized that in order to understand people's perception of trustworthiness toward artificial agents, first I had to understand the psychology behind trust and how that works among humans. Then, I could look at differences in those dynamics when it comes to humans' relationship with automation. As I continued my research, I also found out that trust that is gained through deception or manipulation may work in short periods, but it is an unsustainable trust and extremely fragile. This is another reason why it is so crucial to remain ethical and keep our integrity when it comes to developing AI systems. By doing so, we can be confident that when (and not if!) a trust breach happens, there is still a chance to repair the damaged trust between the users and the AI.

Computational trust models serve as the cognitive architecture for AI systems, allowing them to reason about trust systematically. These models, such as the Online Probabilistic Trust Inference Model (OPTIMo), use various mathematical techniques to estimate trust in real-time. They account for the uncertainty inherent in trust assessments and the dynamic nature of trust itself.

The goal is to create AI systems that can adapt to changing trust dynamics while maintaining consistency and reliability. This requires a delicate balance between responsiveness to user needs and preservation of the system's core identity and purpose. As we continue to refine these technical aspects, we must strive for a natural and unobtrusive integration of trust modeling in human-AI interactions.

Several elements significantly impact trust, and any successful model must consider them. Some we have already discussed but are included here briefly to highlight their importance in the design of trustworthy systems. Going over these components sets the stage for the subsection 4.7 in which I introduce TAVA, a framework for Trust Adaptive Virtual Agents.

Anthropomorphism: The degree to which AI systems present human-like characteristics significantly influences trust dynamics. Many of the works I reviewed for my thesis suggested that embodied virtual agents (EVAs) that display appropriate facial expressions and gestures can inspire trust more quickly than text-based interfaces. This is because humans are inherently social creatures, and we tend to apply social heuristics to entities that exhibit human-like traits. For example, an EVA that maintains eye contact and nods at appropriate times during a conversation may be perceived as more attentive and trustworthy than a text-based chatbot (Lucas et al., 2014). However, this anthropomorphism is a double-edged sword—it can also lead to unrealistic expectations and feelings of betrayal when the system fails to live up to its human-like presentation. Users might expect levels of emotional understanding or contextual awareness that the AI simply cannot provide, leading to disappointment and erosion of trust when these expectations are not met.

Transparency: As AI systems become more complex, the ability to understand their decision-making processes becomes crucial for trust. Explainable AI

(XAI) initiatives aim to make AI systems more transparent, allowing users to understand why a particular decision was made. This transparency can foster trust by demystifying the AI's operations and helping users feel more in control. For instance, a medical diagnosis AI that not only provides a diagnosis but also explains the key factors it considered in reaching that conclusion can help both patients and doctors trust its recommendations. However, this transparency must be balanced against the risk of overwhelming users with too much information. Providing a full technical breakdown of an AI's neural network, for example, would be counterproductive for most users. The challenge here is to find the right level of explanation that informs without overwhelming.

Reliability and Consistency: While perhaps the most straightforward aspect of trust, the importance of consistent performance cannot be overstated. AI systems that perform reliably, even if not perfectly, tend to engender more trust than those with unpredictable performance. This reliability extends beyond just accuracy—it includes consistent response times, consistent availability, and consistent quality of interaction. For example, a virtual assistant that occasionally makes mistakes but always responds promptly and maintains a consistent persona may be trusted more than one that is occasionally brilliant but often unresponsive or inconsistent in its behavior.

Adaptability: The ability of AI systems to learn and improve over time can significantly impact trust. Users may be more willing to trust a system that demonstrates the capacity to correct its mistakes and adapt to new situations. This adaptability can manifest in various ways, such as an AI language model that learns user preferences over time, or a recommendation system that refines its suggestions based on user feedback. However, adaptability must be balanced with consistency—changes should be gradual and understandable to maintain user trust.

Ethical Alignment: As AI systems take on more complex tasks with significant real-world implications, the alignment of their actions with human values and ethical principles becomes crucial for trust. Users need to believe that the AI system will act in a manner consistent with their moral and ethical expectations. This alignment includes considerations of fairness, privacy, and social impact. For instance, an AI system used in hiring decisions must demonstrably avoid biases based on race, gender, or other protected characteristics. Similarly, AI systems handling sensitive personal data must prioritize user privacy and data protection to maintain trust.

Control and Agency: The degree to which users feel they have control over the AI system can significantly impact trust. Systems that allow for user input and override options tend to be trusted more than those that operate as enigmatic black boxes. This sense of control can be fostered through various means, such as customizable settings, clear opt-out mechanisms, or the ability to question and challenge the AI's decisions. For example, a smart home system that allows users to easily review and modify its learned behaviors is likely to be trusted more than one that makes cryptic decisions about home management.

Understanding and effectively managing these forces is crucial for developing AI systems that can build and maintain user trust over time. It requires a holistic approach that considers not just the technical capabilities of the AI, but also the psychological, social, and ethical dimensions of human-AI interaction.

In developing trust in AI systems, our goal is not to maximize trust indiscriminately, but to foster appropriate trust that accurately reflects the system's capabilities and limitations. This approach serves the best interests of users and communities at large. The challenge lies in creating AI systems that are trustworthy to the extent that they are reliable and beneficial, while also being transparent about their constraints.

Research in the field of trust in AI advances our technological capabilities and deepens our understanding of human psychology and social dynamics. By examining how humans develop trust in artificial entities, we gain an understanding of the nature of trust itself and its role in human communities. This research serves a dual purpose: improving human-AI interactions and illuminating the complexities of human trust mechanisms.

As we continue to explore and refine trust in AI systems, we must maintain a balanced perspective, considering both the technological advancements and the broader implications for human-AI relationships and societal structures.

4.6 STRATEGIES FOR BUILDING AND MAINTAINING USER TRUST

In human-AI interactions, building and maintaining user trust is a complicated challenge that requires a nuanced approach. As AI systems become increasingly integrated into our daily lives, the strategies we employ to foster trust must evolve to meet the changing expectations and concerns of users.

Let's explore some strategies designed to cultivate and sustain trust in AI systems. These approaches draw from diverse fields including psychology, human-computer interaction, and ethical AI design (De Graaf et al., 2015). We'll examine how transparency, adaptability, and consistent performance contribute to trust formation, and how these elements can be effectively implemented in AI systems.

We consider both the theoretical underpinnings and practical applications of trust-building techniques. As we do so, we must also consider how these strategies must be tailored to account for individual user differences, cultural contexts, and the specific domains in which AI systems operate.

4.6.1 HEURISTICS

Heuristics serve as mental shortcuts for quick decision-making in trust-related situations. In trust-adaptive agents, these simple rules of thumb guide behavior in specific scenarios. For instance, to combat overtrust, agents may use visual prompts to encourage users to reassess their trust, similar to a car's smart cruise control alerting drivers about over-reliance. In trust repair scenarios, when errors lead to a loss of trust, agents can gradually provide useful information about their capabilities and limitations, allowing users to recalibrate their expectations. While heuristics offer a foundation, they are just the first step toward more sophisticated trust-adaptive interactions.

4.6.2 INTERACTION DESIGN

Interaction design focuses on the nuanced aspects of agent behavior that influence trust. Transparency plays a crucial role; robots demonstrating their limitations through gestures are often perceived as more trustworthy. Clear explanations are equally important, with agents that provide concise rationales for their decisions or mistakes tending to maintain user trust more effectively. Interestingly, expressions of vulnerability and emotion through natural language have been shown to increase trust in robotic agents. However, these techniques must be implemented cautiously to avoid potential manipulation or deception.

4.6.3 COMPUTATIONAL MODELS

Computational trust models attempt to quantify and predict trust in ways that can be implemented in code. The Online Probabilistic Trust Inference Model (OPTIMo) is one such approach, capturing trust as a latent variable in a dynamic probabilistic graphical model and estimating trust in real-time. Other models cluster users into "trust profiles" for more nuanced and personalized trust calculations. Some researchers have incorporated trust estimation into broader decision-making frameworks like partially observable Markov decision processes (POMDPs). These models enable agents to adapt in real-time to the ebb and flow of human trust, but must be balanced with maintaining a consistent agent identity.

4.6.4 THEORY OF MIND APPROACHES

Inspired by developmental psychology, Theory of Mind (ToM) approaches aim to imbue agents with the ability to reason about human mental states. This involves agents attempting to understand and predict users' beliefs, desires, and intentions. With ToM capabilities, agents can recognize user states like frustration or uncertainty and adjust their behavior accordingly. While promising, ToM approaches raise important questions about the extent to which machines can truly understand human mental states and the ethical implications of such capabilities.

4.6.5 PRINCIPLES OF TRUSTWORTHY AI

According to a recent review by Thiebes et al. (2021), trustworthy AI (TAI) is based on five key principles:

- **Beneficence**: AI should be developed, deployed, and used in ways that benefit humanity and the planet, promoting well-being and respecting basic human rights.
- **Non-maleficence**: AI should avoid bringing harm to people, with a focus on protecting privacy, security, and safety.
- **Autonomy**: This principle promotes human autonomy, agency, and oversight, potentially including the restriction of AI systems' autonomy when necessary.

- **Justice**: AI should be utilized to amend past inequities, create and distribute benefits fairly, and prevent the creation of new harms and inequities.
- **Explicability**: This principle calls for the development of explainable AI, producing interpretable AI models while maintaining high performance and accuracy. It also encompasses the creation of accountable AI.

These principles address key concerns about AI's impact on individuals, organizations, and communities, and provide guidance for ethical AI development and deployment.

By integrating these diverse strategies, developers can create more sophisticated trust-adaptive virtual agents. However, the challenge remains to balance technical capabilities with ethical considerations, ensuring that trust-building mechanisms enhance rather than manipulate human-AI interactions. As we continue to refine these approaches, we move closer to creating AI systems that can engage in genuinely trustworthy and meaningful interactions with humans, potentially transforming human-machine relationships.

In the next subsection, I'm sharing a framework that I came up with toward the end of my PhD studies at Drexel University. This framework is designed to serve as a guideline for designing and implementing trust adaptive virtual agents.

4.7 THE TAVA FRAMEWORK: A COMPREHENSIVE APPROACH TO TRUST-ADAPTIVE VIRTUAL AGENTS

The framework that I am planning to introduce in this subsection is my attempt at culminating all the important aspects of creating trustworthy interactions with autonomous agents. As the newer generations see technology differently and AI capabilities change and improve by the hour, we see the need for agents to adaptively change their strategies to improve the trust in their relationship with humans. Unlike traditional AI systems that operate on fixed rules or predefined scripts, systems that follow TAVA are designed to dynamically adapt their behavior based on the user's trust levels, making them more responsive and aligned with user needs and expectations (Figure 4.2).

The TAVA framework is built upon four fundamental pillars that work in concert to create trustworthy AI systems:

The "Fight Bias" pillar goes beyond just acknowledging bias exists. It actively calls for systems to counteract both machine and human biases. This includes addressing the tendency for humans to overly trust initial information (primacy bias) and the counter-intuitive notion that agents making mistakes on simpler tasks may be perceived as less trustworthy overall (easy-error hypothesis). By explicitly tackling these biases, TAVA aims to create more equitable and dependable AI interactions.

"Build Trust" emphasizes proactive measures to foster user confidence. Beyond just being reliable, it advocates for empowering users with easy activation/deactivation options and clear protocols for asking questions when in doubt. The focus on "failing gracefully"—by not just apologizing, but explaining errors and offering solutions - demonstrates a commitment to transparency that goes beyond typical error handling.

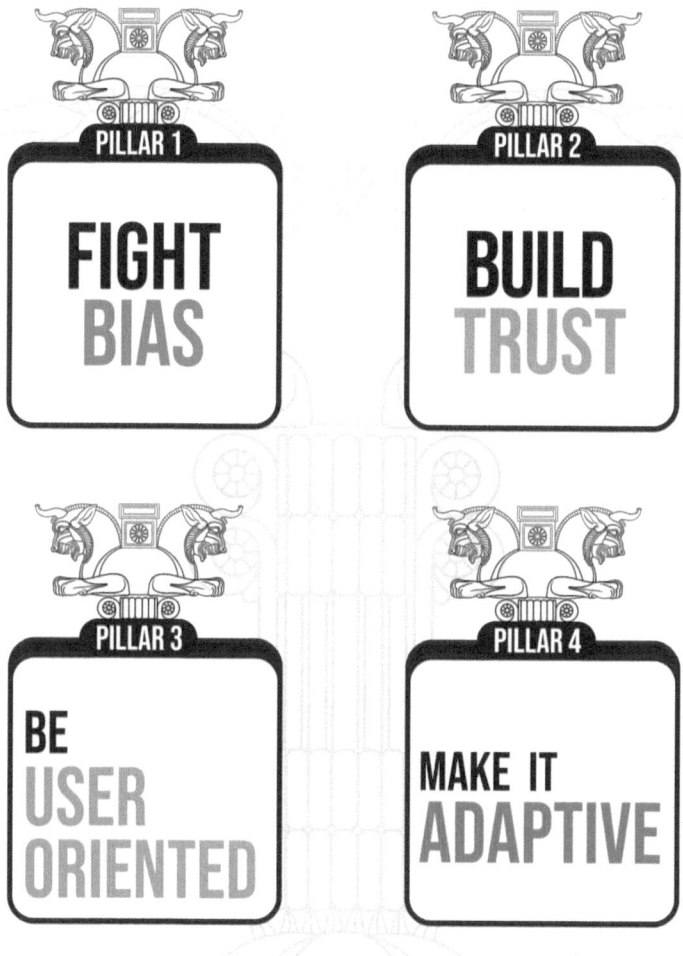

FIGURE 4.2 TAVA: A framework for trust adaptive virtual agents.

The "Be User Oriented" pillar expands on traditional user-centric design. It emphasizes not just ease of use, but also informational depth (providing history and useful context) and emotional intelligence (keeping users in the loop about the AI's decision-making process). The call to "know when to interrupt" shows a nuanced understanding of human-AI interaction dynamics that many systems lack.

"Make it Adaptive" pushes beyond simple personalization. It advocates for systems that can navigate cultural differences, accommodate various accessibility needs, and implement changes gradually to avoid user disorientation. The inclusion of "Clean AI" principles under inclusivity demonstrates a commitment to ethical AI development that considers potential negative impacts on marginalized groups.

4.7.1   EXPLAINING THE TAVA FRAMEWORK

Here, I provide a breakdown of each of the pillars and what they include:

4.7.1.1   Pillar 1: Fight Bias

1. **State the Purpose of the System**
   • What it can, cannot, should, and should not do.
2. **Primacy Bias**
   • Humans have a tendency to prefer what they encounter first in a set.
3. **Easy-error Hypothesis**
   • In cases of equal overall performance, AI agents that make mistakes on easy tasks may be perceived as less trustworthy than those that make mistakes on harder tasks.
4. **State the Capabilities of the System**
   • What is the level of reliability of the agent? What should and should not the user expect from it?

4.7.1.2   Pillar 2: Build Trust

1. **Gradual Changes**
   • Try to minimize the amount of startling and confusing changes by gradually changing over a longer time, not abruptly in a short time.
2. **Accessibility**
   • To succeed in delivering a trusted, quality experience to all users, consider the range of people from different locations, skill levels, and abilities (e.g., people with impairments and those operating under adverse conditions).
3. **Personalized Interaction**
   • Personalize the interaction based on user feedback. This could be learned preferences and direct feedback.
4. **Diversity**
   • Users from different cultural and social backgrounds, local dialects, etc., have different expectations from an intelligent system. Personalize for system expectations and considerations from different backgrounds.

5. **Inclusivity (Clean AI)**
   - Make sure different types of stereotypes and discrimination are not included in the final design of the system. And if they are, measures are being undertaken to ensure that they are in place.
6. **Know When to Interrupt**
   - Choose when an agent must interrupt based on user's performance, trust, skill, and overall context. Stay out of the way the rest of the time.

4.7.1.3 Pillar 3: Be User Oriented

1. **Easy Activation/Deactivation**
   - Make it easy to activate and deactivate the assistant. Give users control and help them explore and cultivate their interactions with the assistant rather than forcing a certain type of interaction on them.
2. **Easy Recovery**
   - The users will be more forgiving toward mistakes if there is an easy and quick recovery or a way to go back to the most recent reliable state.
3. **When in Doubt, Ask**
   - Devise protocols for when to interrupt. Clarify the uncertainty to the user instead of assuming. The cost of tolerance will depend on the nature of task completion and user's trust in the agent. Invest in error protocols, including more contextual examples for tasks.
4. **Fail Gracefully**
   - **Apologize**: Acknowledge and admit responsibility for failures and apologize for users' frustration.
   - **Explain**: If possible, explain the process and tell them where it went wrong. Also, acknowledge suggestions and support to fix the problem.

4.7.1.4 Pillar 4: Make It Adaptive

1. **History**
   - Provide a history (however short) of the interaction to the user so they can see how their interaction with the agent went.
2. **Provide Useful Information**
   - Make information regarding tasks, environment, and performance easily accessible.
3. **Provide Flexibility**
   - Allow the user to manually customize the interaction. Put limits in the system usage bars and manage incomplete and ambiguous reviews and feedback.
4. **Keep User in the Loop**
   - Send appropriate messages when the system's abilities and performance alter. Help users understand how they can support the system better and perform better with it. Explain and update them about the current level and capabilities of the system as and when updated, or removed.
5. **Collect and Receive Feedback**
   - Through unobtrusive methods like thumbs up/down data, audio and speech recognition, etc. Ask the user for feedback at various points (including new thoughts) and not interrupt them.

This framework recognizes that trust is both a cognitive and emotional process, and aims to create a sense of rapport and relatability. What I aimed to do in this framework was to synthesize insights from various disciplines, including psychology, computer science, and anthropology, to create a comprehensive strategy for developing AI agents that can effectively build and maintain trust across diverse user populations and cultural contexts. It incorporates elements from earlier strategies, such as heuristics for quick trust-related decision-making, insights from interaction design for more intuitive user experiences, and computational trust models for real-time trust assessment and adaptation.

It is important to note that there is more to TAVA than the four pillars mentioned above. Implementing TAVA also involves a multi-step process that begins with thorough cultural and user analysis to understand the target user base and relevant cultural contexts. This is followed by adaptive system design, developing flexible AI architectures capable of adjusting to various trust scenarios. The process continues with iterative testing and refinement, continuously evaluating and improving trust-building strategies.

This framework's strength lies in its multidisciplinary foundation, combining principles from psychology, computer science, and HCI to create AI agents that can effectively navigate the complex area of human trust. The emphasis on human-like interaction and empathy further enhances the framework's potential to create more natural and engaging user experiences.

The implementation process, involving cultural analysis, adaptive system design, and iterative refinement, ensures that TAVA-based systems can be tailored to diverse user populations and cultural contexts. This adaptability is crucial in our increasingly globalized world, where AI systems must function across a wide range of cultural norms and expectations.

As we move forward in the development of AI technologies, the TAVA framework provides a strong foundation for creating trustworthy, responsive, and ethically sound AI systems. By prioritizing user trust and cultural intelligence, TAVA paves the way for more meaningful and beneficial human-AI collaborations across various fields, from healthcare and education to customer service and beyond.

The challenge now lies in translating this theoretical framework into practical applications, continuously refining our approach based on real-world feedback and emerging ethical considerations. As we implement these trust-building strategies, we must not lose sight of the foundational importance of system efficiency. In the fast-paced digital world, users' patience wears thin quickly. A system that is trustworthy but slow or cumbersome will quickly find itself relegated to the dustbin of digital history. This efficiency, however, must be balanced with cultural intelligence. Now with this brief introduction to the TAVA framework, let's dive a little deeper into why it is important to be culturally sensitive when designing AI systems.

4.8 IMPORTANCE OF CULTURAL INTELLIGENCE

In the context of AI development, understanding cultural differences is crucial for creating systems that can effectively communicate across diverse cultural backgrounds. We are not building trust in a cultural vacuum, but in a rich, diverse global environment where every interaction is colored by cultural context. An AI system that is efficient but culturally tone-deaf will quickly and efficiently erode trust. Take, for example, the concepts of high-context and low-context cultures. These concepts provide valuable insights into how different societies convey and interpret information, which is crucial for understanding trust dynamics in various cultural settings as culturally familiar communication styles and voices impact trust.

In high-context cultures, communication relies heavily on implicit information and non-verbal cues. Much of the message is conveyed through context, shared understanding, and subtle hints rather than explicit statements. These cultures place a strong emphasis on long-term relationships and group harmony, with personal relationships and social hierarchies being crucial for understanding communication. Messages are often indirect, and people are expected to "read between the lines" to understand the full meaning. Gestures, tone of voice, and facial expressions play a significant role in conveying meaning.

In contrast, low-context cultures feature communication that is more explicit and direct. The message is primarily conveyed through clear, specific language rather than context or non-verbal cues. While relationships are important, they are not as crucial for understanding day-to-day communications. People can effectively communicate without deep personal relationships or extensive shared cultural knowledge. Messages are typically straightforward and explicit, with people expected to say what they mean directly. The spoken or written word carries most of the meaning, with less emphasis on non-verbal cues.

Understanding these cultural differences play a key role in developing trust-adaptive AI systems. AI designed for high-context cultures may need to be more adept at interpreting non-verbal cues and contextual information, while those for low-context cultures might focus on providing clear, explicit information. This distinction is particularly important when developing trust-adaptive AI systems, as trust-building strategies may need to vary significantly between high-context and low-context cultures to be effective and culturally appropriate. By considering these cultural nuances, developers can create AI systems that are more attuned to the communication styles and trust-building mechanisms of diverse user populations. And this can ultimately lead to more effective and culturally sensitive human-AI interactions.

Moreover, cultural intelligence extends to the very foundations of trust itself. What constitutes trustworthy behavior can vary significantly across cultures. In some cultures, consistency and reliability might be the cornerstones of trust. In others, the ability to adapt and show flexibility might be more highly valued. Our trust-adaptive agents must be capable of navigating these cultural nuances and adjust their trust-building strategies to align with the cultural expectations of each user.

4.9 CULTURAL MISREPRESENTATION: A KEY CHALLENGE IN AI DEVELOPMENT

The development of culturally sensitive, trust-building AI systems faces a significant challenge in avoiding cultural misrepresentation. As efforts to make AI more culturally aware intensify, there's a risk of inadvertently reinforcing stereotypes or presenting oversimplified versions of complex cultures.

This issue is present in every modality but is particularly prominent in virtual and augmented reality applications, where AI contributes to creating immersive cultural experiences. The ability to transport users into different cultural contexts brings a substantial responsibility for accurate and respectful representation.

Addressing this challenge requires a culturally humble approach to AI development. This involves:

1. Acknowledging limitations in cultural understanding
2. Actively seeking diverse perspectives
3. Engaging with cultural experts
4. Implementing mechanisms for ongoing feedback and correction

It's crucial to recognize cultures as dynamic, diverse, and evolving entities, rather than static, monolithic constructs. AI systems must be designed with sufficient flexibility to reflect this cultural dynamism and avoid presenting outdated cultural representations.

Building trust in AI systems across diverse cultures requires blending algorithmic precision with subtle cultural understanding. This challenge extends beyond technical considerations, demanding a deeply human approach to AI development.

In essence, AI developers must act as cultural bridge-builders, creating systems capable of earning trust across the spectrum of human cultures. While challenging, this approach holds the potential to develop AI that enhances human interaction and fosters cross-cultural understanding and trust.

4.10   ETHICAL CONSIDERATIONS IN TRUST-ADAPTIVE AI

As we advance in developing trust-adaptive AI systems, we encounter various ethical challenges. These challenges extend beyond technical considerations, touching on fundamental aspects of human interaction, autonomy, and societal structures. Let's briefly go over some of the most important ethical considerations in the development and deployment of trust-adaptive AI.

Anthropomorphism and Authenticity

Trust-adaptive AI often employs human-like characteristics to facilitate trust-building. However, this approach raises critical questions about authenticity and potential deception. We must consider whether we are creating false connections by simulating emotions and vulnerabilities in machines. The "uncanny valley" effect further complicates this issue, as AI that approaches human-likeness without fully achieving it may provoke discomfort or revulsion in users. This phenomenon forces us to reconsider the extent to which AI should emulate human characteristics versus embracing and clearly communicating its artificial nature. The ethical implications of anthropomorphic AI extend beyond the general concerns of deception. Research on conversational AI (Hu et al., 2021) reveals that systems with human-like voices but poor understanding capabilities may inadvertently undermine user trust. This raises ethical questions about the responsible development and deployment of AI systems. Should there be standards for aligning an AI's apparent capabilities (as conveyed through its voice) with its actual capabilities? How can we ensure that anthropomorphic features enhance rather than hinder the development of appropriate trust in AI systems? Striking the right balance between anthropomorphic features and maintaining a clear artificial identity is crucial for building genuine, sustainable trust.

User Autonomy and Informed Consent

The proliferation of AI in our daily lives raises critical questions about its influence on user autonomy in decision-making. While AI's ability to personalize experiences and anticipate needs can be beneficial, it also challenges the preservation of individual agency. This is particularly evident in immersive AI environments where the boundaries between reality and AI-generated content blur. For instance, consider an AI-driven virtual reality health coach that adapts exercise routines based on a user's physiological data. While this personalization can enhance fitness outcomes, it may also subtly shape the user's perception of their capabilities and limits without their full awareness. In such scenarios, ensuring informed consent and maintaining clear boundaries becomes crucial. We must develop strong safeguards against the manipulation of user perceptions and decisions without their explicit agreement. As we advance trust-adaptive AI systems, striking a balance between AI assistance and user autonomy is paramount. This balance is not only ethically necessary but also essential for fostering enduring trust in AI technologies. Our aim should be to create AI systems that augment human decision-making rather than replace it. We should advocate for cultivating a symbiotic relationship that respects user autonomy while benefiting from the potential of AI. This approach will be key to developing AI that users can trust to enhance their lives without compromising their freedom of choice.

Privacy and Data Ethics

Trust-adaptive AI systems rely heavily on massive datasets composed of user data to function effectively. This dependency raises critical questions about data privacy, security, and ownership. We must grapple with how to balance the need for personalized, context-aware AI interactions with the fundamental right to privacy. The potential for data breaches or misuse of sensitive information collected by AI systems could severely undermine user trust and have far-reaching consequences. The use of AI in profiling and predictive analytics based on trust assessments risks perpetuating discriminatory practices, even if unintentional. Trust-adaptive systems may inadvertently amplify existing societal biases. For example, an AI system assessing creditworthiness might use trust metrics that reflect historical inequalities, unfairly disadvantaging certain groups.

These systems often rely on historical data and behavioral patterns that may already contain inherent biases. As they learn and adapt, there's a risk of creating feedback loops that reinforce these biases. The complexity of trust-adaptive AI systems can make it challenging to identify and address these issues, as the reasoning behind trust assessments may not be easily interpretable. This situation underscores the need for constant vigilance and critical examination of trust-adaptive systems.

Accountability and Transparency

As AI systems become more complex and autonomous in their trust-building strategies, issues of accountability come to the fore. When an AI makes a decision that erodes trust or leads to negative outcomes, we must determine who is held responsible—the developers, the company deploying the AI, or the AI itself. Establishing clear lines of accountability is crucial for maintaining ethical standards and public trust in AI technologies. Equally vital is transparency in AI decision-making processes. Users should have the right to understand how and why an AI system has made certain decisions. However, achieving meaningful transparency without overwhelming users with technical details remains a significant challenge. Striking the right balance between disclosure and comprehensibility is key to ensuring informed trust in AI systems.

Cultural Intelligence and Global Ethics

AI isn't just operating in a vacuum. It's being deployed all over the world, in places with vastly different cultural norms and values. What might be considered perfectly trustworthy behavior in, say, New York, could be seen as highly suspicious in Tokyo or Lagos.

Let me give you a concrete example. Imagine you're designing an AI chatbot for customer service. In some cultures, being direct and to-the-point is valued. In others, it might be seen as rude. Your AI needs to be smart enough to navigate these differences.

As another example, consider healthcare AI. In some cultures, involving family in medical decisions is crucial. In others, patient privacy is paramount. Your AI system needs to be sensitive to these differences.

But here's where it gets really interesting - and a bit tricky. As AI becomes more prevalent, it might start influencing cultural norms itself. There's a risk that AI could homogenize how different cultures approach trust. We need to ask ourselves: How do we preserve cultural diversity in a world where more and more of our interactions are mediated by AI?

Long-Term Societal Implications

Perhaps the most profound ethical consideration is the long-term impact of trust-adaptive AI on human relationships and societal structures. As people become more accustomed to interacting with highly personalized, trust-adaptive AI, we must consider how this will affect their expectations and behaviors in human-to-human interactions.

For example, imagine a world where AI personal assistants become so attuned to individual preferences that they can anticipate needs and solve problems more efficiently than any human could. A person might grow frustrated when their human colleague can't match this level of responsiveness or personalization. This could lead to a "trust gap," where the predictability and personalization of AI interactions make human relationships seem less reliable or satisfying by comparison.

Consider a scenario where an AI therapist provides 24/7 emotional support, tailored precisely to an individual's psychological profile. While beneficial in many ways, this could set unrealistic expectations for human relationships, potentially making people less tolerant of the natural inconsistencies and imperfections in human emotional support systems.

In professional settings, AI-mediated performance evaluations or team-building exercises might create environments where employees trust AI feedback more than that of their human managers or peers. This could fundamentally alter workplace dynamics and the development of professional relationships.

The potential for AI to mediate an increasing number of our social and professional interactions also raises questions about the future of human connection and community. For instance, AI-driven social matching algorithms might become so sophisticated that people rely on them exclusively to form new relationships, potentially limiting the serendipitous encounters and diverse connections that often enrich our social lives.

In education, if students become overly reliant on AI tutors and study aids, it might impact their ability to engage in collaborative learning with peers or appreciate the nuanced guidance of human teachers. This could affect the development of crucial social skills and the ability to navigate complex human interactions.

We must strive to ensure that AI enhances rather than replaces meaningful human relationships, preserving the richness and complexity of human social bonds. This might involve designing AI systems that explicitly encourage and facilitate human-to-human interactions, or creating guidelines for "AI-free" spaces and times in various social and professional settings. The goal should be to leverage AI to augment and support human relationships, rather than creating a world where AI becomes the preferred or default mode of interaction. This requires ongoing research, ethical considerations, and potentially new social norms to help society navigate the integration of AI into different communities.

Challenges and Considerations

As AI grows more prominent in our everyday lives, there is a pressing need to address the growing challenges associated with these technological advancements. Let's briefly review some of these challenges here.

Balancing Autonomy and Reliance: As AI systems become more capable and trustworthy, we must balance the benefits of AI assistance with preserving human agency and decision-making skills.

Privacy and Data Ethics: The increasing reliance on personal data for trust-building in AI systems will require strong frameworks for data protection and ethical data use.

Algorithmic Bias and Fairness: Ensuring that AI systems are free from bias and promote fairness will be crucial for maintaining trust across diverse user groups.

Transparency vs. Intellectual Property: Balancing the need for explainable AI with the protection of proprietary algorithms will be an ongoing challenge.

Regulation and Governance: Developing flexible, adaptive regulatory frameworks that can keep pace with rapid AI advancements while ensuring ethical standards will be crucial.

Digital Divide in AI Trust: Ensuring equal access to trustworthy AI systems across different socioeconomic groups will be essential to prevent exacerbating existing inequalities.

The trust we place in these systems will be a reflection of our values, aspirations, and vision for the role of technology in shaping our collective future. In this endeavor, we must remain committed to preserving the essence of human trust while embracing the transformative potential of AI.

Addressing these ethical challenges requires a multidisciplinary approach, bringing together technologists, ethicists, and policymakers. We are challenged to create technology that enhances human potential and societal well-being while respecting individual autonomy and cultural diversity.

The Trust-Adaptive Virtual Agents (TAVA) framework represents a significant advancement in human-AI interaction, offering a comprehensive approach to building and maintaining trust across diverse user populations and cultural contexts. By integrating transparency, reliability, adaptability, and ethical considerations, TAVA imagines a framework for more intuitive and trustworthy AI systems.

However, as we progress in developing these sophisticated AI systems, we must remain vigilant about the ethical implications they bring. The challenges of anthropomorphism, user autonomy, privacy, accountability, and cultural intelligence demand our constant attention. Moreover, the potential long-term impacts on human relationships and societal structures underscore the need for a balanced approach that enhances, rather than replaces, human connections.

The path forward in trust-adaptive AI development requires a delicate balance between technological innovation and ethical responsibility. It calls for interdisciplinary collaboration, cultural humility, and a commitment to preserving human agency and cultural diversity. As we continue to refine these systems, our goal should be to create AI that earns trust while also enriching human experiences and aiding cross-cultural understanding.

Ultimately, the success of trust-adaptive AI will be measured not just by its technical capabilities, but by its ability to integrate seamlessly into communities, respecting our values, enhancing our relationships, and contributing positively to our shared future.

4.11 CONCLUSION

In concluding our exploration of trust in AI, we find ourselves at a crucial intersection of technology and culture. The concept of trust, deeply rooted in human societies and cultural practices, is being redefined as we extend it to our interactions with AI systems.

Throughout this chapter, we've seen how trust in AI is both a technical challenge and a cultural one. The interplay between trust, AI, and culture is complex and nuanced, from the way culture colors our trust in AI to AI's potential to inspire trust and understanding between cultures. The TAVA framework, with its emphasis on cultural intelligence and adaptability, offers one approach to navigating this complexness.

Our examination of trust-adaptive virtual agents has revealed that effective AI systems must do more than simply process data; they must understand and respect the cultural contexts in which they operate. Just as trust varies across cultures, so too must our approaches to building trustworthy AI. The strategies we've explored - from heuristics to Theory of Mind approaches - all require careful cultural calibration to be truly effective.

We envision future AI systems that not only earn our trust but also serve as custodians of cultural knowledge and facilitate cross-cultural understanding. Imagine AI preserving endangered languages, not just in form but in cultural context, or creating immersive experiences that allow us to explore diverse cultural perspectives. These possibilities highlight the potential for AI to enhance rather than erode our cultural heritage.

However, with this potential comes significant responsibility. As AI becomes more integrated into our cultural practices and daily lives, we must pay special attention to making sure our AI systems respect and promote cultural diversity rather than homogenizing it. The ethical considerations we've discussed are not just abstract principles but crucial safeguards for maintaining the integrity of diverse cultural expressions in an AI-mediated world.

The path forward requires a delicate balance. We must leverage the power of AI to build bridges across cultures while being mindful of the unique trust dynamics within each cultural context. This calls for ongoing collaboration between technologists, anthropologists, ethicists, and cultural leaders to create AI systems that are not just technically proficient but culturally intelligent.

As we continue to develop and refine AI technologies, let us remember that trust is fundamentally a cultural construct. By centering culture in our approach to AI development, we can create systems that both earn trust and enrich our cultural worlds. The future of AI lies not just in its technical capabilities, but in its ability to understand and respect human diversity.

The intersection of AI and trust presents a unique opportunity to redefine our relationship with technology. As we've explored, trust in AI is not merely a technical challenge but a cultural and ethical imperative. The future demands AI systems that are proficient but also culturally intelligent and ethically grounded.

Our journey forward requires a multidisciplinary approach, blending technological innovation with deep cultural understanding. The goal is clear: to create AI that enhances human potential while respecting the diversity of global cultures.

The challenges are significant, from ensuring user autonomy to bridging digital divides. Yet, the potential rewards are equally profound. AI could become a powerful tool for cultural preservation, cross-cultural understanding, and global collaboration.

As we navigate this technological evolution, our decisions will shape not just the future of AI, but the very nature of human-machine interaction. By prioritizing trust, ethics, and cultural intelligence in AI development, we can strive for a future where AI serves as a trusted partner in human progress.

The path ahead is complex, but the vision is inspiring. Let us embrace this challenge with wisdom and creativity, working toward a future where AI and human culture flourish together, each enriching the other.

REFERENCES

Baek, T. H. & Kim, M. (2023). Is ChatGPT scary good? How user motivations affect creepiness and trust in generative artificial intelligence. *Telematics and Informatics*, *3*, 102030. https://www.sciencedirect.com/science/article/abs/pii/S0736585323000941?via%3Dihub

Bailenson, J. N., Aharoni, E., Beall, A. C., Guadagno, R. E., Dimov, A., & Blascovich, J. (2004). Comparing behavioral and self-report measures of embodied agents' social presence in immersive virtual environments. *7th Annual International Workshop on PRESENCE*, 1105.

Cassell, J. (Ed.). (2000). *Embodied conversational agents*. MIT Press.

Chandra, S., Shirish, A., & Srivastava, S. C. (2022). To be or not to be …human? theorizing the role of human-like competencies in conversational artificial intelligence agents. *Journal of Management Information Systems*, *39*(4), 969–1005. https://doi.org/10.1080/074212 22.2022.2127441

Cipolle, A. V.. (2022). How Native Americans are trying to debug A.I.'s biases. https://www.nytimes.com/2022/03/22/technology/ai-data-indigenous-ivow.html

Darmody, J. (2021). Can AI be used to preserve cultural wisdom? https://www.siliconrepublic.com/machines/ai-davar-ardalan-ivow-culture

De Graaf, M. M. A., Allouch, S. B., & Klamer, T. (2015). Sharing a life with Harvey: Exploring the acceptance of and relationship-building with a social robot. *Computers in Human Behavior*, *43*, 1–14.

Desai, M., et al. (2013). Impact of robot failures and feedback on real-time trust. *8th ACM/IEEE International Conference on Human-Robot Interaction (HRI)*.

Frith, C., & Frith, U. (2005). Theory of mind. *Current Biology*, *15*(17), R644–R645.

Hakhverdian, A., & Mayne, Q. (2012). Institutional trust, education, and corruption: A micro-macro interactive approach. *The Journal of Politics*, *74*(3), 739–750.

Hu, P., Lu, Y., & Gong. Y. (2021). Dual humanness and trust in conversational AI: a person-centered approach. *Computers in Human Behavior, 119*(C), 106727. https://dl.acm.org/doi/abs/10.1016/j.chb.2021.106727?utm_source=chatgpt.com

Johnson, D., & Grayson, K. (2005, April). Cognitive and affective trust in service relationship. *Journal of Business Research*, *58*(4), 500–507. https://doi.org/10.1016/S0148-2963(03)00140-1

Kok, B. C., & Soh, H. (2020). Trust in robots: Challenges and opportunities. *Current Robotics Reports*, *1*(4), 297–309.

Kramer, R. M., & Tyler, T. R. (Eds.). (1995). *Trust in organizations: Frontiers of theory and research*. SAGE Publications.

Li, Y., et al. (2024). Developing trustworthy artificial intelligence: Insights from research on interpersonal, human-automation, and human-AI trust. *Frontiers in Psychology*, *15*, 1382693.

Lucas, G. M., et al. (2014). It's only a computer: Virtual humans increase willingness to disclose. *Computers in Human Behavior*, *37*, 94–100.

Lukyanenko, R., Maass, W., & Storey, V. C. (2022). Trust in artificial intelligence: From a Foundational Trust Framework to emerging research opportunities. *Electronic Markets*, *32*(4), 1993–2020.

Merritt, S. M., & Ilgen, D. R. (2008). Not all trust is created equal: Dispositional and history-based trust in human-automation interactions. *Human Factors*, *50*(2), 194–210.

Moradinezhad, R. (2022). *Toward trust-adaptive embodied virtual agents* [Doctoral dissertation, Drexel University]. https://doi.org/10.17918/00001112

Moray, N., Inagaki, T., & Itoh, M. (2000). Adaptive automation, trust, and self-confidence in fault management of time-critical tasks. *Journal of Experimental Psychology: Applied*, *6*(1), 44–58.

Novozhilova, E., Mays, K., Paik, S., & Katz, J. E. (2024). More capable, less benevolent: trust perceptions of ai systems across societal contexts. *Machine Learning Knowledge Extraction*, 6(1), 342–366. https://doi.org/10.3390/make6010017

Rheu, M., Shin, J. Y., Peng, W., & Huh-Yoo, J. (2020). Systematic review: trust-building factors and implications for conversational agent design. *International Journal of Human–Computer Interaction*, 37(1), 81–96. https://doi.org/10.1080/10447318.2020.1807710

Thiebes, S., Lins, S., & Sunyaev, A. (2021). Trustworthy artificial intelligence. *Electronic Markets*, *31*, 447–464.

Xu, A., & Dudek, G. (2015). Optimo: Online probabilistic trust inference model for asymmetric human-robot collaborations. *10th annual ACM/IEEE International Conference on Human-Robot Interaction* (pp. 91–100).

Community Voices 4: Insights from Stéphanie Camaréna—Discussing Ethical AI Practices and Community Trust

Our fourth community voice features insights from Stéphanie Camaréna, a strategic leader and expert in sustainable innovation. As the founder of Source Transitions, Stéphanie uses artificial intelligence (AI) for positive societal impact and drives multidisciplinary collaboration to redesign food systems.

With over 15 years of experience across government, corporate, and consulting roles, her pioneering research on AI's role in sustainability positions her as a thought leader in the field. Stéphanie's unique strengths lie in technology, business transformation, and design, making her an invaluable contributor to discussions on AI and cultural preservation.

Growing up in the South of France, Stéphanie's cultural background and professional journey have deeply influenced her commitment to using AI for social good.

Question 1: Share your professional bio

Stéphanie Camaréna is a strategic leader driving sustainable innovation through multidisciplinary collaboration. As founder of Source Transitions, she harnesses AI for positive societal impact. Her pioneering PhD research on AI's role in redesigning food systems positions her as a thought leader. With 15+ years' experience across government, corporate, and consulting roles, Stéphanie has an award-winning track record implementing sustainable strategies. Her unique strengths span technology, business transformation, design, and facilitating diverse stakeholders to co-create responsible, systems-level solutions. A sought-after presenter, Stéphanie empowers organizations to optimize processes and cultivate sustainable mindsets.

Question 2: Share your heritage and family traditions. Where did you grow up? Share a family tradition that you continue to this day.

I grew up in the South of France in the Pyrenees then in the Montpellier region. On my dad's side, there has been a tradition of cooking paella for big family gatherings. This stemmed from the Spanish origins of my grandfather. It's always been a grand affair with preparations starting the day before. Then on the day, the men of the family make a big deal of "orchestrating" the different dishes being added to the

DOI: 10.1201/9781003517115-8

paella pan. Seventeen minutes to cook the rice exactly! Now my husband has taken over the tradition despite having no Spanish origins whatsoever. A real treat.

Question 3: Experience with AI. Have you used AI technologies? If yes, please describe your experience. How do you perceive the role of AI in your professional or personal life?

I started working with AI in 2016. I have been working as a consultant with a company automating information classification. We were using object detection and image recognition to detect specific logos and images and capture them to generate labels or titles for documents. Machine learning was also a big part of what we used. I was involved in the business analysis, functional design, and training of teams who were using the tools. After 20 years of experience in IT and another 15 in design for sustainability, I decided to do a PhD in 2017 with the School of Design at RMIT University in Melbourne. I researched ways of engaging with AI for the benefit of the whole in the transition to sustainable food systems. My PhD was based on action research, and all the projects I conducted were done in the context of business, not for profit and research environments. AI is now central to my professional life as a consultant in AI for sustainability. IT is an integral part of my everyday life, and I see its use in very pragmatic ways.

Question 4: AI and cultural preservation. Can you envision any innovative ways in which AI could be used to safeguard intangible cultural heritage, such as language, folksongs, or storytelling? Are there specific traditions, practices, or aspects of your culture that you believe could benefit from AI technology?

The family stories from previous generations are being lost and with it the knowledge of what brought us to where we are. Young generations are not interested in these stories; they are boring and do not bring anything of value to them. Maybe having ways of recording these stories which would then be played in whatever the latest format is could be of interest, a potential source of pride for younger generations. For example, stories could be stored in a technology-agnostic format that can then be replayed in a format that new generations find engaging.

Question 5: AI and nature. Could you describe a traditional practice from your own culture, or one you've learned about or reported on, that helps in environmental sustainability or climate resilience? Also, how do you think AI could be utilized to support or improve this practice?

There is a danger that AI will be used to further reinforce colonization by extracting further knowledge from indigenous people to gain profits or advantages that are not returned to them. In countryside France, there are still traditions of slaughtering a pig or lamb as a community, or across a couple of families. These practices ensured that 100% of the animal was used for all sorts of different purposes. Nothing was wasted. Nowadays, 30%–35% of all the food produced is wasted. We invest countless efforts and resources (water, fossil fuel, minerals) into growing food that then is thrown away even before it gets to people. AI could possibly help transform food systems to a demand-driven system based on community and local needs and answered by local suppliers. Lower carbon footprint, resilience, economic benefits, and social structure could all benefit.

Question 6: Wisdom of elders and AI. What role do elders play in preserving culture and wisdom in your community? With ethical practices at play, can AI play a role in capturing and disseminating this wisdom? If yes, how?

Elders are the family memory and point of reference. They tell stories, they remind us of what hard times mean, and how lucky we are right now. They are also a voice for what is appropriate or what is not in the way we behave. They remind us of priorities and of the importance of family. Ethics is closer to morality in that context. I am not sure this is something that AI can have a role in. If there was one, it would possibly be for the people who are left behind with no family or friends and could have lots to contribute if they did. AI-powered tools or solutions could help connect knowledge across generations, geographies, and cultural realms.

Question 7: AI and ethics. How important is it for AI systems to be developed ethically, especially in the context of cultural preservation? What steps would you like to be taken to ensure that, as AI expands, it represents diverse cultural perspectives?

How can we expect a team of a few developers to be able to represent culturally diverse ways of thinking and approaches when they have no awareness or contact with that diversity? It is impossible even with the most well-meaning teams. I think this is the end of using empathy maps and personas as they have been used to date. The key to AI ethics is the integration of "realness" into problem framing, design, solution development, and implementation. The need to resolve the issue of cost and time associated with involving real people and navigating cultural perspectives is the main challenge to AI expansion. It's costly and slows down the process. AI ethics needs to be more costly when it is not there than when it is included.

Question 8: AI and personalization. We know that AI systems today don't understand the values and needs of diverse populations. Would you be willing to voluntarily share your family traditions and customs with your personal AI device to improve personalization?

Not really. Mainly because AI systems today are built to generate profits for shareholders. Personalization is only useful to sell more things that we do not need. Unless that changes, I do not think I would be interested in providing more of my personal data and cultural values.

Question 9: Future of AI in community development. What potential risks and benefits should be considered when integrating AI into community initiatives?

The risks are that AI solutions will be developed looking for problems to solve. This is the main approach that has been taken by AI developers to date in the context of communities. There is an issue of trust that could be further damaged when AI systems are imposed onto a community. Benefits appear when AI is jointly imagined with communities who are able to learn from projects and feel empowered by what they learn. AI literacy is built through community involvement when defining the problem that they want to solve and researching possible solutions. Seeing AI projects in multidisciplinary teams as opportunities to learn from each other brings benefits for all and a sense of agency that frees up the thinking of the participants. A codesign approach that allows for the intervention of experts when and if they are needed (on demand) allows people to feel empowered to think and co-create solutions that they need.

Question 10: Final thoughts. Is there anything else you would like to share about your views on AI and its role in preserving cultural heritage and traditions?

I see it more as a human role in preserving cultural heritage and traditions where AI can be used strategically to support what exists, to rejuvenate what has disappeared and to invent new ways that we haven't dared to think about yet because we did not have the tools, capacity, or capability. AI can help us in these ways.

***

Stéphanie Camaréna's survey responses provide a visionary perspective on the transformative potential of AI in cultural preservation and sustainability. Her extensive experience underscores the importance of integrating ethical considerations and diverse cultural viewpoints into AI development.

5 Human Agency and AI

Amir Banifatemi

5.1 INTRODUCTION

As someone deeply immersed in the world of technology, I've witnessed firsthand how artificial intelligence (AI) has moved from the fringes of science fiction to becoming an inescapable force in our daily lives. From healthcare to education, from our workplaces to our homes, AI is seamlessly integrating into the fabric of modern life, offering unprecedented advancements that are pushing the boundaries of what we once thought possible.

Yet, with all this progress, there are real challenges that we cannot ignore. AI's rapid development has the potential to both uplift and disrupt—enhancing privacy while exposing new risks, and promoting fairness while sometimes reinforcing existing biases. This duality demands that we ask tough questions about how we maintain control over these technologies. At this pivotal moment, ensuring that AI empowers rather than diminishes human agency is essential.

This chapter invites the reader to take a high-level look at AI's evolving impact on culture and society. AI is reshaping our world, from the preservation of cultural heritage to the empowerment of communities. We will evaluate the governance and care necessary to ensure AI remains trustworthy and accountable and consider how to prepare communities for an AI-powered future.

My guiding principle throughout this exploration is based on a vision of a future where AI and human agency are not opposing forces but mutually reinforcing pillars of progress. We can envision a future where AI enhances our capabilities, expands our understanding, and empowers us to tackle grand challenges, while celebrating the irreplaceable value of human intelligence and creativity.

It's important to acknowledge that the rapidly evolving nature of AI technology means some emerging areas may not be covered in depth. Topics such as AI's economic implications, its role in addressing climate change, applications in military and security contexts, impact on creative industries, intersection with neurotechnology, and long-term philosophical implications are all critical areas that warrant ongoing consideration. I encourage you to view this discussion as a starting point for further exploration. The field of AI is dynamic and multifaceted, and staying informed about these evolving areas will be crucial as we collectively shape the future of AI in our communities.

> **Transition to Next Section**: As AI continues to shape our world, a fundamental question arises: how do we ensure that these technologies serve to enhance, rather than undermine, our autonomy and decision-making power? This brings us to the critical issue of preserving human agency in an AI-driven world.

DOI: 10.1201/9781003517115-9

5.2   PRESERVING HUMAN AGENCY IN AN AI WORLD

We are witnessing daily how AI is becoming increasingly sophisticated and embedded in various aspects of our lives. Many are warning about preserving human agency as critical to our evolution as humans but also as communities. Let's define human agency in the context of AI weaved in our lives, and sometimes autonomous, where we need to have the ability to understand, influence, and, when necessary, override the decisions made by AI systems. It is common nowadays to refer to AI as a tool for human empowerment rather than a force for disenfranchisement. The challenge lies in ensuring that as AI's role evolves, it does so in a way that enhances rather than diminishes our capacity for independent decision-making (autonomy).

5.2.1   THE NEED FOR AGENCY-PRESERVING AI

The concept of "agency-preserving AI" extends beyond the notion of user-empowerment. It encompasses the design of AI systems that actively enhance human capabilities while respecting human autonomy. Such systems must be transparent in their operations, enabling users to understand the basis of their recommendations or actions. They must be controllable, offering options for users to adjust or override decisions. Crucially, agency-preserving AI should be designed with the explicit goal of augmenting human intelligence, not replacing it.

Consider the realm of healthcare. An agency-preserving AI system might analyze vast amounts of medical data to suggest potential diagnosis or treatment plans. However, the final decision should always rest with the human doctor, who can integrate the AI's insights with their own expertise, intuition, and understanding of the patient's unique circumstances. Here, AI acts as a powerful tool that expands the doctor's knowledge base and analytical capabilities but does not usurp the doctor's role in the decision-making process.

In the financial sector, AI-powered investment platforms offer another example of agency-preserving AI. These systems can process enormous quantities of market data, identify trends, and offer investment recommendations. However, the investor retains control over their financial decisions, adjusting strategies based on personal goals, risk tolerance, and other factors that the AI might not fully capture. The AI provides information and suggestions, but the human user remains the ultimate decision-maker.

Education is another arena where agency-preserving AI can shine. Adaptive learning platforms use AI to tailor educational content to individual students' needs, learning styles, and progress. However, these systems are most effective when they support rather than replace human teachers. The AI might identify areas where a student is struggling and suggest targeted exercises, but it is the human teacher who provides the nuanced guidance, encouragement, and contextual understanding crucial to the learning process.

TABLE 5.1

Comparative Table: AI Applications and Human Agency

Sector	Role of AI	Potential Benefits	Risks to Human Agency	Strategies for Preserving Agency
Healthcare	AI-assisted diagnostics and treatment recommendations	Enhanced accuracy; personalized care	Over-reliance on AI; diminishing the role of human judgment	Keep human decision-making at the center; ensure AI provides explainable insights
Finance	AI-powered investment platforms offering recommendations	Improved financial outcomes; data-driven decisions	Automated decisions without human oversight; potential for bias	Provide users with options to adjust or override AI decisions
Education	Adaptive learning platforms tailored to individual needs	Personalized learning; improved educational outcomes	Reduced human interaction in teaching; loss of critical thinking skills	Use AI to support teachers rather than replace them; maintain teacher-student relationships

5.2.2   RISKS OF DIMINISHED HUMAN AGENCY

While the benefits of AI are significant, the risks associated with diminishing human autonomy must not be overlooked. Without appropriate safeguards, AI systems could inadvertently—or intentionally—undermine individual agency and decision-making power.

One area of concern is the use of AI in hiring processes. While AI has the potential to reduce human biases in recruitment, poorly designed or biased AI systems could perpetuate or even exacerbate discrimination. For instance, if an AI system is trained on historical hiring data that reflects past biases, it may continue to favor certain demographics over others, leading to qualified candidates being systematically overlooked based on irrelevant characteristics. This phenomenon was highlighted in a study by Amazon, where an AI recruiting tool was found to be biased against women.

Another risk lies in the realm of personal privacy and autonomy. AI-powered surveillance systems, while potentially useful for public safety, could also be misused to infringe on personal freedoms. Facial recognition technology, for instance, could enable constant monitoring of individuals' movements and activities, creating a chilling effect on free expression and association. The use of such technologies by authoritarian regimes to suppress dissent underscores the need for stringent ethical guidelines and oversight.

Case Study—COMPAS Algorithm: The case of the COMPAS (Correctional Offender Management Profiling for Alternative Sanctions) algorithm in the U.S. criminal justice system serves as a cautionary tale. This AI system, used to assess the likelihood of a defendant reoffending, has been criticized for potential racial bias. Studies have shown that the algorithm was more likely to incorrectly flag black defendants as high-risk compared to white defendants. This case illustrates how AI systems, if not carefully designed and monitored, can perpetuate and amplify societal biases, leading to unjust outcomes that significantly impact individuals' lives (Wikipedia, n.d.b).

5.2.3 Ensuring Accountability and Transparency

Given these risks, ensuring human oversight and accountability over AI systems is paramount. Effective governance frameworks and regulatory measures are essential to guarantee that AI systems operate transparently, ethically, and in alignment with human values. Here are some mechanisms used for accountability:

Audit Trails: One crucial mechanism for ensuring accountability is the implementation of comprehensive audit trails for AI decision-making processes. These trails should document not just the final output of an AI system but also the data and reasoning that led to that output. This transparency allows for thorough reviews and provides a basis for accountability if issues arise.

Ethics Committees and Review Boards: Ethics committees or review boards play a vital role in overseeing AI development and deployment. These bodies can provide guidance on best practices, monitor compliance with ethical standards, and address potential ethical dilemmas as they arise. Although the effectiveness of such committees depends on their authority and the influence they wield within organizations, their presence is crucial for embedding ethical considerations into AI governance.

Regulatory Frameworks: Governments and regulatory bodies have a crucial role to play in establishing and enforcing guidelines for ethical AI use, including standards for transparency, fairness, and privacy. The European Union's General Data Protection Regulation (GDPR) serves as a benchmark for data protection and privacy in AI, mandating regular audits and impact assessments for systems involved in high-stakes decision-making processes.

Public Involvement in AI Governance: Public involvement in AI governance is another key aspect of maintaining accountability. Engaging the public in AI policy-making ensures that diverse perspectives are considered and that AI development aligns with societal values. Public consultations, citizen assemblies, and participatory design workshops are valuable tools for incorporating public input into AI governance (Table 5.1).

TABLE 5.2
Preserving Human Agency in an AI World

	Key Points
Context	Human agency in AI contexts is crucial to ensure AI serves as a tool for empowerment, not disenfranchisement
The need for agency-preserving AI	AI should enhance human capabilities and decision-making rather than replace them, emphasizing transparency and control
Examples in healthcare, finance, education	AI in these sectors should support human expertise and decision-making, not replace it
Risks of diminished human agency	Discusses risks such as bias in AI systems, privacy issues, and examples like the COMPAS algorithm
Ensuring accountability and transparency	Emphasizes the need for audit trails, ethics committees, and robust regulatory frameworks for AI
Perspective	Advocates for AI that complements human decision-making and preserves human agency

By prioritizing transparency, control, and accountability in AI systems, we can create better environments to allow for human empowerment. As mentioned, the challenge before us is not to choose between human and AI but to find ways for them to work in concert, each amplifying the strengths of the other, to serve the individual, but also the communities in which they live (Table 5.2).

Transition to Next Section: While safeguarding human agency is paramount, it is equally important to consider how we can democratize AI resources to empower a broader range of stakeholders. The AI Commons stands as a pivotal initiative in this regard, creating a collaborative environment where AI tools and opportunity to participate are accessible to all.

5.3   AI COMMONS: A PILLAR OF THE AI FOR GOOD MOVEMENT

The AI for Good movement represents a pivotal moment in the evolution of artificial intelligence, where technology is deliberately directed toward solving the world's most pressing challenges. This movement has grown into a global initiative aimed at ensuring AI technologies are not just tools for economic gain but are leveraged to promote human well-being, social equity, and sustainable development. This chapter explores the origins, key milestones, and ongoing impact of the AI for Good movement, emphasizing its role in shaping a future where AI serves the greater good.

5.3.1   THE ORIGINS: AI XPRIZE AS A CATALYST

The AI for Good movement traces its origins back to the AI XPRIZE competition, which was launched in 2016 by XPRIZE in collaboration with IBM Watson. This $5 million competition sought to inspire teams from around the world to harness the power of AI to address some of humanity's most pressing challenges, with a focus on critical areas such as education, healthcare, the environment, and social justice. The competition aimed to push the boundaries of AI innovation by incentivizing breakthrough solutions that were not only technologically advanced but also capable of delivering significant, measurable impact on a global scale (XPRIZE, 2016).

A key feature of the AI XPRIZE was its emphasis on creating multi-discipline collaboration, bringing together teams from diverse countries and disciplines to tackle complex problems from different perspectives. This collaborative approach underscored the belief that the most effective solutions emerge from a fusion of varied expertise and viewpoints. Moreover, a defining requirement of the competition was that the AI solutions demonstrate tangible demonstrations of AI being used to tackle problems and show positive societal benefits, setting a strong precedent for future AI initiatives aimed at advancing the common good.

The AI XPRIZE served as a crucial starting point for the AI for Good movement by illustrating the potential of AI to contribute positively to humanity. It also laid the groundwork for subsequent initiatives aimed at ensuring AI technologies are developed and deployed ethically and inclusively.

As we explore the role of AI in shaping our future, it becomes evident that democratizing access to AI resources is crucial for ensuring that the benefits of AI are equitably distributed. This brings us to the AI Commons, a key initiative within the AI for Good movement, which exemplifies the power of collaboration in making AI accessible to all, especially those who are often excluded from technological advancements (Gaudiot and Banifatemi, 2016).

5.3.2   AI Commons as a Pillar of the AI for Good Movement

Progress toward a more inclusive and prosperous society, where AI plays a central role, requires dialogue and collaboration among a diverse range of stakeholders. These efforts must include individuals who are most affected by AI technologies yet often the least empowered to engage in their development and application.

Late in the Fall of 2017, Yoshua Bengio and I formed the foundation of an initiative called the AI Commons that started from discussions initiated in 2016 around projects presented to the AI XPRIZE competition and workshops held during the inaugural AI for Good Global Summit. These discussions highlighted a critical need for academic and scientific support, ethical and safety governance, sustainability considerations, and access to data and technical infrastructure to ensure that AI projects could be effectively deployed and have a meaningful impact (AI Commons, n.d.).

The AI Commons was created to establish a collaborative ecosystem where AI resources—such as data, computing power, AI expertise, and domain knowledge—are shared and utilized for AI-enabled problem-solving at the local level. The goal is to democratize, decentralize, and distribute the benefits of AI, ensuring that AI systems are designed and developed with the input of diverse communities and tailored to meet their actual needs.

As a foundational element of the AI for Good movement, the AI Commons goes beyond simply advocating for the ethical use of AI. It actively promotes the creation of collaborative platforms that empower communities—beyond large industrial players or governments—to harness AI's potential for solving global challenges. By providing open access to vital resources like data, algorithms, and expertise, the AI Commons aligns with the United Nations Sustainable Development Goals (SDGs), enabling communities around the world to address both local and global issues through AI-driven solutions.

5.3.3   AI Commons as a Collaborative Framework

In line with the principles of inclusivity and diversity in AI development, the AI Commons identified the creation of collaborative platforms and environments to democratize access to AI resources and promote collaboration across diverse stakeholders. By connecting problem owners with AI practitioners and providing access to data, tools, and expertise, the AI Commons empowers communities to develop AI solutions tailored to their specific needs. This initiative is particularly important for underrepresented regions where access to AI resources has traditionally been limited (Figures 5.1a and 5.1b).

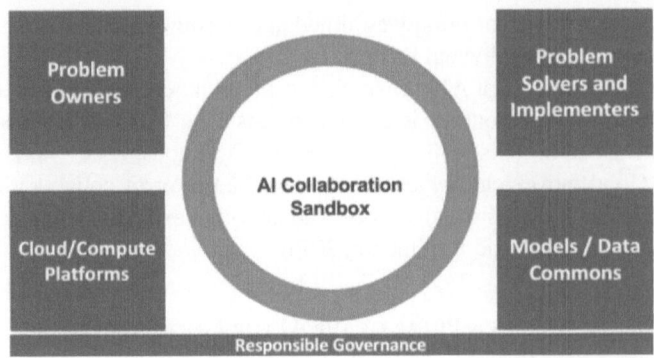

FIGURE 5.1a   The AI Commons collaborative problem-solving framework.

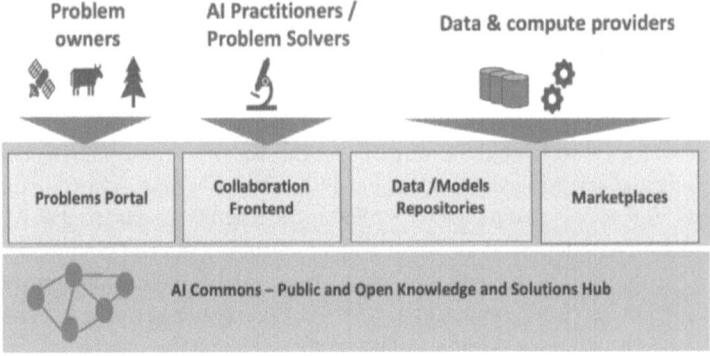

FIGURE 5.1b   The AI Commons community ecosystem.

Example of how it works:

For instance, in regions like Africa and Southeast Asia, where AI development resources may be scarce, the AI Commons facilitates the collaboration between for instance farmers and health care workers with AI practitioners, and contribution of data and algorithms that can be used to address local challenges. This collaborative approach ensures that AI development is not only inclusive but also responsive to the unique needs of different communities around the world.

Data Science Nigeria (2020)

5.3.4   THE BIRTH OF THE AI FOR GOOD GLOBAL SUMMIT

Building on the momentum of the AI XPRIZE, and the AI Commons framing, the AI for Good Global Summit was launched in 2017 by the International Telecommunication Union (ITU) in partnership with XPRIZE, the United Nations (UN), and other global organizations. It was initially conceived as a showcase of teams participating in the AI XPRIZE and discussing the impact of AI on global challenges. The summit was the first international platform dedicated to exploring how AI could be harnessed to achieve the UN Sustainable Development Goals (SDGs) (AI for Good, 2017).

The event placed a strong emphasis on developing AI technologies ethically, ensuring that transparency, human rights, and values were integral to AI's design and application.

Central to the summit's agenda was the potential of AI to contribute to the achievement of the 17 UN SDGs, which range from ending poverty and improving global health to combating climate change and focusing on sustainable development. The summit offered a true multi-stakeholder collaboration, bringing together governments, academia, industry, and civil society to recognize that the complexity of global challenges demands collective action. Furthermore, the event underscored the critical role of public-private partnerships in driving AI for Good initiatives, ensuring that both resources and expertise were effectively pooled to maximize impact.

In 2019, the AI for Good Global Summit featured a full-day track focused on AI and culture. This track explored the intersection of artificial intelligence and cultural preservation, showcasing projects and research aimed at ensuring AI technologies reflect and respect diverse cultural narratives. The discussions highlighted how AI can be used to preserve indigenous knowledge, enhance cultural storytelling, and foster inclusivity in AI development. This unique track underscored the importance of cultural intelligence in AI, ensuring that the technologies of the future not only drive progress but also protect and amplify the voices and stories of underrepresented communities (IVOW, 2019).

Since its inception, the AI for Good Global Summit has grown into an annual event and a key platform for advancing global dialogue on ethical AI. It continues to promote initiatives that leverage AI to address the most pressing challenges facing humanity and works to shape a future where AI is used for the betterment of communities on a global scale.

5.3.5   KEY MILESTONES AND IMPACT

The AI for Good movement has achieved several key milestones that have shaped its trajectory and broadened its influence:

1. **Expanding the Global Dialogue on Ethical AI**: The AI for Good Global Summit has played a crucial role in bringing ethical AI considerations to the forefront of global discussions. It has influenced international policies and inspired the formation of various AI ethics committees and guidelines.
2. **Launch of AI for Good Initiatives Globally**: Inspired by the movement, numerous initiatives have been launched worldwide, focusing on applying AI to solve specific global challenges. These include AI for Earth by Microsoft, which uses AI to address environmental issues, and Google's AI for Social Good, which supports projects focused on healthcare, education, and crisis response.
3. **AI and Data Ecosystems**: One of the outcomes of the AI for Good movement is the emphasis on creating data commons and collaboratives, which democratize access to data and enable more inclusive AI development. These models have been recognized as essential for advancing AI in ways that benefit all of humanity.

5.3.6   THE ROLE OF DATA AND COLLABORATION IN THE AI FOR GOOD MOVEMENT

Data plays a central role in the AI for Good movement, with initiatives emphasizing the need for open, accessible, and high-quality datasets. Collaborative efforts, such as data commons and data collaboratives, are crucial in ensuring that AI technologies are developed in an inclusive and responsible manner.

Data Commons: Data Commons allow for the pooling of data resources to be shared openly for AI research and development. This approach is essential for ensuring that AI solutions are built on diverse and representative datasets, which is critical for reducing bias and improving fairness in AI outcomes.

Data Collaboratives: These initiatives bring together data from various sectors, including government, private companies, and civil society, to address complex public challenges. For example, the COVID-19 Mobility Data Network is a collaborative effort that has shown the power of data sharing in responding to global crises.

5.3.7   THE FUTURE OF THE AI FOR GOOD MOVEMENT

The AI for Good movement has emerged as a significant force in shaping the direction of artificial intelligence, rooted in the belief that these powerful technologies must be harnessed for the collective benefit of humanity. From its early foundations in the AI XPRIZE to the establishment of platforms such as the AI for Good Global Summit and the Global Partnership on AI (GPAI), the movement has laid critical groundwork for AI development that is both ethical and inclusive. These initiatives have set a precedent for how AI can be thoughtfully directed to tackle some of the world's most pressing challenges, from poverty to climate change.

Yet, as the movement continues to grow, it's clear that this is only the beginning. The frameworks and principles established by the AI for Good movement—emphasizing transparency, accountability, and inclusivity—will need to evolve alongside rapid advancements in AI technology. The true test lies in the ability of global stakeholders to maintain these values in the face of increasing technological complexity and economic pressures. While the movement has successfully enabled collaboration among governments, academia, industry, and civil society, the future will demand even more nuanced cooperation. Global collaboration must be strengthened, not just to distribute AI's benefits equitably, but also to navigate the ethical dilemmas and unforeseen risks that accompany new breakthroughs in AI.

One of the most pressing tasks ahead is refining ethical standards that can keep pace with the dynamic nature of AI. As AI systems become more autonomous and embedded in decision-making processes, the movement's emphasis on human agency will be tested. We must question how far AI should be allowed to influence human lives and where the line between augmentation and autonomy lies. This will require not just technical solutions but ongoing philosophical and societal debates that involve diverse perspectives from across the globe.

The AI for Good movement has already shown that AI can be a force for positive change, but its long-term impact will depend on its ability to adapt and scale. As new initiatives emerge, they will need to address an ever-broadening range of challenges, ensuring that AI solutions are contextually appropriate and sensitive to local needs. This expansion will bring with it complexities—how can we ensure that AI initiatives, designed with global goals in mind, remain relevant to the specific needs of communities, especially those that have traditionally been left out of technological advancements?

Looking forward, the movement must also grapple with the tension between technological optimism and pragmatism. While there is great promise in AI's ability to drive progress, the movement must be cautious of overselling what AI can achieve, especially when solutions to deeply entrenched issues require more than just technological intervention. The future of the AI for Good movement lies not only in leveraging AI's capabilities but in recognizing its limitations and working alongside other disciplines to create sustainable and meaningful change.

In essence, the AI for Good movement has opened an important conversation about the future of AI and its role in society. The road ahead is complex and uncertain, but the movement's principles provide a necessary foundation for thinking critically about how we, as a global society, can ensure that AI truly serves the greater good. As we continue to navigate this evolving landscape, we must proceed with both optimism and caution, ensuring that AI remains a tool for empowering humanity rather than diminishing it (Table 5.3).

TABLE 5.3
AI for Good Movement

	Key Points
Overview	The AI for Good movement emphasizes using AI technologies to address global challenges and promote societal well-being
The origins: AI XPRIZE	The AI XPRIZE was a catalyst for the AI for Good movement, inspiring AI innovation aimed at solving humanity's grand challenges
AI for Good Global Summit	The summit serves as a global platform to explore how AI can be used to achieve the UN's Sustainable Development Goals (SDGs)
Key milestones and impact	The movement has expanded global dialogue on ethical AI, inspired numerous initiatives, and promoted the creation of data ecosystems
The role of data and collaboration	Highlights the importance of data commons, collaboratives, and cooperatives in supporting the AI for Good movement's goals
Continuing the legacy: the future of AI for good	The movement will continue to influence AI development, emphasizing global collaboration, ethical standards, and inclusive AI solutions
Perspective	The AI for Good movement has established a framework for using AI to benefit humanity, setting the stage for future ethical AI development

Transition to Next Section: The AI Commons exemplifies the potential of collaborative efforts in making AI more inclusive. Building on this, it's essential to explore how we can further empower diverse stakeholders to actively participate in AI development, ensuring that AI technologies are not only inclusive but also equitable.

5.4 EMPOWERING DIVERSE STAKEHOLDERS THROUGH INCLUSIVE AI DEVELOPMENT

The transformative potential of AI in helping us gain exposure to new knowledge is undeniable. As AI systems are increasingly included in critical aspects of our lives—from healthcare and education to finance and public policy—ensuring that these systems are designed with diverse perspectives in mind is not just a moral imperative but a practical necessity. Inclusivity in AI development helps to mitigate biases, enhance system robustness, and ensure that AI technologies benefit all sectors of society equitably.

5.4.1 THE IMPORTANCE OF CULTURAL INTELLIGENCE IN AI DEVELOPMENT

Cultural intelligence in AI development is a notion that is not discussed enough today and is crucial for creating systems that are effective, fair, and globally applicable. AI systems developed with a narrow cultural perspective risk being ineffective or even harmful when applied in different cultural contexts. For example, voice recognition systems trained primarily on American English have struggled with accents and dialects from other regions, leading to frustration and exclusion for millions of users. A mental assistance using voice bots may not be effective in any cultural environment or geography if built for certain demographics.

Case Study—Voice Recognition: An example of this challenge is the performance disparity in voice recognition systems across different linguistic and cultural groups. Research by the Stanford University Human-Centered AI Institute (hai. standford.edu) found that major speech recognition systems exhibited significant error rates when transcribing speech from African American Vernacular English (AAVE) speakers compared to speakers of Standard American English. This disparity highlights the importance of incorporating diverse linguistic datasets in the development of AI systems to ensure equitable performance across different user groups (HAI, 2021).

5.4.2 DIVERSE DEVELOPMENT TEAMS AND CROSS-CULTURAL RESEARCH

Diversity within AI development teams is essential to identifying and mitigating biases that might otherwise go unnoticed. Teams composed of individuals from various cultural, ethnic, and socioeconomic backgrounds bring a wealth of perspectives to the design process, resulting in more versatile and globally applicable AI systems. Moreover, cross-cultural research plays a pivotal role in understanding how different communities interact with and perceive AI technologies, allowing developers to create systems that are adaptable and respectful of cultural nuances.

Example—Google AI for Indian Farmers: Google's AI initiative in India provides a compelling example of culturally sensitive AI development. By collaborating with local farmers and agricultural experts, Google developed an AI system tailored to the specific needs of Indian agriculture. The system incorporates local weather patterns, soil conditions, and traditional farming practices to provide tailored crop management advice. This project demonstrates the importance of cultural sensitivity in AI.

Example—Te Hiku Media: Another example is the Te Hiku Media project in New Zealand, which uses machine learning to develop speech recognition tools for the Māori language. Recognizing the cultural significance of language preservation, the project collaborates closely with Māori communities to ensure that the AI system aligns with their linguistic and cultural needs. This initiative exemplifies how AI can be used to support cultural heritage preservation while respecting and empowering the communities involved.

5.4.3 Participatory Approaches in AI Development

Beyond cultural sensitivity or cultural intelligence, truly inclusive AI development embraces participatory approaches that actively involve impacted communities in the design and deployment of AI systems. Participatory design ensures that AI technologies are not only technically effective but also socially and culturally relevant. A few examples follow.

Co-Design Workshops: Co-design workshops are a model of participatory AI development that brings together AI developers, researchers, and community members to collaboratively design AI systems. For instance, in the development of AI tools for healthcare in rural areas, co-design workshops might involve local healthcare workers, patients, and community leaders. These stakeholders provide critical insights into the specific challenges and needs of their communities, ensuring that the resulting AI solutions are contextually appropriate and more likely to be successfully adopted.

Participatory Action Research (PAR): Participatory Action Research (PAR) is another powerful approach to inclusive AI development. PAR involves communities in the research process, allowing them to co-create knowledge and solutions with researchers. This approach is particularly effective in developing AI applications that address local issues. For example, in urban planning, PAR could involve residents in data collection, problem definition, and solution design, ensuring that the AI tools developed genuinely reflect and serve community needs (Katell, 2021; Wikipedia, n.d.a)

Example—Barcelona Smart City Initiative: The smart city initiative in Barcelona, Spain, showcases the effectiveness of participatory approaches. The city government engaged citizens through workshops and consultations to gather input on smart city projects. This engagement process prioritized initiatives that residents found most valuable, such as improving public transportation and creating more green spaces. By involving citizens in the decision-making process, Barcelona ensured that its AI-driven urban innovations aligned with community needs and values (Ajuntament de Barcelona, n.d., BABLE Smart Cities, n.d.).

5.4.4 Ensuring Representation of Marginalized Groups

Ensuring the representation of marginalized groups in AI development is not just a matter of fairness; it is essential for creating AI systems that work for everyone. Marginalized communities often have unique needs and perspectives that can be overlooked in mainstream AI development. By actively including these groups, we can create more comprehensive and equitable AI solutions.

Example—Microsoft AI for Accessibility: Microsoft's AI for Accessibility initiative is an exemplary model of how inclusivity can be woven into AI development. The initiative collaborates with advocacy organizations and individuals with disabilities to develop AI solutions that address specific accessibility needs. This project not only creates more inclusive technologies but also empowers individuals with disabilities to actively shape the tools that affect their lives. For instance, AI-driven applications that help people with visual impairments navigate their environments more effectively are developed with direct input from users, ensuring that the technology truly meets their needs (Microsoft Research, n.d.).

5.4.5 POLICY AND INSTITUTIONAL SUPPORT FOR INCLUSIVE AI DEVELOPMENT

Governments and organizations play a critical role in promoting inclusive AI development through policies, funding, and advocacy. Policy initiatives can incentivize diversity in AI development teams and projects, ensuring that inclusivity becomes a standard practice rather than an exception.

Policy Initiatives: Governments can introduce policies that provide grants, tax benefits, or other forms of support for organizations that demonstrate a commitment to inclusive practices. Regulatory standards can also be established to require transparency, fairness, and inclusivity in AI systems, enforced through audits, certifications, and compliance checks.

Example—The Global Partnership on AI (GPAI): The Global Partnership on AI (GPAI) exemplifies the power of collaborative efforts in promoting inclusive AI development. By bringing together experts from various sectors and countries, GPAI facilitates international cooperation and knowledge sharing to ensure that AI technologies benefit all of humanity. The initiative highlights the importance of global collaboration in setting standards and sharing best practices for inclusive AI development (Global Partnership on AI, 2021–2024) (Table 5.4).

TABLE 5.4

Strategies for Inclusive AI Development

Strategy	Description	Expected Outcome
Diverse development teams	Inclusion of individuals from various cultural, ethnic, and socioeconomic backgrounds	Reduces biases in AI systems; produces more versatile AI applications
Cross-cultural research	Study of how different cultures interact with AI technologies	Creation of AI systems that are adaptable and respectful of cultural nuances
Participatory design	Involving community members in the AI development process	Ensures AI systems are relevant, accepted, and beneficial to local communities
Inclusive policy-making	Governments and institutions promote diversity in AI through policies and funding	Encourages broader participation in AI development; ensures equity in AI benefits

Empowering diverse stakeholders through inclusive AI development is not just an ethical imperative; it is a practical necessity for creating AI systems that are truly effective, fair, and beneficial for all. By centering the needs and values of diverse populations, engaging communities in the design process, and ensuring the representation of marginalized groups, we can develop AI systems that reflect the rich tapestry of human experience and serve the global community in all its diversity.

As we move forward, continued collaboration between technologists, cultural experts, and communities will be crucial. Through collective commitment to ethical, inclusive AI development, we can expect AI to help enhance social equity and cultural preservation.

Transition to Next Section: Empowering a diverse array of stakeholders requires robust data ecosystems that support responsible and inclusive AI development. Let's now examine how these ecosystems can be structured to promote fairness, accountability, and access.

5.5 DATA ECOSYSTEMS FOR INCLUSIVE AND RESPONSIBLE AI

5.5.1 INTRODUCTION

At the heart of AI's transformative power lies data. The quality, quantity, and diversity of data available for training AI systems significantly influence their capabilities, biases, and outcomes. As we strive for inclusive and responsible AI development, it is essential to establish data governance models that promote accessibility, fairness, and privacy. By making data ecosystems available, we can democratize AI development, empower communities, and ensure that AI technologies serve the broader public good.

5.5.2 DATA COMMONS: PROMOTING OPEN ACCESS AND COLLABORATION

The concept of data commons represents a paradigm shift in how we approach data sharing and utilization. Data commons are shared resources of data, organized by topic or community interest, that are accessible to a broad range of stakeholders for use in AI model training, research, and other applications. This model promotes open access and collaboration, making high-quality datasets available to a wider audience and lowering the barriers to entry for AI development.

5.5.3 THE EMERGENCE OF DATA COMMONS

The concept of data commons has emerged as a vital tool in democratizing access to valuable datasets, which have traditionally been concentrated in the hands of a few large organizations. Introduced at the 2018 AI for Good Global Summit, supported by XPRIZE and the International Telecommunication Union (ITU), the idea of a global data commons was designed to create repositories that could support AI projects focused on addressing the UN Sustainable Development Goals (SDGs).

This initiative was particularly aimed at enabling diverse actors—including small organizations and researchers from underrepresented regions—to engage in AI innovation and to apply AI technologies to pressing global challenges.

Data commons hold the potential to significantly broaden participation in AI development by making high-quality datasets freely available. The democratization of data access allows a wider range of organizations and individuals to engage in AI research and development, allowing innovation from perspectives that might otherwise be overlooked. Access to open data is crucial in allowing smaller actors to make meaningful contributions to AI's development, thereby increasing its size, diversity, and novel approaches. Moreover, data commons encourage collaboration across sectors and disciplines, facilitating the exchange of knowledge and resources that can accelerate progress on shared goals. By pooling data relevant to issues such as climate change, public health, and education, these commons provide the raw material necessary for AI solutions that can address global challenges more effectively and equitably.

However, while the potential benefits of data commons are vast, several challenges must be navigated to ensure their success. Ensuring the quality and interoperability of the data within these commons is critical. Poor-quality data can lead to unreliable AI models, and datasets that cannot be easily integrated across systems may limit the utility of the commons. Furthermore, sustainable governance structures must be established to manage these resources, including setting clear standards for data usage, access, and contribution. Without robust governance, the integrity and long-term viability of data commons could be compromised.

5.5.4 Data Collaboratives: Bridging Public and Private Data Silos

Data collaboratives represent a new approach to addressing complex public problems by facilitating data sharing across different sectors—government, private industry, and civil society. Unlike traditional public-private partnerships, which often focus on broader resource pooling, data collaboratives are specifically designed around the exchange and use of data to generate insights that no single entity could achieve alone. By combining data from various sources, these collaboratives create richer, more comprehensive datasets that drive AI innovation and enable more precise and impactful solutions.

An example of this collaborative approach can be seen in the COVID-19 Mobility Data Network, where technology companies shared anonymized mobility data with public health researchers to help manage the pandemic response. By analyzing population movements during lockdowns, these shared datasets enabled public health authorities to better predict virus spread and tailor interventions. This type of collaboration demonstrates the immense potential for data collaboratives to overcome the limitations of siloed data, providing more accurate analyses for AI systems to process (COVID-19 Mobility Data Network, n.d.).

Yet, these efforts are not without challenges. One of the primary concerns is the protection of individual privacy, particularly when pooling data from different sectors. Ensuring that data is shared responsibly, with robust privacy protections and ethical guidelines, is essential to maintaining public trust. Furthermore, building and sustaining trust between participants from disparate sectors is critical to the success of data collaboratives. Without a strong foundation of trust, collaboration can falter, and the benefits of data sharing may be lost.

5.5.5   Data Cooperatives: Empowering Individuals and Communities

Data cooperatives offer an alternative model for managing data that emphasizes the empowerment of individuals and communities. Unlike traditional data-sharing models, where large organizations typically hold and control data, cooperatives allow individuals and smaller organizations to pool their data resources and collectively determine how that data is used and shared. This model seeks to address the power imbalances in the data economy by giving data subjects greater control over how their information is managed.

One notable example of a data cooperative is the Driver's Seat Cooperative, which allows gig workers to pool their data in order to gain insights into their work patterns and advocate for better working conditions. In the context of AI, data cooperatives could play a critical role in ensuring that AI systems are trained on more representative datasets, reducing biases and improving outcomes for marginalized groups. By pooling data, cooperatives can generate value for all members, rather than allowing a single entity to benefit disproportionately. This model can also serve as a powerful mechanism for ensuring that AI solutions are aligned with the values and needs of the communities they are designed to serve (Driver's Seat, n.d.).

However, as with other data-sharing models, the success of data cooperatives depends heavily on effective governance. Establishing clear rules for participation and decision-making is essential to ensuring that all members of the cooperative have a fair voice in how their data is used. Additionally, ensuring the long-term

TABLE 5.5
Comparative Table: Data Ecosystem Models

Model	Definition	Key Benefits	Challenges	Example
Data commons	Shared resources of data, accessible to a broad audience for use in AI	Democratizes access to high-quality datasets; allows collaboration and innovation	Ensuring data quality and interoperability; sustainable governance	The AI Commons initiative supporting global AI projects for SDGs
Data collaboratives	Partnerships across sectors (public, private, civil society) to share data for public good	Combines data from multiple sources; responsibly shared data; addresses complex public problems	Privacy protection; building trust among participants	COVID-19 Mobility Data Network pooling anonymized data for public health
Data cooperatives	Individuals or organizations pool their data and collectively govern its use	Empowers individuals and communities; promotes fair data usage; reduces AI bias	Governance and participation; sustainability of cooperative models	Driver's Seat Cooperative for gig workers to control and utilize their data

sustainability of these cooperatives requires careful planning, particularly in terms of resource allocation and management. Without a solid governance framework, data cooperatives may struggle to achieve their full potential.

5.5.6 CHALLENGES AND OPPORTUNITIES IN DATA ECOSYSTEMS

While the models of data commons, collaboratives, and cooperatives present exciting opportunities for more inclusive and responsible AI development, they also pose significant challenges. Ensuring that shared data is accurate, up-to-date, and relevant is crucial to the effective training of AI systems. Equally important is the need for interoperability—standardizing data formats and protocols to ensure seamless integration across systems and sectors. Without this, even the most comprehensive datasets may not be fully utilized.

Privacy protection is another major concern. Balancing the need for data access with robust privacy safeguards is a complex but essential task, particularly when dealing with sensitive personal information. Moreover, developing sustainable governance models that are transparent, inclusive, and adaptable is vital to maintaining trust and ensuring the ethical use of data within these ecosystems. Governance structures must be designed to evolve alongside technological advancements and changing societal expectations.

Despite these challenges, the potential for these data-sharing models to drive innovation in AI is significant. By reducing barriers to entry, these models allow a wider range of actors to participate in AI development, offering diverse perspectives. Additionally, ensuring that AI systems are trained on datasets that reflect the full diversity of communities can help reduce biases and improve fairness in AI outcomes. Furthermore, by pooling data from various sources, these ecosystems can accelerate the development of AI applications that address complex societal challenges—particularly in areas where data has traditionally been scarce or siloed. Data cooperatives, in particular, empower communities to take control of their data, ensuring that AI systems reflect their values and needs.

5.5.7 THE ROLE OF AI COMMONS IN DATA ECOSYSTEMS

The AI Commons plays a crucial role in establishing data ecosystems that are inclusive and responsible. By creating a shared platform where data can be accessed and utilized by a broad range of stakeholders, the AI Commons facilitates the development of AI solutions that are both equitable and effective. This approach not only democratizes access to AI but also helps to mitigate biases by ensuring that diverse data sources are represented (see Table 5.3).

As we advance into an AI-driven future, it is crucial to develop data governance frameworks and policies that support and regulate these innovative data models. By creating data ecosystems that prioritize accessibility, fairness, and privacy, we can fuel AI innovation while respecting individual rights and promoting the public good.

The future of AI depends not only on technological advancements but also on the quality and governance of the data that powers it. By embracing data commons,

TABLE 5.6
Data Ecosystems for Inclusive and Responsible AI

	Key Points
Context	Data is at the core of AI's power, and innovative data governance models are crucial for inclusive and responsible AI development
Data commons	Data commons democratize access to high-quality datasets, enabling broader participation in AI development
Data collaboratives	Data collaboratives facilitate data sharing across sectors to address public problems, with a focus on privacy and ethical use
Data cooperatives	Data cooperatives empower individuals and communities by giving them control over their data, promoting fairer AI systems
Challenges and opportunities	Key challenges include data quality, privacy, and governance, but the opportunities for innovation and inclusion are significant
Perspective	Effective data governance is essential for creating a responsible AI ecosystem that benefits all of humanity

collaboratives, and cooperatives, we can create a more inclusive, equitable, and responsible AI landscape that benefits all of humanity (Table 5.6).

> **Transition to Next Section**: A well-functioning data ecosystem is the foundation, but effective governance frameworks are the pillars that ensure AI systems operate in a trustworthy and accountable manner. These frameworks play a crucial role in guiding the ethical use of AI across various sectors.

5.6 GOVERNANCE FRAMEWORKS FOR TRUSTWORTHY AND ACCOUNTABLE AI

As AI becomes increasingly integrated into various aspects of society, the need for robust governance frameworks to ensure its trustworthiness and accountability has become critically important. These frameworks play a pivotal role in preserving public trust and individual agency in an AI-driven world. Effective AI governance is essential not only for mitigating risks but also for harnessing AI's full potential to benefit humanity.

5.6.1 THE FOUNDATIONS OF AI GOVERNANCE

AI governance refers to the structures, processes, and guidelines established to ensure that AI systems are developed and deployed ethically, transparently, and in alignment with societal values. Several key principles form the foundation of trustworthy and accountable AI systems:

1. **Transparency:** Transparency in AI systems is crucial to build trust and ensure accountability. This principle demands that AI systems be designed and implemented in ways that are open to scrutiny. Transparency involves clear communication about how AI systems work, what data they use, and how decisions are made. For instance, the AI Now Institute advocates for "algorithmic impact assessments" that require public agencies to disclose information about their use of automated decision systems.

2. **Fairness:** AI systems must be designed to treat all individuals and groups equitably. Fairness involves identifying and mitigating biases in both data and algorithms to prevent discriminatory outcomes. The concept of fairness in AI is complex and context-dependent, but tools like IBM's AI Fairness 360 toolkit provide developers with resources to detect and address unfair outcomes in their models.

3. **Privacy:** Given that AI systems often handle vast amounts of personal data, robust privacy protections are crucial. Privacy regulations, such as the European Union's General Data Protection Regulation (GDPR), set high standards for data protection and privacy in the AI context. These regulations include the right to explanation for automated decisions, allowing individuals to understand how and why a decision affecting them was made.

4. **Accountability:** Clear mechanisms for holding AI developers and users responsible for the outcomes of their systems are essential for ensuring accountability. This principle ensures that there are consequences for harmful or unfair AI applications. The IEEE Global Initiative on Ethics of Autonomous and Intelligent Systems provides guidelines for building accountability into AI systems from the ground up (IEEE Global Initiative, n.d.).

5. **Human-Centeredness:** AI systems should be designed to augment and empower human capabilities, not replace human agency. This principle is emphasized by organizations like the Partnership on AI, which promotes the development of AI technologies that benefit people and communities by prioritizing human-centered design.

Table 5.7 provides an overview of several prominent AI governance frameworks, highlighting their approaches to transparency, accountability, fairness, and privacy. However, it is not a comprehensive list. Many other frameworks, guidelines, and initiatives exist worldwide, each contributing to the evolving landscape of AI governance. These frameworks reflect a diversity of perspectives and priorities, underscoring the complexity of governing AI in a global context.

5.6.2 Implementing Governance Frameworks in Practice

Implementing these foundational principles in practice requires a multifaceted approach. One key strategy is the use of impact assessments to evaluate the potential effects of AI systems on individuals and communities before they are deployed.

TABLE 5.7

Comparative Table: AI Governance Frameworks

Governance Model	Key Features	Transparency	Accountability	Fairness	Privacy
European Union's AI Act	Risk-based approach, strict regulation for high-risk AI applications	Requires clear documentation of AI systems, public disclosure	Accountability mechanisms for developers and users	Mandates assessments to prevent discrimination	Strong data protection aligned with GDPR
IEEE's Ethically Aligned Design	Ethical guidelines for autonomous and intelligent systems	Emphasizes ethical transparency in AI system operations	Promotes ethical responsibility among developers	Advocates for fairness in AI decision-making processes	Prioritizes user consent and control over personal data
OECD AI Principles	International guidelines for responsible AI	Encourages openness about AI's societal impact	Recommends frameworks for developer and organizational accountability	Promotes AI that benefits communities as a whole	Supports privacy as a fundamental human right
UNESCO's AI Ethics Guidelines	Focuses on human rights, sustainability, and the promotion of peace	Calls for transparency in AI's purpose and implementation	Stresses the need for accountability at all stages of AI development	Ensures AI systems are non-discriminatory and inclusive	Advocates for robust protections against data misuse

Impact Assessments: Impact assessments are a critical tool for proactive AI governance. These assessments evaluate the potential effects of AI systems on individuals and communities before they are deployed. The European Commission's proposal for an Artificial Intelligence Act includes mandatory impact assessments for high-risk AI systems, setting a precedent for proactive governance. These assessments can help identify potential risks and ensure that AI systems are aligned with ethical standards and societal values.

Ethics Boards and Committees: The establishment of ethics boards or committees is another crucial element of AI governance. These bodies, composed of diverse experts, can provide ongoing guidance on ethical issues in AI development and deployment. While the effectiveness of such boards has been debated, their presence is crucial for incorporating ethical considerations into AI governance. Google's short-lived AI ethics board, for example, highlighted both the challenges and the necessity of having such oversight structures in place.

Regulatory Frameworks: Governments and regulatory bodies have a central role in establishing and enforcing guidelines for ethical AI use. Regulatory frameworks must strike a balance between accelerating innovation and protecting societal interests. Overly restrictive regulations could stifle beneficial AI development, while inadequate oversight could lead to harmful outcomes. The European Union's proposed AI Act is one of the most ambitious regulatory efforts in this space, categorizing AI applications based on their level of risk and imposing corresponding regulatory requirements.

Global Harmonization: As AI technologies transcend national borders, there is a growing need for harmonized global standards. Achieving consensus among countries with diverse values and priorities remains a significant challenge. However, international initiatives like the Organisation for Economic Co-operation and Development (OECD) AI Principles and the Global Partnership on AI (GPAI) are working toward creating a unified global framework for AI governance. These initiatives emphasize inclusivity, sustainability, and respect for human rights, setting a benchmark for responsible AI development worldwide.

5.6.3 Case Studies in AI Governance

Case studies of AI governance in action reveal both the challenges and opportunities in this space. One significant area of focus is the use of AI in policing, a high-stakes application that has raised considerable concerns about fairness and accountability.

Case Study—Predictive Policing: In the United States, predictive policing algorithms have been criticized for perpetuating racial biases. A study by the Royal Statistical Society found that these algorithms often disproportionately target minority communities. The controversy surrounding the use of predictive policing tools highlights the need for rigorous oversight and continuous evaluation of AI systems, especially in sensitive domains like law enforcement.

Case Study—AI in Healthcare: Another area where governance frameworks are crucial is AI in healthcare. AI systems used in medical diagnostics and treatment planning can have life-or-death implications. For example, the use of AI in radiology has shown promise in detecting diseases like cancer more accurately than human doctors. However, the deployment of these systems must be accompanied by strict governance to ensure that they are used ethically and that patients' rights and safety are prioritized. The introduction of AI in healthcare has prompted discussions about the need for industry-wide standards and ethical guidelines to govern its use (Nature Portfolio, 2024; National Library of Medicine, 2024).

5.6.4 The Future of AI Governance: Challenges and Opportunities

As we look to the future of AI governance, several key challenges and opportunities emerge.

Balancing Innovation and Regulation: Governance frameworks must find a balance between encouraging innovation and protecting societal interests. Striking this balance is particularly challenging in the fast-paced world of AI development, where new technologies often outstrip existing regulatory frameworks. Flexible and adaptive governance models are needed to keep pace with technological advancements.

Adaptability: Given the rapid pace of AI advancement, governance frameworks must be flexible enough to adapt to new technologies and emerging challenges. Traditional regulatory models, which can be slow to respond to technological change, may need to be rethought to allow for more agile governance approaches.

Inclusivity: Ensuring that AI governance reflects diverse global perspectives and addresses the needs of marginalized communities is crucial for building truly equitable AI systems. Public participation in AI governance, through mechanisms such as citizen assemblies and public consultations, can help ensure that AI development aligns with societal values.

Enforcement: Developing mechanisms to enforce AI regulations, especially on a global scale, presents complex legal and practical challenges. Effective enforcement will require cooperation between governments, industry, and civil society, as well as the development of new tools and technologies to monitor AI systems and ensure compliance.

Robust governance frameworks are essential for ensuring that AI technologies are developed and deployed in ways that are trustworthy, accountable, and aligned with human values. By emphasizing principles such as transparency, fairness, privacy, accountability, and human-centeredness, we can create AI systems that not only avoid harm but actively contribute to human flourishing.

The path forward requires collaboration among governments, industry, academia, and civil society. It demands ongoing public dialogue to ensure that AI governance reflects societal values and priorities. As we navigate the complexities of AI governance, our ultimate goal must be to harness the transformative potential of AI while safeguarding human rights, promoting equity, and preserving human agency in an increasingly AI-driven world.

Transition to Next Section: With governance frameworks in place, we can turn our attention to how AI can be harnessed for the greater good, such as preserving cultural heritage and empowering local communities.

5.7 AI FOR CULTURAL HERITAGE PRESERVATION AND COMMUNITY EMPOWERMENT

One of its most promising applications of AI lies in cultural heritage preservation and community empowerment. AI could offer unparalleled opportunities to safeguard our past, empower marginalized communities, and bridge generational and cultural divides. By leveraging AI, we can not only preserve cultural artifacts and traditions but also allow—even the smallest- communities to take control of their cultural narratives and futures.

5.7.1 AI Technologies for Preserving and Revitalizing Cultural Heritage

AI's ability to analyze, digitize, and reconstruct historical data has revolutionized the preservation of cultural heritage. From digitizing ancient manuscripts to reconstructing historical sites, AI provides conservationists and historians with powerful new tools to protect and study our shared cultural legacy.

Case Study—Rekrei Project (Formerly Project Mosul): The Rekrei project is a striking example of how AI can be used to preserve cultural heritage. Following the destruction of artifacts in Mosul Museum by ISIS in 2015, the Rekrei initiative used AI and crowdsourced images to create 3D models of the damaged or destroyed cultural artifacts and sites. These digital reconstructions not only help preserve cultural memory but also serve as valuable resources for potential future reconstruction efforts. By leveraging AI, Rekrei has made it possible to virtually restore cultural treasures that might otherwise have been lost forever (Rekrei, n.d.).

Language Preservation: Language is a critical aspect of cultural heritage, and AI is playing a vital role in its preservation. The Te Hiku Media project in New Zealand, for example, uses machine learning to develop speech recognition tools for the Māori language. This technology aids in the preservation of the language by making it more accessible to younger generations, thus helping to keep the language alive and vibrant. The project's collaboration with Māori communities ensures that the AI tools developed are culturally appropriate and serve the needs of the community.

Deciphering Historical Manuscripts: AI is also being used to unlock the secrets of historical manuscripts that have long been inaccessible to scholars. The ALPHABET project in Europe employs AI to decipher and translate ancient texts, making centuries-old knowledge available to modern scholars. This project is expanding our understanding of history by bringing to light previously obscure or unreadable documents. The AI-driven analysis of these manuscripts allows historians to explore new insights and make connections that were previously impossible.

5.7.2 Community-Led AI Initiatives for Sustainable Development

While AI is often associated with high-tech labs and large corporations, some of the most impactful AI initiatives are happening at the grassroots level, led by communities themselves. These community-led initiatives demonstrate how AI can be a powerful tool for sustainable development and social empowerment.

Indigenous Communities and AI: In the Amazon rainforest, indigenous communities are using AI-powered drones and satellite imagery analysis to monitor deforestation and protect their ancestral lands. The Indigenous Peoples Technology Support Project exemplifies how AI can empower communities to maintain traditional land management practices in the face of external pressures. By integrating AI with indigenous knowledge, these communities are able to better protect their environment and assert their rights over their land.

Agricultural AI in India: In India, the Microsoft AI for Earth project collaborates with local farmers to develop AI models that predict crop yields while incorporating traditional agricultural knowledge. This initiative blends cutting-edge AI technology with time-honored farming practices, helping to balance modern techniques with sustainable, culturally appropriate methods. The project empowers farmers by providing them with tools that enhance their productivity and resilience while respecting their cultural practices.

Connecting Rural Artisans with Global Markets: The Handmade in India project is another compelling example of community empowerment through AI. This initiative uses AI-powered image recognition to connect rural artisans with global markets, ensuring fair compensation and preserving traditional craftsmanship. By leveraging AI, the project sustains local economies and cultural practices in an increasingly globalized world. The use of AI to promote traditional craftsmanship not only empowers artisans economically but also helps preserve cultural heritage by making traditional arts more visible and accessible.

5.7.3 AI AND INTERGENERATIONAL KNOWLEDGE TRANSFER

One exciting application of AI in cultural preservation is its potential to facilitate intergenerational knowledge transfer. As societies modernize and younger generations move away from traditional ways of life, there is a risk of losing valuable cultural knowledge and practices. AI can help bridge this gap by preserving and transmitting cultural wisdom across generations:

Interactive Holograms and Storytelling: The StoryFile project is an innovative use of AI that enables intergenerational knowledge transfer. Using AI, StoryFile creates interactive holograms of individuals, allowing future generations to engage in conversations with historical Tables or community elders. Initially used to preserve the testimonies of Holocaust survivors, this technology has broad applications for capturing and sharing cultural wisdom across generations. By creating a living archive of stories and knowledge, AI helps ensure that cultural wisdom is not lost over time but remains accessible to future generations (StoryFile, 2021).

Digital Archives for Indigenous Knowledge: In Australia, the Ara Irititja project uses AI to help catalog and make accessible a vast archive of indigenous artifacts, photos, and audio recordings. This digital archive serves as a vital resource for younger generations to connect with their cultural heritage, learn traditional practices, and understand their history. The use of AI in this context is not just about preserving information; it is about keeping culture alive and relevant for future generations (Ara Irititja, 2020).

Language Learning Tools: AI-powered language learning tools are also playing a crucial role in intergenerational knowledge transfer. By making it easier and more engaging for young people to learn their ancestral languages, these tools help preserve linguistic diversity and the cultural knowledge embedded within languages. Projects like Duolingo's indigenous language courses use AI to tailor learning experiences, making language learning more accessible and effective for new generations.

5.7.4 BALANCING TECHNOLOGICAL INNOVATION WITH TRADITIONAL KNOWLEDGE AND PRACTICES

While AI offers tremendous potential for cultural preservation, it is crucial to approach its implementation as well with sensitivity and respect for traditional knowledge and practices. The goal should be to allow AI development in a way to capture cultural practices, and try to avoid overshadowing them with standardized practices. Here are some approaches as examples.

Collaborative Approaches: Balancing innovation with respect for tradition often involves collaborative approaches that bring together technologists, community members, and cultural experts. For example, in developing AI systems for sustainable agriculture, it is crucial to incorporate traditional ecological knowledge alongside scientific data. This approach not only results in more effective solutions but also ensures that technological interventions are culturally appropriate and sustainable.

AI Decolonization: The concept of "AI decolonization" is particularly relevant in this context. This movement emphasizes the need to develop AI systems that reflect diverse cultural perspectives and do not perpetuate historical biases. The Decolonial AI initiative at the University of Cambridge, for instance, works to ensure that AI development is inclusive and respectful of diverse cultural contexts. By prioritizing inclusivity and cultural sensitivity, AI developers can create technologies that empower rather than marginalize indigenous and other underrepresented communities.

Data Sovereignty: Data sovereignty is another critical consideration, particularly for indigenous communities. The CARE Principles for Indigenous Data Governance (Collective benefit, Authority to control, Responsibility, and Ethics) provide a framework for addressing these concerns. These principles ensure that communities retain control over their data and how it is used in AI applications. By adhering to these principles, AI projects can respect the autonomy and rights of the communities they serve (Tables 5.8 and 5.9).

The intersection of AI with cultural heritage preservation and community empowerment represents a powerful frontier in the application of technology for social good. By enabling the digitization and analysis of cultural artifacts, facilitating intergenerational knowledge transfer, and empowering communities to address local challenges, AI is proving to be a valuable ally in the preservation and revitalization of cultural diversity.

As we move forward, continued collaboration between technologists, cultural experts, and communities will be crucial. By promoting such partnerships and

TABLE 5.8
Comparative Table: AI in Cultural Preservation

Application	AI Role	Benefits	Challenges	Example
Digital reconstruction	AI reconstructs and preserves damaged or lost cultural artifacts	Preserves cultural memory; aids future physical reconstruction	Requires high-quality data and careful curation	Rekrei Project creating 3D models of destroyed artifacts
Language preservation	AI tools for documenting and revitalizing endangered languages	Keeps languages alive; makes them accessible to younger generations	Need for cultural intelligence; data accuracy	Te Hiku Media's AI project for Māori language preservation
Intergenerational knowledge transfer	AI facilitates the preservation and sharing of cultural wisdom across generations	Bridges generational gaps; preserves traditional knowledge	Ensuring authenticity and respect for cultural values	StoryFile's interactive holograms for preserving historical testimonies

TABLE 5.9
Balancing Innovation with Tradition

Aspect	Consideration	Best Practices
AI decolonization	Ensuring AI does not perpetuate historical biases	Develop AI with input from culturally diverse stakeholders; focus on inclusivity
Data sovereignty	Respecting the rights of communities over their data	Adhere to the CARE Principles for Indigenous Data Governance
Collaborative approaches	Integrating traditional knowledge with AI innovation	Engage cultural experts and community members in AI development processes

maintaining a commitment to ethical, inclusive AI development, we can take steps toward a future where technology and tradition work hand in hand, preserving the rich tapestry of human culture (Table 5.10).

> **Transition to Next Section**: As we've seen, AI has the potential to drive significant social change. To fully realize this potential, we must prepare society to navigate the AI-powered future with wisdom and foresight.

5.8   PREPARING COMMUNITIES FOR AN AI-POWERED FUTURE

Preparing communities for an AI-powered future is complex. This preparation extends beyond technological adaptation; it encompasses education, workforce development, ethical design, regulations, and knowledge sharing. Ensuring that

TABLE 5.10
AI for Cultural Heritage Preservation and Community Empowerment

	Key Points
Background	AI offers significant potential for preserving cultural heritage and empowering communities
AI technologies for cultural preservation	AI can digitize and analyze cultural artifacts, aiding in the preservation and revitalization of cultural heritage
Community-led AI initiatives	AI can empower communities through initiatives like environmental monitoring and traditional knowledge preservation
AI and intergenerational knowledge transfer	AI can facilitate the transfer of cultural knowledge across generations, preserving traditions and languages
Balancing innovation with tradition	AI should be used to support cultural traditions, not replace them, with a focus on decolonization and data sovereignty
Perspective	AI can be a powerful tool for preserving cultural diversity and empowering communities when used responsibly

individuals and communities are equipped to navigate and leverage AI technologies is essential for maximizing benefits, minimizing risks, and promoting equitable outcomes across diverse populations.

5.8.1 THE IMPORTANCE OF AI LITERACY ACROSS ALL DEMOGRAPHICS

AI literacy—the understanding of AI concepts, capabilities, and implications—is rapidly becoming as fundamental in the 21st century as traditional literacy. Ensuring that AI literacy reaches all demographics is essential for empowering individuals to engage critically and with awareness with AI technologies, make informed decisions, and actively participate in discussions and policy-making that shape AI's future development and deployment. And equipping people with the ability to understand its capabilities and limitations will be crucial in preparing society to responsibly interact with these technologies. For instance the creation of AI incident databases is allowing to share when and how AI has failed or simply not properly used.

Enabling literacy at scale is not going to be easy and innovative approaches will be needed. AI literacy encompasses a range of knowledge and skills. First, it involves a conceptual understanding of what AI is, how it functions, and the various contexts in which it can be applied. Additionally, AI literacy needs to include the ability to easily and critically evaluate the ethical, social, and economic implications of AI systems for the majority of people. Alongside these conceptual and evaluative skills, individuals must also develop practical abilities to use AI-powered tools effectively and responsibly. Finally, AI literacy demands an awareness of rights and responsibilities concerning data privacy, security, and the broader implications of AI technologies on individual and collective rights.

5.8.2   INITIATIVES PROMOTING AI LITERACY

Several initiatives worldwide are actively working to enhance AI literacy and ensure that knowledge of AI reaches a broad audience. One such initiative is the "Elements of AI" course, developed by the University of Helsinki in partnership with the technology company Reaktor. This free online course, launched in 2018, provides comprehensive AI education for the general public and has since enrolled over 750,000 students from more than 170 countries. The success of the course demonstrates the growing global demand for accessible AI education. Another notable effort is AI4ALL, a nonprofit organization that focuses on increasing diversity and inclusion in AI. AI4ALL provides educational opportunities and mentorship to underrepresented groups, including summer camps and online courses that aim to empower the next generation of AI leaders from diverse backgrounds (Elements of AI, n.d.; AI4 ALL, n.d.).

At the K-12 level, some educational systems are beginning to integrate AI concepts into school curricula. For example, China has introduced AI textbooks into over 100 schools as part of an effort to cultivate AI knowledge from an early age. By teaching AI fundamentals at the primary and secondary school levels, these programs aim to prepare students for the opportunities and challenges they will face in a future increasingly shaped by AI technologies.

5.8.3   ADAPTING EDUCATIONAL SYSTEMS FOR AN AI-DRIVEN WORLD

As AI continues to reshape the workforce and society at large, educational institutions are being called upon to adapt their curricula, teaching methods, and learning environments to reflect the evolving demands of the 21st century. Integrating AI education into the curricula requires an interdisciplinary approach that combines technical AI knowledge with subjects such as ethics, social sciences, and humanities. This holistic approach helps students develop a comprehensive understanding of AI's societal impact. Additionally, project-based learning can encourage students to engage hands-on with AI technologies, building practical skills to participate in the innovation ecosystem (UNESCO, 2024).

Educational systems must also offer continuous learning opportunities for individuals to update their skills as AI technologies evolve. Lifelong learning programs and professional certifications can provide adults with the necessary tools to remain competitive in an AI-driven job market. Crucially, teachers themselves require support to deliver AI education effectively. Professional development programs are essential to providing educators with the training and resources needed to facilitate discussions around AI ethics and applications. Collaborative platforms where educators can share best practices and teaching materials further bolster these efforts, ensuring a more uniform and effective delivery of AI education.

Equity and inclusion must be prioritized in the implementation of AI education. Bridging the digital divide is a key challenge, ensuring that all students— regardless of socioeconomic background—have access to the technology and resources necessary to engage with AI learning. Additionally, culturally responsive teaching methods can help make AI education more relevant and engaging for students from diverse cultural and linguistic backgrounds. Finland, for instance, has adopted a national AI education strategy that includes initiatives aimed at both citizens and public sector employees. Their "AI Challenge" has encouraged other EU countries to educate at least 1% of their population about AI, demonstrating a proactive approach to widespread AI literacy (European Commission, 2020a, b; https://fcai.fi/impact).

5.8.4 Creating a Culture of AI for Social Good

Encouraging a culture that leverages AI for social good requires promoting the development and deployment of AI technologies that address societal challenges and improve the overall quality of life. AI for social good is rooted in several key principles. First, it prioritizes human-centric design, ensuring that AI solutions are built to serve human needs, values, and well-being. Second, it emphasizes ethical responsibility, ensuring that AI applications adhere to rigorous ethical standards, respect privacy, and promote fairness and justice. Third, the culture of AI for social good depends on collaborative efforts that bring together technologists, policymakers, and community stakeholders to co-create solutions. Finally, sustainability is a core principle, as AI systems must be designed to contribute to SDGs and environmental conservation.

Several prominent initiatives illustrate how AI is being applied for social good. For instance, Google's AI for Social Good program supports projects that address challenges such as healthcare access, environmental conservation, and crisis response. One notable application includes using AI to predict flood patterns in India, providing early warnings to vulnerable populations. Microsoft's AI for Good initiative also focuses on environmental sustainability, accessibility, humanitarian action, and cultural heritage, using AI to monitor endangered species and develop tools for individuals with disabilities. Additionally, the United Nations' Global Pulse initiative leverages big data and AI to support sustainable development and humanitarian efforts, analyzing social media data to track public health trends and inform crisis response strategies (Google AI, n.d.; Microsoft Research, n.d.; United Nations Global Pulse, n.d.) (Table 5.11).

TABLE 5.11
Key Areas for AI-Driven Education

Area	Description	Expected Outcome
Interdisciplinary approach	Integrating AI with ethics, social sciences, and humanities	A well-rounded understanding of AI's societal impact
Project-based learning	Encouraging hands-on AI projects in educational settings	Enhanced practical skills and innovation in students
Teacher training	Providing educators with resources and training in AI	More effective AI education; improved student engagement
Equity and inclusion	Ensuring access to AI education for all students, regardless of background	Reduces the digital divide; promotes equity in AI opportunities

TABLE 5.12
Preparing Communities for an AI-Powered Future

	Key Points
Foundation	Communities must be prepared for AI's impact through education, ethical considerations, and a culture of AI for social good
Importance of AI literacy	AI literacy is crucial for empowering individuals to engage with AI technologies and make informed decisions
Adapting educational systems	Educational systems must evolve to integrate AI learning, emphasizing interdisciplinary approaches and lifelong learning
Promoting AI for social good	AI should be developed and used in ways that address societal challenges and promote public good
Case studies of AI for social good	Examples include AI applications in healthcare, environmental conservation, education, and disaster management
Addressing ethical and social challenges	Ethical challenges such as bias, privacy, and accountability must be proactively addressed in AI adoption
Perspective	Preparing communities for AI requires concerted efforts in education, policy, and promoting a culture of responsible AI

Preparing communities for an AI-powered future is a multifaceted endeavor that requires concerted efforts across education, policy, industry, and civil society. By enhancing AI literacy, adapting educational systems, promoting a culture of AI for social good, and addressing ethical challenges proactively, we can expect that AI technologies be used to improve lives and create equitable opportunities worldwide.

The path forward involves collaboration, innovation, and a sustained commitment to human-centric values. As we continue to integrate AI into the fabric of society, it is imperative that we do so thoughtfully and inclusively, empowering individuals and communities to shape and benefit from the technological transformations of our time (Table 5.12).

Transition to Next Section: The journey we've taken through the realms of human agency, inclusivity, data ecosystems, governance, and societal readiness highlights the multifaceted challenges and opportunities that AI presents. Let's conclude by reflecting on the path forward.

5.9 CONCLUSION

5.9.1 ENVISIONING A FUTURE WHERE AI AND HUMAN AGENCY ARE MUTUALLY REINFORCING

This chapter has explored the profound impact of AI across various domains, from cultural preservation and community empowerment to the need for robust governance frameworks and the preparation of communities for the inevitable AI transformation.

The journey through these topics reveals both the immense potential and the complex challenges that lie ahead. Now, as we conclude, it is vital to synthesize these insights and chart a path forward.

5.9.2   VISION FOR THE FUTURE: AI AND HUMAN AGENCY AS COMPLEMENTARY FORCES

The vision we must strive for is one where AI and human intelligence are not competing forces but complementary strengths that together push the boundaries of what is possible. In this envisioned future, AI serves as a powerful tool that amplifies human creativity, augments our decision-making capabilities, and frees us to focus on uniquely human endeavors that require empathy, ethical reasoning, and complex problem-solving.

Empowering Healthcare Professionals: Imagine a world where AI systems work alongside healthcare professionals, not to replace their judgment but to provide them with unprecedented insights and support, leading to more accurate diagnoses and personalized treatments. AI's ability to analyze vast amounts of medical data can help doctors identify patterns and make connections that would be impossible to discern with the human eye alone. However, the final decision-making power remains with the human practitioners, who bring their expertise, intuition, and understanding of the patient's context to the table.

Transforming Education: Envision educational systems where AI-powered adaptive learning platforms tailor instruction to each student's needs, while human teachers focus on nurturing creativity, critical thinking, and social-emotional skills. In this scenario, AI serves as an enabler of personalized learning, providing students with customized resources and feedback while allowing teachers to engage more deeply with students on a personal level. This approach not only enhances educational outcomes but also ensures that the human elements of teaching—such as mentorship, inspiration, and moral guidance—are preserved and amplified.

Preserving and Revitalizing Cultural Heritage: Picture a global community where AI helps preserve and revitalize endangered languages and cultural practices, bridging generational gaps and diverse cultural landscape. AI-driven initiatives could digitize and analyze cultural artifacts, enabling communities to maintain and share their heritage in ways that were previously unimaginable. By working hand-in-hand with cultural experts and community members, AI can help ensure that these efforts are respectful of and aligned with the values of the communities they aim to serve.

Enhancing Civic Engagement: Contemplate a society where AI-driven civic engagement platforms facilitate more inclusive and informed democratic processes, empowering citizens to actively shape their communities and governments. These platforms could leverage AI to analyze public opinion, identify pressing issues, and present information in accessible ways, enabling citizens to participate more effectively in decision-making. AI could also help ensure that all voices are heard, particularly those of marginalized groups, thereby promoting equity and justice in governance.

5.9.3 SUMMARY OF KEY POINTS DISCUSSED IN THE CHAPTER

Throughout this chapter, we have explored several critical aspects of AI's impact on culture and communities:

1. **Preserving Human Agency:** We examined the need for "agency-preserving AI" that empowers rather than replaces human decision-making. Transparency, interpretability, and human oversight emerged as key principles in ensuring that AI serves as a tool for human empowerment.
2. **Empowering Diverse Stakeholders:** We delved into the importance of inclusive AI development, emphasizing the need for participatory approaches and the representation of marginalized groups. These efforts are essential for creating AI systems that are effective, fair, and globally applicable.
3. **Governance Frameworks:** We explored the necessity of robust governance frameworks to ensure that AI technologies are developed and deployed in ways that are trustworthy, accountable, and aligned with human values. Principles such as transparency, fairness, privacy, accountability, and human-centeredness were highlighted as foundational to ethical AI development.
4. **Cultural Heritage and Community Empowerment:** We showcased how AI can be leveraged to preserve cultural heritage and empower communities. Through examples such as AI-driven language preservation and community-led AI initiatives, we demonstrated the potential of AI to support cultural diversity and local development.
5. **Preparing Communities for an AI-Powered Future**: We discussed the importance of AI literacy, educational reform, and creating a culture of "AI for social good." By promoting widespread understanding and responsible use of AI, we can prepare individuals and communities to navigate the challenges and opportunities of an AI-driven world.

5.9.4 THE NEED FOR ONGOING PUBLIC DIALOGUE AND PROACTIVE GOVERNANCE

As we move forward, it is clear that realizing the positive potential of AI while mitigating its risks requires ongoing public dialogue and proactive governance. The rapid pace of AI development demands that our ethical frameworks, regulatory systems, and societal understanding evolve in tandem.

Public Dialogue: Public dialogue is crucial for building trust, understanding societal concerns, and ensuring that AI development aligns with public values. This dialogue should be inclusive, involving diverse stakeholders from technologists and policymakers to educators and community leaders. Initiatives like citizen assemblies, public consultations, and community forums can play a vital role in engaging in these dialogues.

Proactive Governance: Proactive governance is equally important. Rather than reacting to problems after they arise, we need governance structures that anticipate challenges and guide AI development in beneficial directions. This includes developing adaptive regulatory frameworks, establishing ethics review boards, and creating mechanisms for ongoing assessment and adjustment of AI systems.

International Cooperation: International cooperation will be crucial in this endeavor. As AI transcends national borders, we need global standards and collaborative efforts to ensure that AI benefits humanity as a whole. Initiatives like the Global Partnership on AI (GPAI) represent important steps in this direction, but much more needs to be done to create a truly global framework for responsible AI development.

5.9.5   A Call to Action: Developing AI That Empowers Global Communities

As we conclude this exploration of AI's potential benefits and risks to culture and society, it is clear that we stand at a critical juncture. The decisions we make now about how we develop, deploy, and govern AI will shape the future of human society for generations to come.

To AI Developers and Companies: Prioritize the development of agency-preserving AI that enhances rather than replaces human capabilities. Commit to transparent and ethical AI practices and actively seek diverse perspectives in your development processes.

To Policymakers and Governments: Develop proactive, adaptive governance frameworks for AI that protect public interests without hindering innovation. Invest in AI literacy programs and in preparing your workforce for an AI-driven future.

To Educators: Integrate AI literacy into curricula at all levels and adapt educational approaches to prepare students for a world where human-AI collaboration is the norm.

To Community Leaders and Civil Society Organizations: Engage actively in public dialogues about AI, ensuring that diverse voices are heard. Explore how AI can be leveraged to address local challenges and preserve cultural heritage.

To Citizens: Educate yourselves about AI and its implications. Participate in public discussions about AI governance and hold developers and policymakers accountable for responsible AI development.

5.9.6   Additional Considerations in the AI Landscape

While this chapter has provided an overview of AI's impact on culture and society, the rapidly evolving nature of AI technology means that there are always new areas of consideration emerging. We acknowledge that several important topics warrant further exploration, and we encourage readers to critically engage with these as they continue to develop:

1. **Economic Transformations**: The AI revolution is reshaping economic structures globally. While we've touched on workforce changes, the full economic impact of AI—including job displacement, new job creation, and shifts in global economic power—deserves ongoing attention. Readers should consider how AI might reshape industries and labor markets in their own contexts.

2. **Global Inequalities**: AI has the potential to either exacerbate or reduce global inequalities. As AI technologies proliferate, it's crucial to consider their differential impacts on developed versus developing nations and how we can ensure equitable access to AI benefits worldwide.
3. **Environmental Applications**: While we've discussed AI for social good, the specific application of AI to climate change and environmental challenges is a critical area for further exploration. AI's potential to model climate systems, optimize resource use, and drive sustainable practices could be transformative in our fight against climate change.
4. **Military and Security Implications**: The use of AI in warfare and cybersecurity raises complex ethical and strategic questions that warrant careful consideration. Readers should stay informed about developments in this area and engage in debates about the responsible use of AI in defense and security contexts.
5. **AI and Creativity**: As AI systems become more sophisticated in generating art, music, and literature, we must grapple with questions about the nature of creativity and the role of AI in creative industries. This intersection of technology and artistry opens up fascinating avenues for exploration.
6. **Neurotechnology and AI**: The convergence of AI with neurotechnology presents both exciting possibilities and ethical challenges. As these fields progress, it will be important to consider the implications for human cognition, privacy, and the very nature of human-machine interaction.
7. **Mental Health Applications**: AI is increasingly being applied in mental health contexts, from chatbot therapists to predictive models for mental health crises. The potential benefits and risks of these applications deserve careful scrutiny.
8. **Philosophical Implications**: The development of AI continues to raise profound philosophical questions about the nature of intelligence, consciousness, and what it means to be human. Engaging with these questions is crucial as we navigate the future of AI.
9. **Evolving Regulatory Landscape**: As AI technologies advance, so too must our regulatory frameworks. Staying informed about current and proposed AI regulations across different regions is essential for anyone involved in AI development or implementation.
10. **Long-term Scenarios**: While predicting the future is challenging, considering long-term scenarios of how AI might shape society can help us make more informed decisions today. Readers are encouraged to engage in thoughtful speculation about potential future trajectories of AI development.
11. **Impact Measurement**: As we deploy AI systems, developing robust methods to measure and evaluate their societal impact becomes increasingly important. This includes considering both quantitative metrics and qualitative assessments of AI's effects on individuals and communities.

The future of AI is not predetermined; it will be shaped by the choices we make today. As you reflect on the content of this chapter, we encourage you to explore these additional areas and to remain curious and critical in your engagement with AI technologies. The future of AI will be shaped by our collective decisions and actions. By staying informed, engaging in public dialogue, and approaching these complex issues with nuance and ethical consideration, we can work toward a future where AI truly serves the best interests of humanity.

REFERENCES

AI Commons. (n.d.). https://ai-commons.org/

AI for Good Global Summit: Xprize & ITU, Accelerating progress on the SDGs. https://www. itu.int/en/ITU-T/AI/Pages/201706-default.aspx

AI in the Global. (2023). *South*. https://www.brookings.edu/articles/ai-in-the-global-south-opportunities-and-challenges-towards-more-inclusive-governance/

AI Now Institute. (2018b). *Algorithmic accountability: A primer*. https://ainowinstitute.org/ publication/algorithmic-accountability-for-the-public-sector-report

AI4 ALL. (n.d.). https://ai-4-all.org/

Ajuntament de Barcelona. (n.d.). *Digital Barcelona*. https://ajuntament.barcelona.cat/digital/en/

Ara Irititja. (2020). *Preserving indigenous knowledge through AI*. https://irititja.com/

BABLE Smart Cities. (n.d.). *City: Barcelona*. https://www.bable-smartcities.eu/connect/cities/ city/barcelona.html

Banifatemi, A. (2017). Preparing for an AI driven society. https://www.telecomtv.com/content/ industry-announcements/itu-blog-preparing-for-an-ai-driven-society-26750/

Banifatemi, A. (2019). *Can we use AI for global good*. https://dl.acm.org/doi/ pdf/10.1145/3264623

Brynjolfsson, E., & McAfee, A. (2014). *The second machine age: Work, progress, and prosperity in a time of brilliant technologies*. W.W. Norton & Company. https://wwnorton. com/books/9780393350647

Cath, C., et al. (2018). Artificial intelligence and the 'good society': The US, EU, and UK approach. *Science and Engineering Ethics*, *24*, 505–528. https://link.springer.com/ article/10.1007/s11948-017-9901-7

COVID -19 Mobility Data Network. (n.d.). https://www.covid19mobility.org/

Data Science Nigeria. (2020). *AI Commons*. https://datasciencenigeria.org/wp-content/ uploads/2024/01/Data-Science-Nigeria-Annual-Report-2020.pdf

Driver's Seat Cooperative. (n.d.). https://driversseat.co/

Elements of AI. (n.d.). https://www.elementsofai.com/

European Commission. (2019). *Ethics guidelines for trustworthy AI*. https://ec.europa.eu/ futurium/en/ai-alliance-consultation.1.html

European Commission. (2020a). *Finland leads the way in AI education*. https://ai-watch. ec.europa.eu/countries/finland/finland-ai-strategy-report_en

European Commission. (2020b). *White paper on artificial intelligence: A European approach to excellence and trust*. https://ec.europa.eu/info/publications/white-paper-artificial-intelligence-european-approach-excellence-and-trust_en

European Union. (2016). General data protection regulation (GDPR). *Official Journal of the European Union*. https://gdpr-info.eu/

Finland AI Education Strategy. https://fcai.fi/impact

Floridi, L., & Cowls, J. (2019). *A unified framework of five principles for AI in society*. Harvard Data Science Review. https://hdsr.mitpress.mit.edu/pub/l0jsh9d1/release/8

Gaudiot, J. L., & Banifatemi, A. (2016). Engineering the new boundaries of AI. *Computer*, *49*(11), 77–79. https://ieeexplore.ieee.org/document/7742229

Global Partnership on AI (GPAI). (2021–2024). https://gpai.ai/

Google AI. (n.d.). *AI for social good.* https://ai.google/responsibility/social-good/

IEEE Global Initiative. (n.d.). *Industry connections activities.* https://standards.ieee.org/industry-connections/activities/ieee-global-initiative/

IVOW. (2019, July 3). AI for good 2019 report. *Issuu.* https://issuu.com/ivowai/docs/ivow_aiforgood_report_2019

Microsoft. (n.d.). *AI for good.* https://www.microsoft.com/en-us/ai/ai-for-good

Microsoft Research. (n.d.). *Accessibility and assistive technology.* https://www.microsoft.com/en-us/research/project/accessibility-and-assistive-technology/

Mohamedali, E. Federated Grassroots Community Model for Catalyzing AI for Common Good. https://www.academia.edu/51013030/Federated_Grassroots_Community_Model_for_Catalyzing_Artificial_Intelligence_for_Common_Good

NAACP. (n.d.). *Artificial intelligence and predictive policing issue brief.* https://naacp.org/resources/artificial-intelligence-predictive-policing-issue-brief

National Library of Medicine. (2024). *The potential of AI in healthcare.* https://www.ncbi.nlm.nih.gov/pmc/articles/PMC6616181/

Nature Portfolio. (2024). *AI in healthcare.* https://www.nature.com/collections/dbfcjjigbi

Obermeyer, Z., Powers, B., Vogeli, C., & Mullainathan, S. (2019). Dissecting racial bias in an algorithm used to manage the health of populations. *Science, 366*(6464), 447–453. https://www.science.org/doi/10.1126/science.aax2342

Organization for Economic Co-operation and Development (OECD). (2019). *OECD principles on artificial intelligence.* OECD. https://www.oecd.org/going-digital/ai/principles/

Pentland, A., & Hardjono, T. (2020). *Data cooperatives: Digital empowerment of citizens and workers.* MIT Connection Science. https://ide.mit.edu/sites/default/files/publications/Data-Cooperatives-final.pdf

The Future Society. (2019). Report on AI Commons Summit at GFAIH. (2019). https://thefuturesociety.org/the-ai-commons/

Selbst, A. D., Boyd, D., Friedler, S. A., Venkatasubramanian, S., & Vertesi, J. (2019). Fairness and abstraction in sociotechnical systems. *Proceedings of the 2019 ACM Conference on Fairness, Accountability, and Transparency.* https://dl.acm.org/doi/10.1145/3287560.3287598

Stanford University Human-Centered AI Institute. (2021). *About HAI.* https://hai.stanford.edu/

StoryFile. (2021). *Interactive storytelling with AI holograms.* https://www.njamemorial.org/storyfile

Topol, E. J. (2019). High-performance medicine: The convergence of human and artificial intelligence. *Nature Medicine, 25*(1), 44–56. https://www.nature.com/articles/s41591-018-0300-7

UNESCO. (2021). *AI and ethics: Global insights.* UNESCO. https://unesdoc.unesco.org/ark:/48223/pf0000374174

UNESCO. (2024). *Future of education.* UNESCO. https://www.unesco.org/en/articles/use-ai-education-deciding-future-we-want

United Nations. (2018). *AI for good: Harnessing AI for the global goals.* UN Report on AI and SDGs. https://www.itu.int/en/ITU-T/AI/2018/Pages/default.aspx

United Nations Global Pulse. (n.d.). *UN innovation lab.* https://www.unglobalpulse.org/

Wachter, S., Mittelstadt, B., & Floridi, L. (2017). Why a right to explanation of automated decision-making does not exist in the general data protection regulation. *International Data Privacy Law, 7,* 76–99. https://academic.oup.com/idpl/article/7/2/76/3860948

West, D. M. (2018). *The future of work: Robots, AI, and automation.* Brookings Institution Press. https://www.brookings.edu/events/the-future-of-work-robots-ai-and-automation

Wikipedia. (n.d.a). *Participatory action research.* https://en.wikipedia.org/wiki/Participatory_action_research

Wikipedia. (n.d.b). *COMPAS (Software)*. https://en.wikipedia.org/wiki/COMPAS_(software)

XPRIZE. (2016). *AI XPRIZE: $5M AI for good competition*. https://www.xprize.org/prizes/ai

Zuboff, S. (2019). The age of surveillance capitalism: The fight for a human future at the new frontier of power. *PublicAffairs*. https://www.publicaffairsbooks.com/titles/shoshana-zuboff/the-age-of-surveillance-capitalism/9781610395694/

Community Voices 5: Insights from Nishan Chelvachandran— Considering AI's Broader Societal Implications

Our fifth community voice features insights from Nishan Chelvachandran, the founder of Iron Lakes, a consultancy specializing in the intersection of technology and humanity. Nishan is a cybersecurity advisor, strategist, and researcher with a rich background in advising state governments, non-profits, and international organizations on cyber resilience and ethical AI.

His work focuses on creating holistic innovation ecosystems, especially for rural and isolated communities. Nishan's deep commitment to promoting ethical uses of technology, and his extensive experience in the public and private sectors make him a crucial contributor to our exploration of AI's impact on cultural preservation and community development.

Question 1: Share your professional bio

Nishan is the founder of Iron Lakes, a bespoke cyber impact consultancy specializing in providing expertise from the conflux of technology and humanity. He is a C-Suite professional, Cybersecurity adviser and influencer, strategist, published author, and researcher, with years of experience built on the strong foundations of bespoke operational and technological activity in the UK Public Sector. He has advised municipal and state governments in Finland on their cybersecurity strategies, The Vatican on AI and Peace, and the Canadian Nonprofit sector on cyber resilience. He is spearheading emerging work in Rural Futures, creating holistic innovation ecosystems that address bespoke challenges faced by rural and isolated communities. He is also on IEEE's Global Expert Advisory Panel on Children Experiences with Technology. He is a special adviser to the British and Commonwealth Chamber of Commerce in Finland and a Fellow of the RSA and the Network lead for the RSA in Canada.

His current focus is on regenerative and resilient systems (re)design in public, private, and third sectors, and empowering the democratization and representative reimagining of collective futures through AI and future technology. In the little spare time he has, Nishan is an Olympic Trap Clay-Pigeon and sustenance hunter.

DOI: 10.1201/9781003517115-10

Question 2: Share your heritage and family traditions. Where did you grow up? Share a family tradition that you continue to this day.

As a child of empire, I grew up in the UK, with Tamil heritage (from Sri Lanka and Mauritius). However, my visible heritage did not play a big part in my upbringing, in that for all intents and purposes, my family and I assimilated into an anglo community dynamic. However, elements of cultural influences from ancestral heritage likely shaped my upbringing differently to those in my physical and social immediacy. My immediate family are extremely close, and we keep in contact almost daily, despite geographic challenges/limitations. Access to technology has made this easier to maintain.

Question 3: Experience with AI. Have you used AI technologies? If yes, please describe your experience. How do you perceive the role of AI in your professional or personal life?

Yes. More recently, I have been using ChatGPT, Dall-E, Midjourney, and similar for assistance in content creation, be that for videos, drafting documents, or speeches. The AI for me is an augmentation or assistive process, as I can generate a few variations on themes when I figure out how to realize a creative idea or thought that I have. After I see some iterations, it is far easier for me to then develop and flesh out the draft into something fully fledged. Essentially, the AI saves me the time and frustration of either not knowing where to start, or spending a lot of time missing the mark. I can accelerate that learning curve and spend the same amount of energy creating something far better. In my previous line of work, I developed algorithms to data mine/scrap and collate open-source intelligence profiles of individuals for the government/law enforcement. Working in this more nefarious application of AI/technology was the precursor to my later journey of promoting ethical uses and safeguards for technology.

Question 4: AI and cultural preservation. Can you envision any innovative ways in which AI could be used to safeguard intangible cultural heritage, such as language, folksongs, or storytelling? Are there specific traditions, practices, or aspects of your culture that you believe could benefit from AI technology?

Language, knowledge, and cultural expression could be safeguarded by an AI technology. There are many languages and practices that are lost to time and generations. Paradoxically, humanity is more connected now than at any other time in history, yet societally, we are perhaps the most isolated; and generational knowledge, heritage, and experience is lost. Humans have become short-form drones, lacking nuanced experiences that are considered Too Long, Didn't Read (TLDR). Having an app like Duolingo for language, or other gamification or immersive experiences where culturally significant stories and knowledge could be transferred in a meaningful way, is perhaps one of the most powerful potentials of AI technology.

Question 5: AI and nature. Could you describe a traditional practice from your own culture, or one you've learned about or reported on, that helps in environmental sustainability or climate resilience? Also, how do you think AI could be utilized to support or improve this practice?

AI in this instance could be used as a knowledge sommelier of sorts, to share isolated and unknown cases that might be buried in research or esoteric reports. For people who are trying to figure out how to make an impact change environmentally, but are unsure how, AI could help them with examples of initiatives from around the world, which may apply to the end user's ideated use case. This accelerated learning/knowledge sharing means that changemakers can spend more time and energy on actually applying meaningful initiatives rather than getting stuck in an ideative feedback loop.

Question 6: Wisdom of elders and AI. What role do elders play in preserving culture and wisdom in your community? With ethical practices at play, can AI play a role in capturing and disseminating this wisdom? If yes, how?

Elders traditionally have been knowledge keepers, sages of wisdom and guidance. However, as nuance has been lost in our accelerated society, this wisdom has been seen as antiquated or outdated: leaning on canceling or ignoring sage wisdom, relegating elders to play a more distant and disconnected/disengaged role in our communities. AI could not only capture this wisdom for preservation and posterity but also disseminate and draw comparisons between wisdom from otherwise disconnected communities: drawing communal truths and understanding for younger generations to assimilate and make good on.

Question 7: AI and ethics. How important is it for AI systems to be developed ethically, especially in the context of cultural preservation? What steps would you like to be taken to ensure that, as AI expands, it represents diverse cultural perspectives?

It needs to be developed together with people from outside of the technological/developer space: people with diverse experiences, heritage, and values. It needs to be developed with different-minded people. Google's Gemini is a good example of what happens if you completely design something with a group of homogenous-values individuals; where the output is skewed and not representative of reality.

Question 8: AI and personalization. We know that AI systems today don't understand the values and needs of diverse populations. Would you be willing to voluntarily share your family traditions and customs with your personal AI device to improve personalization?

In principle yes, although we are not at that stage, and clarity is needed as to how those traditions and customs will be used and who the beneficiary of that data will be. Historically, the very people whose diverse information is needed are the same people who have been exploited for gain not of their own; and so I would be appre-hensive to openly share such intimate information without some safeguards and accountability processes in place as well as a clear framework to beneficiaries and uses of the data.

Question 9: Future of AI in community development. What potential risks and benefits should be considered when integrating AI into community initiatives?

As referred to above: that this is used as another mechanism to potentially exploit and harm marginalized communities.

Question 10: Final thoughts. Is there anything else you would like to share about your views on AI and its role in preserving cultural heritage and traditions?

[no response]

***

Nishan Chelvachandran's survey responses offer a profound exploration of AI's potential to both benefit and harm communities. His insights highlight the impor-tance of developing AI technologies that respect and incorporate diverse cultural per-spectives and ethical considerations. Nishan emphasizes the need for community-led development of AI tools to ensure that they serve to empower rather than exploit marginalized communities.

6 Key AI Concepts for Communities

Fernando Gonzalez

As a Cuban-American, my journey with AI began long before it became the widely applied tool it is today. Growing up, I was deeply curious about science and how it could be used to benefit society. This passion led me to pursue a career in engineering, eventually becoming Chair of the Computing and Software Engineering Department at Florida Gulf Coast University. In 2024, we launched an AI Institute, a pioneering initiative that reflects our commitment to advancing AI research and supporting real-world applications. We also introduced new degree programs centered on AI and data science, aiming to prepare future generations to use AI in ways that benefit and empower communities.

Over the years, I have watched AI evolve from a specialized scientific pursuit to an everyday tool across nearly every profession. My own work began with automated control systems and gradually expanded into developing collaborative intelligent agents. Through this evolution, I have seen how AI has the potential to drive societal progress, especially when it is accessible, inclusive, and tailored to community needs.

As a person with dyslexia, I've found it immensely helpful to ground myself in the foundational science before tackling more advanced AI concepts. Similarly, for AI to be fully integrated into our communities, its concepts must be clearly articulated and accessible to everyone. Today, AI is embedded in our daily lives, from the devices we use at home to the systems powering industries and public services. Yet, many still struggle to grasp what AI truly is and how it can enhance communities in meaningful ways. In this chapter, I aim to provide an overview of AI's core technologies, its limitations, and the potential benefits and challenges as we move forward in an AI-driven world.

6.1 AI AND COMMUNITY

Computers have certain strengths, like their vast memory, high computational accuracy, and speed. However, they lack the human ability to experience emotions, develop common sense, or act with morality and ethics. For instance, while people use emotions like happiness, sadness, and pride to make decisions, AI lacks this level of understanding. Consider laughter, computers will never laugh and do not understand what that is. Humans also tend to make choices based on cultural and ethical standards—such as respecting certain traditions or practices that reflect their beliefs, even when they're not purely logical. For example, the decision to preserve and celebrate cultural practices, even if they are outdated or impractical, reflects human

DOI: 10.1201/9781003517115-11

attachment to heritage and identity, something AI does not inherently understand. The human brain is very complex and decision-making involves many other factors besides simple logic.

AI is also not creative. It only regurgitates or interpolates existing material to form new material. Consider making an artistic pottery. In 1918, Maria Martinez, the famous potter from San Ildefonso Pueblo in New Mexico and her husband, Julian, created the black-on-black pottery style that is now famous in the Santa Fe art community and beyond. New Mexico is known for its artistic pottery, however what made Maria famous was her then unique black-on-black style they created. In contrast, AI is not creative. It can combine different types of art to make new art, but it cannot create new styles like what Maria Martinez and her husband were able to accomplish.

Take, for example, AI's role in language preservation. AI can be trained to recognize and replicate elements of endangered languages, capturing dialects or unique phrases from a community. However, while AI can help in preserving these languages through documentation or translation support, it lacks the understanding of cultural nuances. An AI can store words and rules but cannot grasp the context or emotional depth that native speakers bring to a language. AI may, for instance, struggle with translating idiomatic expressions that convey deeply cultural or emotional meanings.

Similarly, consider a historical documentation project. AI tools can assist communities in cataloging artifacts or digitizing archives, which is invaluable for preserving histories that might otherwise be lost. However, an AI system cannot evaluate the cultural significance or emotional weight of an artifact—knowledge that often comes only from a deep human connection with history. While AI can efficiently classify and organize, it doesn't replace the role of cultural scholars or community members who provide meaningful interpretations.

Author Beba Garcia is known for writing books that capture Latin cultures, including the history of Puerto Rican television. Though she does not use AI in her writings, she raises concerns that AI-generated content may lack the emotional resonance needed to authentically tell cultural stories. Like me, Garcia relies on stories from family and community to deeply understand and convey her culture. AI may be able to replicate factual elements, but the subtleties of culture—rooted in emotional and experiential understanding—remain beyond its reach.

Automation in general has a profound impact on communities and society at large. Whenever work becomes automated, there is a shift in employment needs. Jobs may change rather than disappear, with new opportunities emerging in fields that support and manage AI technologies. For example, in the public sector, automation and AI might streamline administrative tasks, but this allows community workers to focus on complex, human-centered needs, like social services and community engagement, that AI cannot address. This shift also means that education and upskilling for such new roles are critical for community growth and stability in an AI-driven world.

Automation allows societies to accomplish the same amount of work with less human effort, leading to questions of wealth distribution rather than job scarcity. Automation is generally good for society meaning less effort is needed to maintain the existing wealth. However, when less human labor is needed, owners of automated systems may accumulate wealth, while displaced workers see reduced income opportunities. Given that much AI research was publicly funded, we might consider whether the economic benefits of AI should be more equitably shared with the communities that helped fund its development through taxes. This question of fairness will be essential as communities navigate the social impacts of increasing AI adoption.

6.2 NEW AI EDUCATION FOR CULTURAL PRESERVATION

Educators are essential in training future AI experts who will work with technology to serve society's diverse needs. It's vital for AI education to emphasize cultural preservation, ethics, and professional responsibility alongside technical skills. This emphasis shifts the focus from purely technical advancements to creating systems that respect and integrate cultural values.

Bias in AI training is one of the main challenges that educators must address. Suppose, for instance, an AI system is trained on data primarily from dominant cultural groups but is used in communities with unique languages, practices, or social norms. This system could produce outputs that do not accurately represent or serve these communities, potentially erasing cultural identities in the process. For example, if an AI model trained on standard American English is used to understand regional dialects or Indigenous languages, it may misinterpret or ignore these languages, leading to underrepresentation in AI-driven language tools. A solution here involves creating synthetic data that amplifies underrepresented dialects or cultural expressions, helping to achieve a balanced dataset that truly reflects community diversity.

This synthetic data must be carefully constructed to avoid reinforcing stereotypes. For example, if creating data for a group of speakers from a minority language, it's important not to overrepresent any one feature—such as certain phrases or traditional attire that might not be universally representative. Synthetic data should capture diverse expressions without creating a monolithic view of any culture, ensuring that AI tools do not perpetuate inaccuracies.

Educators have a responsibility to introduce these principles early, so AI professionals recognize that cultural and ethical considerations are integral to system design. An AI model must be evaluated not only for its technical performance but also for how well it serves and respects the cultural contexts in which it operates. The more AI students learn to integrate these practices into their designs, the more capable they will be of creating systems that positively contribute to cultural preservation and community needs.

6.2.1 AI Concepts for Community and Cultural Applications

Next, together with co-author Iran Davar Ardalan, we turned to her AI Assistant (ARC-AI) to review our book and identify where the following six AI definitions are relevant to AI for Community:

6.2.1.1 Artificial Intelligence (AI)

Definition: Artificial intelligence refers to machines and software systems that can simulate aspects of human intelligence such as learning, problem-solving, and pattern recognition. Unlike traditional programs that follow rigid, pre-set algorithms, through machine learning, AI can adapt and refine its performance based on data and experiences. Most of the recent advancements in AI involve the use of neural networks. These networks are created using machine learning techniques which rely on processing labeled data in supervised learning or unlabeled data in unsupervised learning. Initially used in specialized industrial settings like manufacturing for optimizing processes and supporting design, AI has expanded into everyday life, contributing to fields such as healthcare, autonomous vehicles, and generative tools like ChatGPT. These advancements underscore AI's evolution from niche applications to essential components in various sectors.

Application: AI can transform community services and cultural preservation by enhancing accessibility, inclusivity, and cultural understanding in various sectors. AI tools can streamline public resources, like organizing library systems and digitizing local archives, making information more accessible and tailored to community needs.

6.2.1.1.1 Examples from AI for Community

In Chapter 1, examples like Laleh AI showcase how AI preserves a scholar's legacy, allowing users to engage interactively with Dr. Laleh Bakhtiar's work. This approach to AI shows its potential for maintaining cultural and intellectual heritage, making a scholar's insights accessible through AI-driven conversations.

The chapter also features MEXICA, an AI developed by Rafael Pérez y Pérez that generates narratives centered on Mexica (Aztec) culture by embedding culturally resonant emotions, such as friendship or animosity, between characters to produce authentic storytelling. Chapter 1 also describes a project at the AI for Good Summit utilizing AI to process The Shahnameh, a Persian epic. This model required cultural adjustments to interpret elements like the hero Rostam and his horse Rakhsh correctly, underlining the importance of culturally specific AI algorithms.

Finally, Chapter 1 introduces CulturaFX, a research project led by TulipAI, which aimed to bridge advanced AI and cultural authenticity by ethically sourcing global sounds to enrich AI-generated audio with cultural specificity. Although funding challenges limited the project, the research contributed valuable insights into building ethically sourced and culturally resonant AI audio.

In Chapter 2, the AI application highlighted is Project Elevate Black Voices, a collaboration between Google and Howard University. This project aims to create a high-quality dataset for African-American Vernacular English (AAVE), improving speech recognition technology's inclusivity and accuracy for Black communities. The initiative addresses the common difficulties Black users face with voice-activated devices, ensuring these tools better understand and respond to Black speech patterns without requiring code-switching. The project also emphasizes ethical data collection and aims to establish a framework that protects the interests and agency of Black communities in AI development.

In Chapter 2, we present the WhatsApp chatbot developed for social-emotional assessments in early childhood development programs in South Africa. This automated tool allows home visitors to complete assessments on young children, streamlining the evaluation process and improving access to essential developmental insights. By automating these assessments, the chatbot reduces the manual workload, enabling a consistent and scalable approach to gathering vital data for child development in low-income communities.

In Chapter 3, AI's role in language preservation is emphasized, featuring natural language processing (NLP) tools tailored to minority languages like Basque, Angika, and Amazigh. These tools document and digitize endangered languages, capturing cultural nuances to ensure linguistic heritage endures for future generations.

Chapter 4 highlights the importance of transparent and inclusive AI to foster community trust.

In our book's Conclusion, we highlight NVIDIA's support for Te Hiku Media in New Zealand, an example of AI used to preserve the Māori language and heritage. Also, NVIDIA's AI Nations initiative that assists countries in building sovereign AI infrastructures.

6.2.1.2   Generative AI

Definition: Generative AI refers to systems capable of creating new data, such as text, images, or audio, by leveraging existing data. While it seems to produce novel content, generative AI typically recombines and interpolates from its training data. For instance, it can generate a realistic image of a cat that wasn't in its training set by iterating adjustments until the desired output aligns with learned characteristics. Although generative AI can produce convincing results, it lacks true creativity; it cannot originate concepts beyond its training data's scope.

Application: Generative AI can support cultural preservation by generating authentic cultural content, such as traditional stories or language simulations. Our book highlights the importance of ensuring that such use is ethical, focusing on sourcing culturally significant data responsibly and involving communities to avoid misrepresentation or exploitation.

6.2.1.2.1   *Examples from AI for Community*

In Chapter 1, Laleh AI—a customized generative AI—preserves and conveys Dr. Bakhtiar's knowledge by training on her writings and letters, demonstrating generative AI's application in cultural preservation.

Chapter 3 demonstrates how this aligns with the vision of enhancing minority language visibility through culturally grounded content.

In Chapter 5, the **Rekrei Project** (formerly known as Project Mosul) exemplifies the use of generative AI to digitally reconstruct and preserve cultural artifacts destroyed or damaged during conflict. This initiative began in response to the 2015 destruction of the Mosul Museum's artifacts by ISIS. Leveraging crowdsourced photographs and AI-powered generative technology, the project successfully created 3D models of the lost items, enabling virtual restoration and ensuring that the cultural memory of these invaluable artifacts is maintained. Such efforts demonstrate how generative AI can support digital heritage conservation, allowing future generations to access and learn from reconstructed historical treasures.

And, in the Conclusion, we are introduced to John Smith's environmental engineering assistant. Based on the engineer's past work, this custom AI supports sustainable resource management by providing insights into previous infrastructure and landfill projects. It demonstrates generative AI's value in environmental engineering, helping professionals access tailored information relevant to current challenges.

6.2.1.3 Machine Learning (ML)

Definition: Machine learning is a subset of AI that involves systems modifying their algorithms to enhance future results based on new data. This capacity allows ML systems to improve tasks such as medical diagnostics, sales forecasting, and image recognition, which contrast with the fixed logic of conventional programs. Through techniques such as neural networks, ML provides adaptive solutions that evolve with usage, making them more efficient over time.

Application: ML models can predict health trends based on community data, allowing local clinics to anticipate health needs and tailor services for cultural groups.

6.2.1.3.1 Examples from AI for Community

ML can support language preservation by focusing on high-risk languages and dialects, as seen in Chapter 3 discussions on endangered languages like West Polesian.

In Chapter 5 and the Conclusion Te Hiku Media: An example from New Zealand where ML is used to develop speech recognition tools for the Māori language. This initiative illustrates how ML can be leveraged for cultural preservation, enabling language accessibility for future generations while collaborating with local communities to ensure cultural alignment.

6.2.1.4 Supervised Learning

Definition: Supervised learning is a type of machine learning where an AI system is trained using labeled data. This approach requires that the training dataset consists of input-output pairs, with each pair accurately labeled to guide the learning process. The model adjusts its weights during training to improve the classification or prediction of new data, based on the patterns it has learned from the labeled examples. This process ensures that the model can make more accurate predictions when exposed to new, unseen data.

Application: In the context of language preservation, supervised learning can help train AI models to recognize and generate specific linguistic patterns in minority languages.

6.2.1.4.1 Examples from AI for Community

By tagging data with cultural nuances and idiomatic phrases, linguists can work with native speakers to create accurate educational tools for endangered languages. In Chapter 3, this approach is applied in Angika, where native speakers manually verify translations to ensure they reflect authentic use, reinforcing cultural and linguistic accuracy in AI outputs.

6.2.1.5 Trust-Adaptive AI

Definition: AI systems designed to dynamically build, maintain, and adapt trust by aligning with user values, cultural contexts, and transparency standards.

Application: Building trust and as a result participation among groups that are not well represented in today's AI models is critical to increasing the training data from members of these groups. Their participation directly increases the cultural knowledge AI models have from such groups.

6.2.1.5.1 Examples from AI for Community

Chapter 4 explicitly discusses Trust-Adaptive AI and introduces the Trust-Adaptive Virtual Agents (TAVA) framework, which is designed to build and maintain trust in AI systems across various cultural contexts. Trust-Adaptive AI can be applied in community and cultural contexts to support initiatives like language preservation, heritage archiving, and local resource management. These AI systems can enhance decision-making in healthcare, social services, and public platforms, making them more responsive, culturally aligned, and ethically sound in meeting community needs.

In Chapter 5, the Barcelona Smart City Initiative demonstrates how community-driven participatory design was integrated into AI solutions for urban planning. This approach involved residents in the decision-making process to ensure that AI systems were transparent and aligned with the specific needs and priorities of the local population. By engaging citizens directly, this initiative built trust between the community and AI, showcasing how trusted AI can support collaborative urban development while respecting and empowering local voices.

6.2.1.6 Unsupervised Learning

Definition: Unsupervised learning does not rely on labeled data; instead, it explores and identifies patterns within input data on its own. This learning method is akin to the way children intuitively recognize language rules before formal education. Unsupervised learning can group data into natural categories based on inherent similarities without external labels. While it requires large datasets, it facilitates broad, general learning and can uncover structural insights within data, such as distinguishing between basic categories like birds and fish.

Application: Unsupervised learning is instrumental in organizing and analyzing dialectal variations within minority languages.

6.2.1.6.1 Examples from AI for Community

In Chapter 3, this method is useful for capturing informal linguistic patterns across dialects of languages like Amazigh, where distinct regional differences exist. By identifying clusters of linguistic data, unsupervised learning helps create more nuanced AI tools that cater to the diversity within a single language, respecting its inherent complexity.

6.3 WHERE TO GET HELP

Local Universities/Community Colleges: Many universities offer community outreach programs or workshops in AI, especially if they have AI research centers or data science departments.

Local Libraries and Community Centers: Some libraries now host AI literacy programs to help residents understand and use basic AI tools.

Online Courses: Free online courses (e.g., Coursera, Udemy) offer introductions to AI, often supported by partnerships with universities.

Local Startups and Small Businesses: Research startups focusing on automation tools for small and community-based organizations. They may provide affordable consulting or workshops on automating simple tasks.

Local Economic Development Offices: These offices sometimes offer small business support, including guidance on integrating affordable automation.

Civil Rights Organizations: Many civil rights groups have task forces on AI fairness and can offer guidance or resources on how to identify and challenge AI bias.

Regional Tech Meetups or Hackathons: These events provide a hands-on environment to learn the basics of ML, often with a focus on solving local community issues.

Nonprofit Tech Support Services: Organizations like TechSoup provide low-cost tech support for community nonprofits interested in automation.

6.4 TRY THESE AI PROMPTS FOR COMMUNITY AND EDUCATION

With the help of our AI Assistant, ARC-AI, we developed this section to inspire community and educational leaders to leverage AI effectively. Use these prompts to create impactful, community-focused projects. Be sure to replace the specific details about your community for a tailored approach:

1. **Community Engagement Prompts**:
   - "Create a weekly newsletter outline featuring local events, cultural stories, and interviews with community leaders in Albuquerque, New Mexico."
   - "Develop a plan for a community workshop on basic AI literacy, including hands-on activities that reflect the interests and needs of different generations in Albuquerque, New Mexico."

2. **Cultural Preservation Prompts:**
   - "Generate questions for an oral history project to capture stories from elders in Albuquerque, New Mexico about local traditions and heritage."
   - "Suggest methods for digitizing and cataloging artifacts that represent the cultural significance of Albuquerque, New Mexico."

3. **Educational Prompts:**
   - "Develop prompts for students to explore ethical questions in AI, such as 'How can AI be used responsibly to benefit the people of Albuquerque, New Mexico?'"
   - "Create a quiz on the history and applications of AI, incorporating examples that are specific to Albuquerque, New Mexico."

4. **Local Problem-Solving Prompts:**
   - "Propose AI-based solutions for challenges commonly faced in communities such as organizing volunteer efforts or improving public services. Tailor this to Albuquerque, New Mexico."
   - "Outline a student project where they collaborate with local nonprofits to create an AI tool that addresses a specific need in Albuquerque, New Mexico."

Next Steps:

To get your community aligned on AI, start by asking key questions: What challenges and opportunities do we see with AI in our daily lives? How can AI align with our cultural values and local needs? What skills or knowledge do we need to better understand and use AI responsibly?

These questions can help initiate meaningful dialogue, ensuring that everyone operates from the same level of understanding and contributes to thoughtful, community-centered AI practices. Good luck, and make sure to have fun too!

Community Voices 6: Insights from Leandro de Castro—Analyzing AI's Potential in Community-Driven Initiatives

Our sixth survey features the insights of Leandro de Castro, a distinguished academic and expert in artificial intelligence and data science. Dr. de Castro holds an impressive array of qualifications, including a BSc in Electrical Engineering, MSc and PhD in Computer Engineering from Unicamp, Brazil, along with an MBA in Strategic Business Management.

His extensive career spans teaching and research positions at prestigious institutions worldwide, including the University of Kent, Malaysian Technological University, and the University of Salamanca. With over 250 scientific publications and recognition as one of the top 2% most influential researchers globally, Dr. de Castro brings a wealth of knowledge and experience to our exploration of AI's role in cultural preservation and community development.

His work on artificial neural networks, natural computing, and machine learning provides a foundation for understanding the potential and challenges of integrating AI into diverse cultural contexts.

Question 1: Share your professional bio

BSc in Electrical Engineering from the Federal University of Goias (1996), MSc (1998) and PhD (2001) in Computer Engineering from Unicamp, and an MBA in Strategic Business Management from the Catholic University of Santos (2008), all in Brazil. He was a Research Associate at the University of Kent at Canterbury, UK (2001–2002), a Visiting Professor at the Malaysian Technological University (2005), a Visiting Professor at Unicamp (2012), and a Visiting Research Professor at the University of Salamanca (2014). He was an Assistant Professor at the Master's Program in Informatics at Unisantos (2003–2008), an Associate Professor at the Graduate Program in Electrical Engineering and Computing at Mackenzie Presbyterian University (2008–2022), and the Chief Executive Officer at In.lab (Center for Research, Development, and Innovation of AI Applied to Health) (2022–2023). Dr. de Castro has

DOI: 10.1201/9781003517115-12

4 authored books, more than 250 scientific papers published, and over the past four years (2020–2023), he was recognized as among the 2% most influential researchers in the world based on scientific impact indices monitored by PLoS Biology. He has already served as Research Chair and also as Chief Innovation and Entrepreneurship Officer in previous universities. He is currently an Artificial Intelligence and Data Science Professor at FGCU.

Question 2: Share your heritage and family traditions. Where did you grow up? Share a family tradition that you continue to this day.

I was born in Goiania, GO, Brazil, where I lived until I finished my BS in Electrical Engineering in 1996. I then moved to Campinas, SP, Brazil, where I did my MSc and PhD in Electrical Engineering, concluding in 2001. A family tradition that we keep until today is to travel together once a year.

Question 3: Experience with AI. Have you used AI technologies? If yes, please describe your experience. How do you perceive the role of AI in your professional or personal life?

My journey in AI began in 1994 during my BS in Electrical Engineering. I was awarded an undergraduate research grant to develop a computational tool for current transformers. This sparked my interest in AI, leading me to apply artificial neural networks to predict soybean crops and develop neural classifiers for short-term load prediction in electrical power systems. During my Master's degree, I focused on improving learning algorithms for multilayer neural networks. In my Doctorate, I explored computational tools inspired by the immune system and their applications in data analysis and optimization. My postdoctoral work at the University of Kent at Canterbury in the UK allowed me to investigate theoretical aspects of artificial immune systems, culminating in the publication of the world's first textbook on the subject. At Unicamp, I taught courses on artificial neural networks and evolutionary computing and introduced a novel course on Natural Computing. As an Assistant Professor at the Catholic University of Santos, I contributed to the accreditation of the MS Program in Informatics and established the Laboratory of Intelligent Systems (LSIn). Later, at Mackenzie, I founded the Natural Computing and Machine Learning Laboratory (LCoN). I authored the publication of several textbooks, including one on Data Mining. My influence in the field was recognized with my inclusion among the top 2% of the most influential researchers in the world.

Question 4: AI and cultural preservation. Can you envision any innovative ways in which AI could be used to safeguard intangible cultural heritage, such as language, folksongs, or storytelling? Are there specific traditions, practices, or aspects of your culture that you believe could benefit from AI technology?

AI presents innovative solutions for safeguarding intangible cultural heritage such as language, folksongs, and storytelling. Through automatic transcription and translation, AI can preserve endangered languages and facilitate language learning. AI-driven music analysis and generation can help preserve folk songs by recognizing melodies and creating new compositions. Similarly, AI-powered storytelling chatbots and recommender systems can engage users in interactive storytelling experiences, preserving oral traditions and recommending folktales based on individual preferences. In my own culture, where oral histories and folktales are rich and diverse, AI technology could be invaluable in transcribing, analyzing, and sharing these stories, ensuring their preservation and accessibility for future generations.

Question 5: AI and nature. Could you describe a traditional practice from your own culture, or one you've learned about or reported on, that helps in environmental sustainability or climate resilience? Also, how do you think AI could be utilized to support or improve this practice?

One traditional practice from Brazilian culture that contributes to environmental sustainability and climate resilience is agroforestry, particularly the practice known as "sistema agroflorestal" (agroforestry system). This practice involves the deliberate integration of trees, crops, and livestock on the same piece of land. Trees are strategically planted alongside crops and pastures, creating a diverse and symbiotic ecosystem. The trees provide shade, regulate water flow, and enrich the soil with nutrients, which benefits crop growth and soil conservation. Additionally, agroforestry helps mitigate climate change by sequestering carbon dioxide from the atmosphere.

AI could be utilized to support and improve agroforestry practices in several ways:

1. **Predictive Analytics:** AI algorithms can analyze environmental data such as soil moisture, temperature, and rainfall patterns to predict optimal planting times and locations for different tree and crop species within the agroforestry system. This can maximize productivity while minimizing water usage and environmental impact.
2. **Precision Farming:** AI-driven precision farming techniques can optimize resource use within agroforestry systems by monitoring plant health, detecting pests and diseases early, and providing targeted interventions. For example, drones equipped with AI can monitor tree health and identify areas requiring additional nutrients or pest control measures.
3. **Decision Support Systems:** AI-powered decision support systems can assist farmers in planning and managing their agroforestry systems. These systems can provide personalized recommendations for tree-crop combinations based on local conditions, market demand, and environmental goals.

Question 6: Wisdom of elders and AI. What role do elders play in preserving culture and wisdom in your community? With ethical practices at play, can AI play a role in capturing and disseminating this wisdom? If yes, how?

In my community, elders play a vital role in preserving culture and wisdom. They are the custodians of traditional knowledge, stories, and practices passed down through generations. Elders serve as teachers and mentors, imparting valuable lessons about history, culture, and moral values to younger generations. Their wisdom and experience are highly respected and sought after, shaping the identity and cohesion of the community. AI can play a significant role in capturing and disseminating the wisdom of elders in communities by digitizing oral histories, creating virtual elders or chatbots, integrating cultural knowledge into educational tools, and preserving indigenous languages. Through AI-powered technologies like natural language processing and speech recognition, the wisdom and teachings of elders can be recorded, organized, and made accessible to future generations. However, ethical considerations are essential to ensure informed consent, respect cultural sensitivities, and protect privacy and intellectual property rights. Overall, AI serves as a tool to complement the role of elders in preserving cultural heritage, fostering intergenerational dialogue, and ensuring the continuity of traditional knowledge and wisdom.

Question 7: AI and ethics. How important is it for AI systems to be developed ethically, especially in the context of cultural preservation? What steps would you like to be taken to ensure that, as AI expands, it represents diverse cultural perspectives?

Ethical development of AI systems is necessary in the context of cultural preservation to ensure respect for diverse perspectives, avoidance of bias and stereotypes, and empowerment of communities. It is crucial to obtain informed consent, respect privacy, and promote transparency in data collection and decision-making processes. To represent diverse cultural perspectives, steps such as fostering diversity in AI development teams, collecting inclusive datasets, and engaging with communities are essential. By adhering to ethics guidelines, promoting transparency, and empowering communities, AI can play a positive role in preserving cultural heritage while respecting the values and traditions of different cultures.

Question 8: AI and personalization. We know that AI systems today don't understand the values and needs of diverse populations. Would you be willing to voluntarily share your family traditions and customs with your personal AI device to improve personalization?

I might be willing to voluntarily share my family traditions and customs with it to improve personalization. Sharing this information could help the AI better understand my cultural background, preferences, and values, leading to more personalized and relevant recommendations or interactions. However, I would also want assurances regarding data privacy and security to ensure that my personal information is protected and used responsibly. Transparency about how the AI uses this information and the ability to control what is shared would also be important factors in my decision to share my family traditions and customs with a personal AI device.

Question 9: Future of AI in community development. What potential risks and benefits should be considered when integrating AI into community initiatives?

Integrating AI into community initiatives offers potential benefits such as increased efficiency, personalization, and informed decision-making but also poses risks, including exclusion, bias, and privacy concerns. To maximize the benefits and mitigate risks, it is crucial to involve community members in all stages of AI implementation, ensuring transparency, accountability, and respect for privacy. Addressing potential biases in AI algorithms and data, as well as promoting accessibility and inclusivity, are essential for ensuring that the benefits of AI are realized by all members of the community.

Question 10: Final thoughts. Is there anything else you would like to share about your views on AI and its role in preserving cultural heritage and traditions?

[no response]

***

Dr. Leandro de Castro's survey responses offer a profound and detailed exploration of AI's capabilities in preserving cultural heritage and enhancing community initiatives. His extensive background in AI and commitment to ethical considerations provide a critical perspective on the responsible development and deployment of AI technologies. Dr. de Castro highlights the importance of involving community members in the design and implementation of AI solutions, ensuring that these technologies respect and enhance cultural diversity.

Conclusion
Honoring Roots, Shaping the Future

Iran Davar Ardalan

It is remarkable to live in times when artificial intelligence is becoming more and more a part of our lives, especially with the significant investments being made in AI today. Throughout this book, our perspectives aim to champion an AI-for-community model, where technology is designed to amplify human strengths, safeguard cultural identity, and address pressing global needs responsibly.

My time in Tonga in 2017 brought this to light, as I met Uili Lousi, a Tongan artist whose work is deeply intertwined with his community's heritage. Uili's intricate Tongan patterns, depicting the ancient art of Fata-'o-Tu'i-Tonga, are not just visually stunning but also imbued with sacred geometry and movements inspired by his surroundings—the cosmos, the ocean, and the land (Ardalan, 2017).

When I invited Uili to Geneva for the AI for Good Summit in 2019, his words resonated deeply: "AI is now part of the evolution of human beings—there is no way around it." He emphasized that AI could bring us together to address significant challenges, such as climate change, by leveraging data and algorithms for meaningful action. His closing plea to recognize the importance of AI and connect through knowledge sharing underlined a crucial point: the relevance of AI to all communities.

This reflection on Uili's love for his community and his visionary approach to AI reminds us of our responsibility. Creating modern tools that bring education, joy, and economic prosperity to every corner of the world, including Tonga—where time begins (Ardalan, 2017).

During my time with SecondMuse and the Australian InnovationXchange, I also had the opportunity to meet Chef Rob Oliver in Australia, where I learned about his incredible work with the Pacific Island Food Revolution. This initiative exemplifies how community engagement around healthy eating can lead to significant, positive outcomes (Pacific Island Food Revolution, 2024).

By utilizing the power of reality TV, radio, and social media, the Pacific Island Food Revolution has successfully encouraged Pacific Islanders to embrace local, indigenous foods, transforming perceptions and dietary habits across the region. With viewership rates reaching 85% in Tonga and 84% in Samoa, the program has driven an impressive 42% of participants to report positive changes in their diets. More importantly, it has helped shift the perception of local food from "village food" to something trendy and desirable, highlighting the power of culturally relevant, community-centered interventions (Pacific Island Food Revolution, 2024).

DOI: 10.1201/9781003517115-13

While no AI models have been applied to the Pacific Island Food Revolution at this time, this example demonstrates that AI tools, when developed with community consent and for community benefit, can ensure the knowledge embedded in these movements is preserved and disseminated to serve those who contribute to them.

In New Zealand, Te Hiku Media is using trustworthy AI to preserve and revitalize the Māori language, te reo. With the support of NVIDIA's open-source NeMo toolkit and A100 Tensor Core GPUs, Te Hiku Media has developed automatic speech recognition (ASR) models that transcribe te reo with 92% accuracy (Lee, 2024).

These models are not only preserving the language but also amplifying the stories and cultural heritage of the Māori people. By employing ethical, transparent methods of data collection, Te Hiku Media ensures that the data sovereignty of the Māori people is maintained. The success of this initiative is inspiring other indigenous groups, such as Native Hawaiians, to embark on similar projects, demonstrating that AI can be a powerful tool for cultural preservation and empowerment when guided by the communities it serves.

We have come a long way since 2017 when I first tested IBM's Chef Watson, no longer accessible online. Companies like NVIDIA have initiatives like the AI Nations initiative that are helping countries build sovereign AI capabilities (Strier, 2024). Communities are getting involved so that AI isn't yet another tool that leaves out the very people it should be supporting, ignoring local values, needs, and diverse perspectives. Sovereign AI refers to a nation's ability to develop and operate AI using its own infrastructure, data, workforce, and business networks, ensuring that these systems reflect and serve their social and cultural contexts (Strier, 2024).

In practice, sovereign AI means building physical and data infrastructures that serve local needs, including foundation models and large language models. These models, developed by local teams and trained on regionally sourced datasets, promote inclusivity by reflecting specific dialects, cultures, and practices. For example, speech AI models can play a crucial role in revitalizing indigenous languages, and next-generation AI factories—advanced data centers designed to support AI—are fast becoming essential for achieving this independence (Strier, 2024). Now, keep in mind that some say focusing heavily on sovereignty in technology could undermine efforts to govern AI transparently and protect rights, potentially reducing global safety, prosperity, and democracy (Digital Forensic Research Lab, 2024).

As sovereign AI evolves beyond technical infrastructure, it must also encompass values of ethics, equity, and sustainability, reminding us of the shared responsibilities we have in advancing AI. Sustainability, in this context, extends beyond environmental concerns to include cultural and social dimensions.

For instance, inscribed in 2023 on UNESCO's Representative List of the Intangible Cultural Heritage of Humanity, *traditional irrigation* practices across regions in Europe—such as Austria, Belgium, and Switzerland—are prime examples of this interconnectedness. Using gravity-fed channels and hand-built ditches, these systems distribute water from natural sources like springs and glaciers to the fields.

This practice requires a deep understanding of the landscape, water flow, and seasonal conditions, along with close cooperation among farmers, landowners, and local cooperatives. For practitioners, traditional irrigation is not only a technical skill but also an identity marker, passed down informally through generations and accompanied by community gatherings that celebrate the watering seasons (UNESCO, 2023).

Practices like traditional irrigation reflect a bond, where cultural knowledge aligns with ecological stewardship. With its specific vocabulary and rich knowledge base—including awareness of lunar cycles and woodworking skills—traditional irrigation exemplifies how cultural heritage can foster resilience and environmental guardianship. AI, when developed with community input, could play a transformative role in documenting and supporting these practices, ensuring that this rich knowledge is preserved and adapted for future generations.

This connection becomes especially pertinent as we face the environmental challenges of AI itself. For instance, data centers powering large AI models like ChatGPT consume significant water for cooling—a reminder of the urgency for eco-friendly practices in AI development (Associated Press, 2023).

This issue resonates with the work of my husband, John Oliver Smith, an environmental engineer who has dedicated his career to sustainable resource management. To support John's work, I developed a custom GPT model based on his previous engineering projects. Though still in beta and based on limited data, this model serves as a tailored AI assistant, helping John access insights on his past work, sustainable conservation, and infrastructure. When we showcased this model at the 2024 Florida Engineering Summit and the Chesapeake Tricon Association, it sparked interest as a practical example of AI's potential in environmental engineering.

Just as AI can support heritage practices like irrigation, it can also empower professionals with specialized knowledge to address today's pressing environmental challenges. This approach brings us back to the heart of *AI for Community*, where technology nurtures both cultural and natural heritage for a sustainable future.

In closing, we've curated a set of resources to accompany this book, available on our website. You'll find links to projects like the Māori Speech AI Model, which helps preserve New Zealand's indigenous language, and AI and Media Insights on Spotify, both examples of how AI can empower communities with cultural intelligence, sensitivity, and respect. This collection of podcasts, videos, and articles provides practical frameworks and insights for anyone interested in fostering a responsible and inclusive AI landscape.

REFERENCES

Ardalan, D. (2017, November 10). Reactivating the hidden wisdoms of Tonga. *HuffPost*. https://www.huffpost.com/entry/reactivating-the-hidden-wisdoms-of-tonga_b_5a05fe5 2e4b0cc46c52e6a26

Associated Press. (2023, September 9). *Artificial intelligence technology behind ChatGPT was built in Iowa—With a lot of water*. Associated Press. https://apnews.com/article/ chatgpt-gpt4-iowa-ai-water-consumption-microsoft-f551fde98083d17a7e8d904f8be822c4

Digital Forensic Research Lab. (2024, July 17). *The sovereignty trap*. DFRLab. https://dfrlab. org/2024/07/17/the-sovereignty-trap/

Lee, A. (2024, January 16). Māori speech AI model helps preserve and promote New Zealand indigenous language. *NVIDIA Blog*. https://blogs.nvidia.com/blog/te-hiku-media-maori-speech-ai/

Pacific Island Food Revolution. (2024). https://www.pacificislandfoodrevolution.com/

Strier, K. (2024, February 28). What is sovereign AI? *NVIDIA Blog*. https://blogs.nvidia.com/ blog/what-is-sovereign-ai/

UNESCO. (2023). *Traditional irrigation: Knowledge, technique, and organization*. UNESCO. https:// ich.unesco.org/en/RL/traditional-irrigation-knowledge-technique-and-organization-01979

Index

Note: **Bold** page numbers refer to tables and *italic* page numbers refer to figures.